VANISHED HERO

VANISHED HERO

The Life, War, and Mysterious Disappearance
of America's World War II Strafing King

JAY A. STOUT

C CASEMATE | publishers
Philadelphia & Oxford

Published in the United States of America and Great Britain in 2016 by
CASEMATE PUBLISHERS
1950 Lawrence Road, Havertown, PA 19083, USA
and
10 Hythe Bridge Street, Oxford OX1 2EW, UK

Hardcover Edition: ISBN 978-1-61200-395-5
Digital Edition: ISBN 978-1-61200-396-2 (epub)

A CIP record for this book is available from the Library of Congress.

Printed and bound in the United States of America.

For a complete list of Casemate titles, please contact:

CASEMATE PUBLISHERS (US)
Telephone (610) 853-9131
Fax (610) 853-9146
Email: casemate@casematepublishers.com
www.casematepublishers.com

CASEMATE PUBLISHERS (UK)
Telephone (01865) 241249
Fax (01865) 794449
Email: casemate-uk@casematepublishers.co.uk
www.casematepublishers.co.uk

Especially for the fiercest of our fighting men—those who actively seek out our enemies, find them and kill them.

CONTENTS

INTRODUCTION: "I'LL SEE YOU WHEN I GET BACK"

The jeep squeaked to a stop. The pilot sat motionless in the passenger's seat and stared straight ahead, drawing slow, weary breaths. All at once he grunted, sat upright, grabbed his flying gear and stepped onto the damp ground. The jeep immediately crunched into gear and scooted away as he started toward his aircraft.

Block letters across the sleek fighter's nose marked it as *Katydid*. It was named after his wife, Cathryn. Next to the name, a voluptuous, green caricature of a winged katydid struck a pose. Bare-breasted, long-legged, and high-heeled, the implausible but undeniably sexy figure conveyed a distinctly flirtatious look.

A crew chief fussed with a balky set of fasteners on the P-51's under-side. The pilot watched him for a moment before moving unhurriedly around the aircraft to confirm that everything was as it should be. Satisfied, he leaned over and checked once more on the enlisted man.

A brisk English breeze chilled the morning and the pilot stood upright and zipped his jacket against it. He reached for his leather helmet and pulled it on. After so many months of combat it was stiff with dried sweat and it stank, but the snugness of it was nevertheless familiar and comforting. He pulled the goggles that were fastened to the helmet over his eyes to make certain they were clean. Through them, across the airfield, he saw dozens of other pilots and ground crews readying for the day's mission.

He lifted the goggles back onto his helmet, stepped onto the fighter's left wing and up to the cockpit. There, he grabbed the top of the windscreen, stepped over the canopy sill and eased his athletic frame down into the seat. A quick glance at the myriad gauges, switches, knobs and levers confirmed to him that the aircraft was ready to start.

He waited a moment for the crew chief to come out from under the airplane to help him with the buckles and straps of his parachute. The man didn't appear and the pilot tired of waiting. He sighed and called out, "Sergeant! Sergeant, come help me with my parachute."[1]

The crew chief, Don Downes, was still busy with the fasteners. "If you can't put on the goddamned chute, you can't fly the plane," he shouted.

The pilot's request changed to a demand. "Sergeant! Come up here and help me with my parachute!"

Exasperated, Downes scrabbled out from under the P-51. His eyes widened when he looked up to the cockpit. Rather than a fresh-faced, shavetail lieutenant, he discovered that the pilot wore "oak leaves as big as basketballs," and packed a .45 caliber pistol in a shoulder harness. The man to whom he had just mouthed off was the 55th Fighter Group's commander, Lieutenant Colonel Elwyn G. Righetti. Righetti, a celebrated ace, was in charge of not only the 55th and its airfield at Wormingford, but virtually everything and everyone on it, including Downes.

Downes leapt onto the wing and apologized as he bent over and helped his commander settle into the cockpit. Finished, he stood upright. Righetti fixed him with a look that left no doubt that his displeasure had not passed. "I'll see you when I get back."

The deep-throated thrum of the P-51's engine vibrated the airframe with a gentle tremble that made it feel as if it were a living thing. Righetti loved the Mustang and especially liked how it seemed to wrap itself around him as if it were a bespoke suit, custom tailored by artisans. No other aircraft had cradled him so perfectly and there was no other fighter in the world he wanted to fly. Aside from the feel of it, the gas and oil and metal reek of the muscular little fighter comprised a unique perfume. And no flying machine could match its sleek good looks—a striking balance of purposeful power and aerodynamic efficiency.

Righetti looked across the airfield where dozens of other P-51s also sat idling. They waited for his lead. Some of the fighters, like his own silvery aircraft, wore scarcely any paint at all. Their propeller spinners were circled with green and yellow stripes and the fronts of their engine cowlings wore similarly colored, checkered bands. These were identification markings specific to the 55th. But a few of the aircraft were partially painted with a sweeping olive drab pattern that covered the wings and ran back from the engine cowling, and then stretched down the top of the fuselage to the empennage. The unsanctioned scheme accented the aircraft's trim lines and was unique to the 55th. The tails of a few of the Mustangs wore the profile of a rearing stallion on their rudders.

Righetti checked his wristwatch against the slip of paper strapped to his knee. It was marked with important particulars about the day's mission such as the takeoff and rendezvous times, the route, the markings of the bomber units that were to be escorted and the expected weather— among other important information. The slip was marked with the date, April 17, 1945. It was his thirtieth birthday and he reflected for a moment on his wife and young daughter. They would be asleep now, at home near San Luis Obispo on the ranch where he had been born and raised.

The 55th was assigned to escort B-17s of the Eighth Air Force's 3d Air Division across targets in Dresden, not far from Germany's border with Czechoslovakia. In fact, the war was nearly over and there was little promise of air combat as the Allies had beaten the German Air Force—the Luftwaffe—nearly out of existence. Indeed, the Nazis were expected to surrender, or be completely overrun, during the next few weeks. It was a timeframe that neatly corresponded with the end of Righetti's combat tour as he had to fly only a few more missions before reaching the three hundred combat hours required to rotate back to the States. Regardless, he had been growing increasingly exhausted and was ready for it all to be over.

Righetti nodded at Downes who, careful to stay away from the spinning propeller, ran under the aircraft and dragged the wheel chocks clear. Checking ahead and behind him, Righetti released the fighter's brakes, added power and rolled from the hardstand onto the airfield's perimeter track. He returned the salute that Downes threw at him and started for the runway.

The P-51's nose blocked his view forward and Righetti stepped on one rudder pedal, then the other, fishtailing the little fighter back and forth across the track so that he could better see what was in front of him. Other aircraft left their hardstands, likewise weaving, as they fell into a long, snaking line behind him. Crew chiefs, armorers and other support personnel held tightly to their hats and shielded their eyes against the blast of propeller-blown dust and debris.

Nearing the runway, Righetti finished his takeoff checks and cranked the canopy closed. The growl of his engine changed timbre to a muted rumble. Behind him he saw the three squadrons that made up the 55th—the 38th, the 338th, and the 343rd—readying for takeoff. He checked his wristwatch once more and watched Paul Reeves and his wingman pull past him and onto the runway. Reeves was flying his last mission. "At the briefing, Righetti called me aside," said Reeves, "and told me that I would lead the group, form it and take it to enemy territory, and at that point he would assume the lead and I was to return to base. He pointed out that we had lost too many guys on their last scheduled mission and that we were not going to lose any more ... it seemed like a very thoughtful and considerate thing."[2]

A few seconds passed and a flare arced skyward from the control tower. The flagman posted at the edge of the runway pointed at Reeves's ship and whipped his flag over his head with a dramatic flourish. Reeves and his wingman advanced their engines and started down the runway together. The prop wash from the two aircraft rocked Righetti's fighter as he pushed up his own throttle and rolled onto the runway.

Carroll Henry, Righetti's wingman, taxied into position next to *Katydid*, raised a thumb and flashed a smile. The rumble of *Katydid's* engine grew into a popping roar as Righetti eased the throttle forward. At the same time he stepped on the right rudder pedal to counter the powerful torque that tried to swing the aircraft left and off the runway. More power produced more torque but Righetti reflexively kept it under control and soon he and Henry were accelerating down the runway.

At just more than a hundred miles an hour the tails of the two aircraft lifted clear of the ground and seconds later they were airborne. Righetti and Henry raised their landing gear simultaneously and climbed straight ahead after Paul Reeves. Behind them the group's other aircraft chased each other down the runway and into the sky. As the distance between him and the airfield grew, they looked to Righetti like a long stream of silvery-green minnows.

Several miles out, he followed Reeves and his wingman into a gentle turn back toward the airfield as the last elements of the group got airborne and joined the formation in three distinct squadrons. Righetti, with Reeves, headed the 338th, while the 38th and 343rd followed in trail. With the airfield a few miles ahead, the pilots tightened the formation and accelerated in a gentle descent. This low pass over the airfield not only made it easy for the 55th to pick up an exact heading from Wormingford to the first point on the assigned route, but more importantly it was a morale booster for the men who maintained the aircraft and otherwise made it possible for the group to fly.

Those same men squinted into the sky as the 55th's aircraft roared overhead. The noise from so many powerful engines rattled their chests and thundered for miles across the East Anglian countryside. Don Downes was among those men. As the last of the group's P-51s passed and started a climb to the east, he set off to find his boss. He wanted to take a three-day furlough, starting immediately.

Nearing Freiberg, over eastern Germany, Righetti leaned forward and peered past his gunsight and through the aircraft's windscreen. Straight ahead, at 24,000 feet, he spotted a series of specks at the head of a great carpet of white, fluffy contrails. The specks were nearly indistinguishable from the tiny nicks and bug carcasses and motes of dirt that spotted his windscreen, but they grew in size as he led the 55th closer. Finally, he recognized the bright white squares that were painted on the tails of each of the big B-17s—the squares marked them as 3d Air Division bombers. The 55th had made the rendezvous a few minutes early, but he suspected that the bomber crews wouldn't mind.

In truth, however, the early rendezvous probably wouldn't make much difference as it was doubtful that the much-beleaguered Luftwaffe would make an appearance. Still, regardless of whether the enemy showed or not, Righetti and his fighter group had a job to do. He checked to see the 38th and the 343rd separate from him and the rest of the 338th to take up their assigned positions. Spread apart, the 55th's three squadrons—flying a few thousand feet above the bomber stream—could provide better coverage than if they stayed together in one huge, unwieldy formation.

At the same time, Reeves's aircraft arced up and away toward Wormingford. Righetti watched a second aircraft follow Reeves. He knew this was Frank Birtciel who, like Reeves, was flying his last mission. Birtciel had arrived in England with the 55th in September 1943 and completed one combat tour flying P-38s before the group made its transition to the P-51 during July 1944. "I really liked and respected Righetti," Birtciel said. "He might have saved my life during that last mission. We had lost two other guys during the previous week who were also flying their last missions. Righetti didn't want to see that same thing happen, so he ordered me to go home as soon as we rendezvoused with the bombers."[3]

Through the occasional breaks in the clouds below, Righetti checked his chart against his position over the ground and his fuel gauge. Likewise, he glanced at his engine instruments every minute or so; a sour engine so deep over enemy territory was no small matter. And, as did every other pilot in the 55th, he scanned the sky for enemy fighters. But he gave no thought to the actual act of flying his aircraft. After so many years of experience his hands and feet directed it automatically.

The mission was a grueling one not because of enemy action but simply because—at more than five hours—it was so long. Protracted flight at high altitudes in an unpressurized cockpit was exhausting. It numbed the senses and the bitter cold often overpowered the cockpit heating system and worked its way through the layers of clothing that the men wore. At a minimum the missions were boring and frigid. At their worst—when beset by enemy fighters and heavy flak—they were terrifying.

On this particular mission, up to that point, it was the former. Bored and cold, Righetti and the rest of the 55th took the bombers across the target and started them on their way back to England. Below them, under attack by more than a thousand bombers, Dresden's citizens were anything but bored and cold. The bombs bounced and burned the rubble that their city had already become after a number of previous raids. Those raids killed more than twenty thousand. On this day more than five hundred additional civilians were killed.

The responsibility for escorting the bombers was passed to another fighter group on schedule and the 55th's individual squadrons descended to look for targets of opportunity. The weather through the entire region was poor, and heavy cloud cover and haze made formation-keeping difficult. Consequently, the men tightened their formations as they dropped through the clouds.

Righetti, with Henry still on his wing, took the 338th down to just a few thousand feet and trolled the area to the north and west of Dresden. The pilots looked for whatever merited killing—aircraft, trucks, troops, trains or anything else that might be useful to the Germans. As they motored through the poor visibility, calls over the radio made it apparent that other elements of the 55th were heavily engaged with enemy fighters.

There is little doubt that this information sharpened Righetti's lookout. Competitive and chronically keen for a fight, there were few missions during which he didn't fire his guns. He spotted an airfield near the town of Riesa, about twenty miles northwest of Dresden. There were a number of enemy aircraft parked at various points around the airfield and Righetti ordered the flight to stay at altitude while he dropped down to check for antiaircraft fire. Henry asked for, and received, permission to follow him. "He wanted me to stay up there with the other guys," Henry said. "But when I requested, he let me go."[4]

Righetti dove almost to the ground and leveled off to set up for a firing run from the east. He cranked in a touch of rudder trim to center the ball in the fluid-filled tube of his turn-and-bank indicator; an aircraft that was out of trim sprayed bullets everywhere but where they were aimed. Next he twisted the gunsight's rheostat to adjust the brightness of the aiming pipper that was projected onto its small glass plate. Too bright and it would wash out whatever he aimed at. Too dim and he couldn't see where *Katydid*'s guns were pointed. Finally, he checked that his gun switch was set to "Guns, Sight & Camera."

With Henry on his wing, Righetti spotted an Me-109 parked at the edge of the airfield. He banked slightly left and lowered the aircraft's nose until the gunsight's pipper rested on the fuselage just below the canopy. He held it there with slight forward pressure on the control stick as *Katydid* swiftly closed the range.

Righetti squeezed the trigger at the front of his control stick. The six, .50 caliber machine guns—three in each wing—responded with a bucking roar that actually slowed his aircraft. Each of the guns sent armor-piercing projectiles toward the enemy fighter at a rate of eight hundred rounds per minute.

Righetti released the trigger after only a couple of seconds. An instant passed before great clots of earth and grass erupted from the ground around the German fighter. The rounds which found their mark twinkled and flashed and tore pieces from the Me-109 before turning it into a fireball just as Righetti passed overhead. He looked up and immediately caught sight of an FW-190 approaching to land. Henry was closer to the enemy aircraft than he was, and Righetti called out its position and told Henry, "Go get it."

"He had eyes like an eagle," Henry said. "I didn't see it." A few seconds of frantic searching later, Henry spotted the enemy aircraft and made a quick heading correction. Slow as he was—and with his landing gear extended—the German fighter pilot was virtually helpless. Henry framed the FW-190 in his gunsight, fired his guns, and watched his rounds knock the hapless German out of the sky. "I killed him I guess, because he just hit the runway and rolled over. The plane was on fire when he hit the ground."

Righetti saw the German aircraft crash in flames. He wrenched his own ship around in a sequence of sharp, treetop-level turns while enemy gun crews, fully alert now, tried to shoot him down. Puffs of light antiaircraft fire burst around him as he lined up for another run. More antiaircraft fire crisscrossed his flight path, and smoke from the aircraft he and Henry had already set ablaze drifted skyward. Notwithstanding the efforts of the German gun crews, Righetti set several more aircraft afire.

This wasn't the artful, twisting, aerial ballet that was air-to-air combat. That sort of fighting demanded superb gunnery and a deft touch on the controls. Indeed, the skill required to cause a stream of bullets fired from an aircraft moving in three dimensions to arrive at the exact same point in the sky—and at the exact same instant—as another aircraft moving in those same three dimensions, was not easily acquired. Very few pilots were good at it. Righetti was one of them and had proven it during the previous months by single-handedly downing seven German aircraft.

But strafing parked aircraft was different. The targets didn't move and consequently the physics necessary to achieve a satisfactory firing solution were relatively simple. A pilot only had to hold his aircraft steady and put the gunsight's pipper on the target until he flew into range. Then, just a few seconds on the trigger delivered enough rounds to tear any aircraft apart.

But it took big guts. Indeed, there was no more dangerous mission for a fighter pilot. This was a fact borne out by the records as many more fighters over Europe were lost to ground fire than to enemy fighters. This was primarily because an aircraft flying a straight, predictable flight path low to the ground was vulnerable to the batteries of guns that typically protected important targets. The enemy gunners needed only to shoot far enough ahead of an attacking aircraft to stand a reasonable chance of hitting it. Or—together with other gun crews—they could simply create a curtain of fire through which an aircraft had to fly. These types of concentrated barrages became especially deadly as the Germans retreated into an ever-shrinking area and brought their antiaircraft guns with them. Indeed, as the war drew to an end, the concentration of antiaircraft guns on the Luftwaffe's remaining airfields was devastating.

Righetti and Henry made their attacks at speeds that were considerably less than what their aircraft were capable of flying. "If you flew too fast you didn't have time to see anything," Henry said. But slower speeds made them more vulnerable. So did making repeated passes against a well-defended airfield. It was a practice that went against common sense and tactical dictums, but it was perfectly consistent with Righetti's outsized ferocity in the face of enemy fire.

Indeed, by the time he started his third run, the gun crews at Riesa were fully ready. He picked out another enemy aircraft, lowered the nose of his aircraft and held it down. Finally in range, he squeezed the trigger and saw his bullets arc over the airfield and into the German fighter.

An instant later Righetti heard a loud bang and felt *Katydid* shudder.

Don Downes finished packing his bag. It was a cinch that he'd be off the base before Righetti landed back at Wormingford.

"I NOW HAVE CANCER"

I love to hear from people who have read my books. Truly, we history writers never get the attention we think we deserve. Who does? So, naturally, I was gratified upon reading the first line of the e-mail: "I am a big fan of your outstanding work on USAAF fighter pilots and have read and reread your books, *Fighter Group*, and *The Men Who Killed the Luftwaffe*." And then, the bombshell. "I now have cancer and want to find someone to whom I can donate my library and research archive."

This admirer I didn't know, Tony Meldahl, was dying. An Army veteran and German linguist, he was a researcher rather than a writer and had worked with renowned authors Iris Chang and Joe Galloway. And for more than two decades he had been fascinated with the Elwyn Righetti story. He had conducted interviews, collected stacks of obscure books, translated dozens of documents, collaborated with aviation experts around the world and visited with the Righetti family. The products of all those efforts were boxed into an enormous stack of cartons and additionally captured on two, massive hard drives.

And although he had once planned to write a book on Righetti, he now wanted to give the material he had collected to me. "My first choice is you. Your depth of understanding, quality of research, and extraordinary writing skills make you, in my opinion, the best writer in this field. I feel you have the right stuff to write a mainstream book [about Righetti] on par with Galloway's *We Were Soldiers Once, and Young*."

I felt simultaneously prideful and guilty. Such praise! But life was leaving Tony and there was little hope that he would see his dream of a

Righetti biography realized. Still, I reminded myself to be wary of gift horses. I didn't know Tony and wasn't exactly certain what he wanted. I responded very tentatively, but with compassion for a dying man whose interests were so similar to mine.

I offered this stranger a few lines filled with words of comfort but he hadn't contacted me for solace and I soon turned to the subject at hand. "Do I understand correctly that you are suggesting this because you simply want to see the story brought to light? Because you've done so much work and you don't want to see it go to nothing? I ask because I've had no experience with collaborative writing or sharing of work that has worked out well. Collaborative writing is just not something that works for me." It was mostly true. Aside from working with Hamilton McWhorter—the world's finest gentleman—to write *The First Hellcat Ace*, all my other attempts at collaboration had produced nothing.

"I do not want to do a collaborative book," Tony replied. "I'd just like to give you everything I have with no strings attached … if you would consider some day to write on the Righetti topic." There it was. Tony wanted to pass his work and material to me.

But the very real question remained. Tony's passion and heartbreaking situation aside, did I want to start this project? I had a passing familiarity with Righetti but wasn't certain if there was enough of a story to justify a book. Although he had earned his commission and wings before the war, Righetti arrived late to the fighting and had missed many of the most famous battles. But after arriving in England during the fall of 1944 he threw himself into the war like a star athlete who had been kept on the bench until the final few minutes of the game. He flew and fought like a banshee and quickly became an aerial ace, while also destroying more aircraft on the ground than anyone else.

Sadly, despite his spectacular accomplishments, he has been largely overlooked by history—not often mentioned in the ranks of great fighter aces and leaders. This is curious as he was awarded the Distinguished Service Cross, the second highest military honor the nation can bestow. And he shot his way to aerial acedom during a time when many men never even saw an enemy aircraft.

Most impressive was his ground strafing record. Aside from a couple of dozen or more locomotives and a multitude of other important ground targets, he set the Eighth Air Force record by destroying 27 German aircraft in strafing attacks. It was incredibly risky work, recognized to be more dangerous than the type of aerial combat popularly known as dogfighting. But perhaps the most noteworthy of his achievements was the spirit of professional aggressiveness he imparted to the 55th Fighter Group. After languishing in near-anonymity since starting combat operations, it emerged as one of the Eighth Air Force's "hottest outfits."

Why he faded into relative obscurity is difficult to determine with certainty. However, one reason is that the number of aerial victories he achieved did not match up with the tallies of the highest scorers. But what those lists don't take into account is that Righetti scored them when the "hunting" was lean. That he scored as highly as he did—7.5 officially credited aerial victories—so late in the war is remarkable. In fact, no one during the entire history of the 55th Fighter Group knocked down more enemy aircraft while flying as part of the group.[1]

There were other reasons why his celebrity faded. Although his achievements and those of the 55th were much celebrated during the closing months of the war in Europe, the public's attention shifted to the Pacific and Japan after Germany surrendered. And once the fighting was over altogether, the nation busied itself creating a postwar society. People were weary of war and the talk of war.

But perhaps the most important reason for the gradual forgetting of his achievements was the way in which he was lost. He was alive after his aircraft was shot down during the mission of April 17, 1945, but was never heard from again. For years, no one knew if he was alive or dead. Live men can't be memorialized and men aren't generally declared dead without substantive proof of their demise. And for its part, Righetti's family didn't beat the drum of his fame. Rather, they prayed for his safe return. As they did, the nation turned to other things. Righetti, and what he accomplished, gradually disappeared from America's collective memory.

After much deliberation—but with all of this in mind—I decided to accept Tony's offer. To my way of thinking the worst that could happen was that I might discover the project was not worthwhile. But even in that case, Tony's considerable archive would be saved. On the other hand, the best possible outcome, the one I obviously hoped for, was that the book would be a success and that Righetti's story would become deservedly better known.

Tony was pleased by my decision and immediately started shipping his material—much of it personally annotated to me. In the meantime we kept up a steady correspondence. His notes usually started or ended with some version of: "I'm at chemotherapy now." His body was failing, but still he worked.

I was stunned at the volume of it all. Tony was obviously a collector and the dozen or so boxes—arriving two or three at a time—quickly took over my study and garage. Even my wife, The Most Unflappable Woman in the World, raised an eyebrow. But, sympathetic to Tony's condition, she didn't say a word.

During the next few months I triaged Tony's treasure trove which included much of the material I needed. But I knew I couldn't write the book without working with the Righetti family. Approaching them was a prickly undertaking. More than seven decades after he left for the war, it was obvious they still missed him. Two of his sisters, Doris and Lorraine, were both in their nineties and lived not far from the ranch where they grew up with Elwyn and the rest of their siblings—the ranch was still in the family and prospering. Hard work, loyalty and commitment are enduring Righetti traits.

But where their celebrated hero Elwyn was concerned, they had been misled too many times. When I approached them I was only the latest in a string of people who had declared they were going to preserve his legacy with a book. Most of these people were well-meaning but few if any were capable of completing such a project. And none of them did. Consequently, after I contacted them, the Righettis quite understandably did not raise their hopes just because I promised that I was going to do what others had also promised and failed to do.

And I also had been forewarned by one of the quite extensive family that the clan could be an actively "opinionated bunch" that "didn't always agree." In other words, the Righettis were a normal family. Still, they were kind enough to meet with me. Righetti's daughter Kyle allowed me to copy the considerable collection of letters that were so important to the book. She additionally set up a nice lunch and arranged for a gathering that included more than a handful of relatives. After introducing my wife and myself, I explained who I was, what I wanted to do and how I planned to approach the project. And I solicited their help. The initial circumspection and tension dissipated and we relaxed into a nice conversation that included important recollections and an interview with Righetti's sister Doris.

The project was well and truly underway. With the family's blessing, I launched into the effort with an enthusiasm that was tempered by the promises I had made to both Tony and the Righetti family. That tempering was heightened when the notes from Tony slowed to a trickle. There finally came a message from his wife Gina that he had died. "Tony peacefully passed away at 3:48 this morning. I was by his side. My daughters have been with me. He looks so peaceful with a big smile."

Although I had never met him, I felt sad at Tony's passing. Nevertheless, I pressed on. For reasons I still don't understand, the book developed to be the most difficult of the many I have written. My subject had perished long before, as had most of his peers. Getting the story right was consequently more difficult. And always there in various degrees was the pressure to succeed where others had not. Worse, was the fact that the book wasn't immediately put on contract by the first few publishers I approached; it was a story that did not have a happy ending. Perhaps more problematic was the fact that the end might not ever be knowable.

So, with no immediate commitments from any of my publishing contacts, I almost panicked. I feared becoming another of those Righetti enthusiasts who had made promises they could not keep. Happily, it wasn't too long before my anxiety was salved. Casemate's managing editor, Steve Smith, recognized the story's excellent potential and we immediately negotiated a publishing agreement.

Now, with the manuscript complete, the notion that small gestures can create outsized effects has been reinforced to me. Had Tony Meldahl not reached out to me this book would never have happened. And that would have been sad as it is one of which I am especially proud. It is a unique story, unfiltered by its subject and untainted by modern sensibilities. Indeed, it is honestly told and preserves as much as possible the context of the world as it was more than seven decades past. And finally, it captures the heart and essence of one of the USAAF's most complex and aggressive fighting men.

"HE LOVED FLYING MORE THAN ANYTHING"

He let go of the two teats, flexed his fingers and sighed. Her udder dry, the cow stood stoically above him, breath steaming into the early morning cold. Across the barn, his brother Ernie finished with one Holstein and moved to another. The single leg of the milking stool strapped to his backside wig-wagged with each step. Pop squatted nearby atop his own little stool and squeezed jets of milk into a pail—zip, zip, zip. Young Maurice, wrapped in a jacket that was too big for him, scraped with a shovel at a pile of manure in the barnyard.

Elwyn Guido Righetti grabbed the nearly full pail from under the cow, stood up and rubbed his lower back. He loved his father and his brothers. And he loved his mother and his sisters who were doing their own chores in the house beyond the barnyard. He even loved the ranch and the backbreaking work that it demanded—nothing could compare to the way it looked and felt, or to its sounds and smells. It was home.

But despite all his feelings, Righetti did not want to make his life here. Cows and fields and fences and everything else about the place—and there was plenty of "everything else"—were enough for his father, and maybe his brothers, but not him. He wanted to go into the wider world to do bigger and more exciting things. He *needed* something more.

The Spanish preceded the Righettis to the central California coast by a hundred years. The golden rolling hills and the verdant valleys that characterized the area were initially visited by explorers during 1769, and Franciscan priest Junípero Serra founded the mission of San Luis Obispo soon after, on September 1, 1772. Located approximately ten miles inland, it was the fifth of an eventual twenty-one missions established in California.

The area's moderate Mediterranean climate featured soft, soaking, winter rains, and dry, bright summers. The gentle weather, together with the region's rich soils and a generally docile native population, encouraged a prosperous ranching and agricultural community. This community eventually grew into the town of San Luis Obispo. As part of Alta California—or upper California—the region passed from Spain to Mexico at the end of the Mexican Revolution in 1821, and subsequently to the United States in 1848 following the Mexican-American War. However, its history was generally as placid as its weather, with no remarkable events or turmoil.

Righetti's paternal grandfather, Francesco "Robertino" Righetti, arrived in the area from Switzerland in 1873. Born in 1858, he immigrated with a brother from the Italian-speaking canton of Ticino in southern Switzerland where political discord, a series of crop failures and a general lack of opportunity drove citizens out of the insular nation—many to California. At the time, San Luis Obispo numbered just more than two thousand inhabitants including a relatively large Swiss population.

Like many of his countrymen, Robertino took a variety of odd jobs, including work as a hired hand on the area's dairy farms; dairying was a way of life that many Swiss knew well. He eventually saved enough to buy a small ranch in the nearby Edna Valley to which he added acreage over time. He built a house and married Ermenia Bonetti who bore him a son, Guido, in 1882. Three other children followed. One of them, Lorinda, died in 1891 and Ermenia was taken by typhoid a few months later, that same year.

Guido grew up dairying with Robertino who eventually remarried. He attended the local public schools where he did well enough to study at Armstrong Business College. Following several years of work in the oil industry he returned to his roots, married Elizabeth Mary Renkert—a local girl of Swiss and French heritage—and returned to his father's ranch. This couple, as their children were born, became Mom and Pop Righetti, Elwyn's mother and father.

The first child, Elizabeth, or "Betty," came in 1913. "I was born in a little board and batten, mud sill, unpainted house," she said.[1] Elwyn was born in that same house a year and a half later on April 17, 1915. The other four children, Ernest, or "Ernie," Lorraine, Doris and Maurice—pronounced "Morris"—likewise followed in measured intervals of a year and a half.

Disease was a regular danger during that time, and the Spanish flu laid Mom Righetti low during the fall of 1918. She survived, but lost her sense of smell. "We always knew breakfast was ready," said Elwyn's sister Doris, "because we could smell toast burning."[2] Polio was also a threat during this time before an effective vaccination. Ernie, Doris and Maurice were exposed and quarantined. "I remember we talked to our parents through the hospital windows," Doris said. Ultimately, neither she nor Maurice exhibited any symptoms.

Ernie was not so lucky. "They put sand bags on my legs to keep them straight," he said. "That was all they could do."[3] It wasn't enough and Ernie walked with a slight limp for the remainder of his life. On the other hand, unlike thousands of children, Ernie survived. And, likely to the relief of Mom and Pop, the mild disability exempted him from military service later, during World War II.

But notwithstanding polio and other childhood diseases, ranching and farming were dangerous in their own right. They always had been. A kick from a horse could kill in an instant. Lightning struck men down in the blink of an eye. Razor-sharp tools slashed, or punctured, or took fingers and hands in accidents. And during this time when powered machinery was only just becoming commonplace on the farm, unguarded belts and gears and chains—combined with ignorance or carelessness or plain, bad luck—tore away scalps, ripped off arms and pulled men into their mechanicals where they were ground to death.

In fact, long before Elwyn was born, his father Guido was so badly injured that he nearly died. An account was carried by the local newspaper:

> Yesterday morning Guido Righetti, the fifteen-year-old son of Robertino Righetti of Edna, was brought to this city and placed in the care of Doctors Nichols and Dial at the Grutli hotel. The little fellow had started out to ride a horse on his father's ranch, minus a bridle and relying solely upon a rope which he placed about the horse's nose. He allowed the rope to become slack and the animal stumbled, throwing the boy heavily to the ground. Injuries were sustained about the left side of the head and upon the left shoulder. The boy remained insensible for fully an hour after being picked up by his father.[4]

Ultimately, the family patriarch was lost to an accident. On September 6, 1929, Robertino—who had come to the area from Switzerland more than five decades earlier—felled a tree on his ranch. As he trimmed the limbs, it rolled over, pinned him to the ground, broke his back and killed him.[5]

Still, those sorts of dangers existed on nearly every farm and ranch across the country. The truth was that there were few places better suited for ranching and dairying than the area around San Luis Obispo. Although nature was occasionally stingy with rain, the temperatures were idyllic. The region's settlers were never forced to endure the bone-numbing cold that blanketed much of the nation during the winter, nor did they suffer from the sopping, stinking heat that stifled the Midwest, the South and much of the East during the summer.

Indeed, the rural upbringing of the Righetti children was almost a Rockwellian cartoon. "Oh, it was a good life," said Doris. "There was lots of love in the family and everyone did their part. Pop was the disciplinarian and Mom looked after us. If we did something to get Pop mad, Mom would always step in and say, 'Oh, go easy, that's not so bad,' or 'Don't get mad, they didn't mean for it to go wrong.' So, our parents were well balanced."

"Sometimes the neighbors seemed too far away," said Doris, "And then there were times when they seemed too close. Our parents played cards with other parents in the area and that's how we got to know a lot of the other kids." Doris noted that the Righetti children occasionally picked up bad habits from their neighbors. "And I'm sure we passed some of our own on to them."

"We were almost two sets of kids," Doris said. "The oldest, Elizabeth, Elwyn and Ernie, ran together, while Lorraine and Maurice and I did what we did together." The Righetti children varied in their temperaments. Elizabeth, the oldest, was smart, strong-willed and self-sufficient. The others paid attention when she spoke. "Elwyn was always the adventurous one," said Doris. "He loved to be outside and he loved to hunt. Sometimes he didn't like working on the ranch too much. And Ernie was serious and reliable and a very hard worker. He and Elwyn were very close and Ernie really looked up to him."

The girls did most of their chores inside the house. Among Elizabeth's jobs was washing the dishes and cleaning kerosene lamps; electrical service didn't reach the house until 1941. "I washed those old lamp chimneys because they would get sooty and not shed any light." Immediately after high school Elizabeth went to work in a dentist's office. "I wore white uniforms but we had to heat the irons on the old stove. And if you got even a speck of soot from the stove onto the iron it would streak the uniform. My mom and I cried over those uniforms sometimes."

"The other girls and I loved horses," said Doris. "In the evening, when it came time to bring in the cows, we raced the boys to the horses. The first ones there got to ride, and we usually beat them. And Maurice, the youngest, was at the tail end," she said. "He was so sweet. He didn't like hunting as much as Elwyn and Ernie."

A good part of the family's income came from the dairy cows—about twenty head of Holsteins—that demanded near-constant attention. Dairying was a never-ending job and it was mostly done by Pop and the boys. The cows required milking twice each day, and everything that came into contact with the milk required fastidious cleaning or sterilization. "The milk was put into pans on racks," said Elizabeth. "And they would let the cream rise and skim it off. Then they put the milk into cans that were furnished by the creamery, and take it down to San Luis Obispo. From there it was sent via railroad to Avila, and then transshipped to San Francisco."

Another source of income was the herd of beef cattle—and sometimes sheep—that the family raised on the ranch's pastureland. By the

1930s the ranch had grown to more than a thousand acres with fences that needed regular repair; the boys became experts with barbed wire and cutters and posthole diggers. Although not so needy as the dairy cows, the other animals still had to be watched and cared for as there was seldom a time when one or more of them was not sick or lame or otherwise needful of attention. Both the girls and the boys regularly canvassed the ranch on horseback and reported to their father. "He believed the livestock needed to be counted often," recalled Elizabeth. "It was important to know where they were and how they were doing."

Then there was the hay and grain—barley, wheat, oats, and corn—that supplemented the grass in the pastures. In helping to tend these crops the children learned not only how to operate such varied machinery as tractors, spreaders, binders and bailers, but they also grew savvy about how to maintain and repair them. Later, during World War II, instructors in the technical disciplines were surprised to discover that America's country bumpkins were more mechanically astute than their supposedly sophisticated city cousins.

The family bought some foodstuffs from stores in town, but much of what they ate was produced on the ranch. "Mom baked all the bread," said Doris. "And she had Rhode Island Red chickens for eggs and for the table. And there were hogs—Poland China hogs. I disliked them. They were huge and they smelled bad, and were mean and nasty. It was my job to slop them."

Cows and pigs were occasionally butchered and their hides were scalded in a massive steel kettle near the barn. Canned and dried vegetables from the household garden and fruit from various trees supplemented the family's fare. "There was always a big pot of pink beans on the stove," Doris said. "They were just lightly seasoned and always there for anyone whenever they wanted. Next to them there was always a pot of applesauce. The two were always just there together—always a part of our lives."

Aside from hard work, the ranch was a place that rewarded—even demanded—teamwork, well considered and timely decisions, and good, plain commonsense. As he grew, Elwyn came to understand all of this and more, even if he didn't always practice it. As a young man, he often wished to be elsewhere. "Sometimes," Doris allowed, "Elwyn tried not to work too hard."

Still, he learned not only how to work with and around machinery, but also with beasts, crops and especially people. And the work made him strong; it suited a body that was muscled and lean, but still big enough to shoulder heavy loads. Ultimately, the value of the family's hard work was apparent to him everywhere. It was on the dinner table, it was in the bank account, it was in the neat fences that crisscrossed the property, and in the barn, corral and silo. And most important, it was apparent in his father's smile—a smile that signified approval of a job well done.

"Elwyn was my hero," said Elizabeth. "He and I started grammar school together and walked all the way from the home place down to the Independence Grammar School—just more than a mile. It was a one-room school with an anteroom for the boys and a separate one for the girls. The boys came in the south side and the girls entered on the north side. We left our hats and coats and lunches in the anterooms and had class in the big room."

"Elwyn and I sat in the same seat for a while and then the teacher, Emelia Lewis, sat us with older children so that they could help teach us." Mom and Pop emphasized the importance of schoolwork and education. "Mrs. Lewis was a disciplinarian," said Elizabeth. "And my dad used to say that if we got a licking at school and he heard about it, then we were going to get another licking when we got home. Dad believed in school. You went to school to learn and not to fool around. I think he whopped the boys with a razor strop once or twice."

There were rarely more than twenty students at any one time and both Elizabeth and Elwyn excelled through good instruction, familial support, and their own, innate intelligence. They also, as did all their siblings, became active participants in 4-H, which sought to better connect public school learning with rural lifestyles and skills. When they came of age, a bus took them to San Luis Obispo High School where Elwyn performed well ahead of his peers. In fact, he graduated with Elizabeth in 1931 when he was just sixteen.

"And then he found girls," said Doris. "He wasn't around nearly as much after that, unless he had to be." It is likely that there were plenty of girls only too willing to be found. Elwyn was good-looking; he had an even-featured face, straight, white teeth, a thick shock of brown hair and an athletic build. He was smart and charming and came from a respectable family that operated a fair-sized ranch. Photos from the period show a smiling young man who carried himself with grace and confidence.

On the other hand, he was inexperienced, was not regularly employed, and owned nothing. And the early 1930s were the worst years of the Great Depression. Steady jobs were difficult to find and hold, especially for a boy still in his teens. Although Mom and Pop fed and clothed him and put a roof over his head, he and Ernie received little else. "I never did draw a salary," said Ernie.

Exacerbating the employment realities were Steinbeck's Okies, displaced farmers from Oklahoma and elsewhere who flooded California in search of a better life. They hunkered down in squalid camps and followed the truck crop harvests, working as pickers and packers. In fact, famed photographer Dorothea Lange's iconic photo, *Migrant Mother*, was captured only ten miles south of the ranch, near Nipomo. It showed a woman seemingly devoid of hope, a small child clinging to her shoulder. Certainly, the plight of these people affected Elwyn and the rest of the family.

However, except for drops in dairy and beef prices, the Great Depression had no significant impact on the day-to-day lives of the family. "We just went on as we always had," Doris said. "We had always been land rich and dollar poor." In fact, Mom and Pop were frugal by nature, and the family's income, before and after the crash, was typically spent on improvements or to buy more land to enlarge the ranch. Clothes and shoes were handed down, or altered, or mended rather than thrown out. "Mom had a friend in San Francisco who used to send down clothes she didn't wear anymore," said Elizabeth. "Some of our clothes came from her."

Likewise, equipment was repaired until it simply gave out. Consequently, the collapse of the nation's economy and the government's reactionary machinations in far-away Washington, D.C. made little difference to the Righettis. "We still had pink beans and applesauce," said Doris. "You can do a lot with pink beans."

And ammunition. There was always plenty of ammunition for target practice, plinking pests and hunting. "Elwyn loved to hunt," said Doris. "He loved to hunt about as much as anything else." Indeed, whenever possible, Elwyn and Ernie disappeared into the scrub and oaks of the surrounding canyons to hunt whatever counted as food: rabbits, ducks, dove and quail, and especially deer. "Their hunting was always done legally and always in season," Doris said. "Well, maybe not always." The deer indigenous to the area were blacktails, closely related to mule deer. They seldom exceeded two hundred pounds, but were a welcome addition to the dinner table.

Elwyn grew to be an exceptional shot with both rifle and shotgun. He especially looked forward to the hunting trips that Pop arranged to northern California and Idaho for mule deer and elk. Pop and the boys packed a truck and trailer with camping gear, rifles, food and a pack horse, and then drove a day or more to favorite hunting areas. "Dad used a .25-35 Winchester, Model 94," said Ernie, "and Elwyn had a .32 Winchester Special, Model 94."[6]

When Elwyn enrolled in the California Polytechnic College in San Luis Obispo in 1933, he likely did so as much out of boredom as for any other reason. Since graduating from high school he had done little more than work on the ranch; his early graduation had served him no real purpose. Although he still lived at home, college exposed him to something other than the sameness that had been his life to that point. Moreover, he met new people.

"Oh, he loved school," said Doris. "He made a lot of friends and became very involved in a lot of activities." Doris did not exaggerate. The school's annual, El Rodeo, showed that Elwyn, whose course of study was Meat Animals, was a member of the Future Farmers of America, the Boots and Spurs club and the manager of the El Rodeo itself. Moreover, he was made a member of Gamma Pi Delta, a fraternity that emphasized service and leadership. Aside from their stated charters, the highlight of service with these clubs was the social activities—dances, barbeques, beach parties and other events. In fact, he was made the king of Poly Royal, the annual festival that became the hallmark of the school's social calendar. "He was so handsome," said Doris.

Elwyn's course of study lasted two years and he scored good grades, graduating in 1935. But still, the nation was in the grips of the Great Depression and employment was difficult. He found work during the next couple of years driving trucks and working as a salesman for both Swift Creamery and Golden State Creamery. It did not satisfy his ambitions. "He came home one day after smashing his hand working on a truck," said Doris. "He told me that there had to be a better way to make a living."

He also tried retail sales in town, and additionally went to work for a Buick dealer. There, the owner was unable to collect payments against a considerable list of customers. Elwyn established an arrangement whereby he kept half of any defunct debt he was able to collect. Exercising considerable charm and persuasiveness, he laid out realistic payment plans for the delinquent parties. These were people he knew, or knew of, and he enjoyed a good deal of success. Noting that success, and the methods that made it possible, the owner took Elwyn's plan as his own and relegated him to the lot as a used car salesman.

Tragedy masquerading as opportunity came to the central California coast when the Norwegian lumber freighter, *Elg*, ran aground at Oceano near San Luis Obispo on September 9, 1938. When the rising tide failed to lift the ship free, the captain ordered its cargo jettisoned. That cargo was nearly half-a-million linear feet of finely milled Canadian lumber.

During the next few days, as tugs worked to free the ship, and as the lumber was dumped into the ocean, the surrounding area was swept by a gold rush mentality. Virtually every able-bodied man went down to the cold, choppy water to claim what he could under the law of salvage. The San Luis Obispo *Daily Telegram* recorded the scene: "Trucks, trailers and tractors arrived from points as far away as Paso Robles and Santa Maria to carry away loads of lumber varying from a few hundreds of board feet to thousands of board feet. Stories circulated regarding men being hired by contractors at $1 and even $1.50 an hour to salvage the lumber as it washed ashore."[7]

A line of trucks stretched nearly a mile, waiting to gain access to the beach. Opportunism and greed were everywhere. One man set his daughter up in the back of his truck to sell hotdogs to famished salvagers. Disputes over ownership of the errant rafts of boards were common and shoving matches and fistfights broke out. "Weary watchers who had stood by piles of lumber along more than a mile of beach through Sunday night, waiting for trucks to arrive had difficulties galore. A man, red-eyed from sleeplessness, said he had left his wife to watch his salvaged lumber while he left to find food and on his return his wife weepingly reported that strangers with a truck had pushed her aside and taken the lumber." The sheriff and his deputies were able to do little more than try to control the chaos.

The salvaging was dangerous and many of the men had no business being in the frigid, wave-wracked currents. During a period of several days, seven men drowned. Others lost fingers and suffered cuts and broken bones. Many men were rescued from certain death. The *Daily Telegram* noted one of these: "Hero stories also marked Monday. Elwyn Righetti, 22 [23], Edna Road, San Luis Obispo, was rescued early Monday and revived with artificial respiration. He was reported in good condition Monday evening."

That Elwyn was at the center of the frenzy surprised none of his family or friends. "But my parents had a talk with him," said Doris. "I wasn't allowed to hear, but I know they had something to say." As it developed, Elwyn recovered from his near-drowning with no lasting ill effects. And the lumber that was salvaged during that period was used in the construction of many local houses and businesses, some of which still stand.

It was also during 1938 that Elwyn, like many young men, was bitten by the flying bug. Lindbergh's crossing of the Atlantic a decade earlier in 1927—when Elwyn was twelve—fired the public's imagination as nothing had before. Tickertape parades were almost commonplace, and newspapers and radios trumpeted every new achievement as intrepid aviators went higher, faster and farther. In so doing they made the world a smaller place.

But many of them did so at the cost of their lives. Amelia Earhart went missing only the year prior, in 1937, and Wiley Post, the first person to fly solo around the globe, was killed in 1935. Nevertheless, the advances that were pioneered by these luminaries and the thousands of scientists and engineers who made their achievements possible, culminated in an aviation industry that was more accessible than ever. No longer was it the exclusive domain of heavily financed daredevils, or military men flying government machines. In fact, anyone with the desire and talent, and a reasonable amount of cash, could learn to fly. That accessibility, together with preparations for the coming war, marked the waning days of the golden age of aviation.

Still, flying was expensive. At that time and place, flying lessons averaged 7 dollars per hour.[8] This was during a decade when laborers averaged 50 cents per hour. Still, Elwyn scrimped, saved, bartered and charmed, and was certified as a private pilot by the summer of 1939. During that time he logged 170 flying hours—a considerable achievement considering his age, the cost, and the fact that most flights averaged under an hour.

He flew primarily from the San Luis Obispo county airport, and at Hancock Field in nearby Santa Maria, at the controls of whatever was available. His logbook noted flights in Aeronca, Great Lakes, Taylorcraft, Rearwin, Piper and Porterfield aircraft—among others. They made up the colorful panoply of small aircraft that increasingly put-putted across the nation's skies. They would be joined, in only a few short years, by hundreds of thousands of war machines that would make them look like the flying toys they were.

"He loved flying more than anything," said Doris. "Even more than he loved hunting." Still, once the novelty wore thin, Elwyn realized that the sort of recreational flying he was doing offered no real career prospects. The budding airline industry was where a pilot could earn a real living, but gaining the experience required to qualify for such a job took time and money. And the competition was stiff; there were literally thousands of young men like him who had a dream, a few hundred flight hours, and little else.

The United States Army Air Corps, or USAAC, offered another option. For much of its existence after World War I it had been a very small organization of just a thousand pilots or so. It typically trained only a few new pilots each year and had its choice of the most qualified—and sometimes, well-connected—young men in the nation. Graduates from West Point were given first priority, but a four-year college degree, at a minimum, was a must. And education aside, successful candidates were as nearly physically perfect as possible. Even then, many of the newly trained men who survived the high-attrition training were sent to reserve or National Guard units.

Such a life was attractive to Elwyn. A commission as a second lieutenant would provide him with a paycheck well beyond what he could earn peddling used cars, or hauling dairy products. A commission would also put him at the controls of some of the world's most sophisticated aircraft. That experience could help him punch the tickets necessary to fly as an airline pilot—as far from squeezing cow teats as he could wish. Still, the Air Corps requirement for a four-year college degree meant that Elwyn was at least two years from being qualified. And two more years of school would have to come at the cost of money he didn't have.

However, political frictions and armed clashes in Europe and Asia compelled the USAAC to develop expansion plans. In order to enlarge the pool of qualified men, it dropped its requirement for a four-year college degree. Instead, young men with two years of college would be accepted for flight training, presuming they could pass a challenging battery of academic and physical tests.

Elwyn could and did.

"MY FLYING HAS BEEN PRETTY
GOOD LATELY"

The family was as keen for Elwyn to stay as he was to leave. He was their oldest son, and Mom and Pop hoped that he would remain at home and help with the ranch; at least part of it would eventually pass to him. Nevertheless, Elwyn couldn't resist the opportunity to fly. "He didn't want to have anything to do with the ranch," brother Ernie said.[1]

His parents worried. They worried that he might stumble and fail to realize his dream. On the other hand, they worried that he might make the Air Corps a career and never return home. And, of course, they worried that he might be hurt or killed. In the end, they didn't press him to stay on the ranch; they had always told their children they were free to choose their own way in life.

"Mr. Prescott told me today that if I continue to go as I have been, I'll be at the top of my class when I get out of here," Righetti wrote in early December 1939. "He's really pleased with my progress, and so am I."

Bob Prescott was an instructor at the Ryan School of Aeronautics in San Diego, California, where Righetti was working his way through the primary phase of flight training. Ryan's operation, self-proclaimed as "America's most modern school of aviation," had been in service since 1932, and was one of nine that the United States Army Air Corps, or USAAC, had contracted to provide initial flight training to the unprecedented numbers of cadets it was busy recruiting.[2] At that point the service counted fewer than three thousand pilots in its ranks. It was a number that was desperately short of what Major General Henry "Hap" Arnold—the tireless and visionary head of the Air Corps—knew the nation needed.

By late 1939 the Germans and Soviets had been consolidating their conquest of Poland for more than two months, and Arnold was in a race to create a world-class air force capable of prevailing in the event the United States was pulled into the new world war. Well-trained pilots were critical to such an organization and the USAAC was not yet equipped to produce them. "Right now, we needed to train 100,000 pilots and the most we were turning out were about 750 a year," he said.[3]

"I invited some of the best civilian flying school people in the country to my office," Arnold said. "I made them a proposal." He asked the flying schools to house, feed and train cadets in the primary phase of training. And he asked them to do it on their own dime until he could get Congress to appropriate the necessary funds. "We would furnish them the planes and the small supervisory personnel necessary; they would be paid so much a head for graduated students and a smaller flat sum for each washout." It was an audacious request but the power of Arnold's personality prevailed. Moreover, the promise of business on a scale that the schools' owners never imagined possible was compelling. "Late that afternoon they came in to see me again, and told me there was no doubt about it—they could do it!"[4] For their trouble, the schools were to be paid $1,170 for each student they successfully trained.[5]

When Arnold initially made the deal with the flying schools during 1939, they were told to expect to produce a total of 2,400 primary phase graduates per year. By the end of that year, the quota was raised more than twelve-fold to thirty thousand.[6] It would grow even more.

Righetti and his thirty-six classmates at Ryan were among the very first of the nearly half-million young men who eventually started pilot training during the wartime period. Although much of the rest of the world was at war, the fighting was still far away and the pace of the training, although demanding, was not as frenetic as it would eventually become. Consequently, Righetti found time to enjoy himself outside of training. "I went riding back in the hills Sunday with Mr. Prescott and had a keen time. I really get along swell with him and his wife, Ruth [Grace] Prescott, who's a nationally known aviatrix—she won a transcontinental race [Chatterton Air Derby] in 1935, and she really likes me."

Notwithstanding these sorts of diversions, Righetti worked hard and it showed. "Boy, I've been so darn busy lately that I just couldn't write—and that's a fact," he wrote in mid-December. "I've managed to catch up a little tonite so I feel that I do owe you a letter. My flying has been pretty good lately. I got the best grade in the class last Friday when I flew my first stage. I've got about 15 or 16 hours now and really think I'm doing a pretty good job."

Righetti flew the PT-13 Kaydet at the Ryan school. Originally designed by Stearman, and most often known by that name, its manufacture was continued by Boeing when it bought Stearman in 1938. It was a single-engine, two-place biplane that ultimately became an iconic trainer—in different variants—for both the Air Corps and the Navy. Simple and rugged, it was easy to maintain and capable of absorbing the different sorts of abuse that neophyte fliers were so imaginative in delivering. More than ten thousand in a number of variants were eventually produced.

Certainly Righetti's considerable flying experience—relative to most of his peers—was an advantage during this early stage of flight training. However, that experience could be a double-edged sword as the Air Corps' style of flying was not always consistent with what was taught by civilian instructors. Consequently, habits previously learned often had to be unlearned—and in a hurry. Habits being second nature, this wasn't always easy. Indeed, it was not unusual for students with many hundreds of civilian flying hours to be eliminated, or "washed out," because they simply could not adapt to military instruction.

In fact, it wasn't unusual for *anyone* to wash out. Through the war, only just more than half of the carefully screened and selected men who started flight training successfully completed all three phases: primary, basic and advanced. As might be expected, most of the eliminations occurred during the primary phase where a cadet's inability to physically and mentally adapt to the dynamism of flight usually became quickly apparent.

Certainly that was the case with Righetti's class. "We've had a little tough luck with some of our planes lately. There have been two freak accidents and two ground loops," he wrote. "Outside of lost fabric, the loops weren't serious, but three planes were washed out [destroyed] in the other catastrophes. One, a grandstand pilot, dipped a wing in and nosed over when he looked out at a crowd. The other, a Stearman, came down and landed right on top of a Ryan [PT-16] that was landing. It is a miracle that no one was hurt. Both of these ships were pretty well torn up. The guys, a student and the instructor, ducked when they saw it coming and just saved their necks. The side of the Stearman tore off enough of the top of the Ryan to start a good junk yard."

"Each one of these wrecks washed out a man—'lack of judgment,'" Righetti recounted. "Six fellows have now been eliminated and more are expected daily." This represented a failure rate approaching twenty percent after only a month of training. It was a typical trend that held steady to the end of the war. Ultimately, Righetti finished the primary phase with good marks and was sent to Randolph Field, near San Antonio, Texas, in February 1940.

Randolph was the seat of the Air Corps training establishment. Although the Army taught pilots at 27 different airfields during World War I, those bases were shuttered immediately following the cessation of hostilities in 1918. During the next several years, such flight training as was done by what was then known as the Air Service was performed at various locations in an almost haphazard fashion. Eventually, the course of training achieved some stability with primary flight training conducted at Brooks Field in San Antonio, while advanced training was taught at nearby Kelly Field. At that time there was no middle, or basic, phase of training.

However, it was recognized that the service—renamed as the Air Corps in 1926—needed a proper, purpose-built "schoolhouse." Construction of a new airfield was begun in 1929 according to plans that melded the latest in city planning to the most advanced ideas in airbase design. Concentric streets with connecting spokes ringed the hangars and other flight-related buildings that lined three sides of what was then a circular landing area.

The installation was dedicated as Randolph Field. It was named after William M. Randolph, a member of the naming committee who, ironically, was killed in a plane crash. When it opened for the primary phase of training during November 1931, Randolph was already recognized as a masterpiece. Not only was the blend of Spanish Colonial Revival and Art Deco architectural styles done to perfection, but the layout of the airfield and its supporting infrastructure proved to be every bit as efficient as its designers had hoped. From that point, Randolph Field was known as the "West Point of the Air."

And it made quite an impression on Righetti when he arrived less than ten years later. Among its many features, he was particularly taken by the meals. "I thought Ryan fed well," he wrote, "but Randolph makes Ryan grub look like dog food. In the first place, we enjoy officers' mess. Every meal is a formal occasion—table linen, including cloth napkins, a long string of silverware, soft lights and salads (individual), soup, at least two main courses to choose between, and several vegetables. Cake and ice cream are common desserts but we always have strawberries or chocolate sauce for the ice cream. On Washington's Birthday we were given two-pound boxes of chocolate-covered cherries, and day-before-yesterday a carton of cigarettes apiece (I sold mine for a buck)."

The aircraft Righetti flew during the basic phase was the North American BT-9 Yale. The BT-9 was a good example of how Arnold primed the aviation industry's pumps during this period by contracting for existing designs that were, at a minimum, "good enough" for the task at hand. "I felt that every factory must be given orders for maximum production, whether it had won a design or flight-test competition or not, whether it built planes of its own design or some other firm's."[7]

This practice served several purposes. Firstly, it kept manufacturers afloat so that if America entered the war, there would be factories and a trained workforce available to build the needed aircraft. Those factories and workforces could then be expanded as required. Also, Arnold's approach obviously got aircraft into the hands of the men who needed them. And it additionally gave the Air Corps an opportunity to try out different types before selecting the one or two that were best capable of performing specific missions or tasks.

First flown only a few years earlier in 1936, the BT-9 was a single-engine, two-place, low-wing monoplane with fixed landing gear and enclosed cockpits. It was an iteration of a line of trainers that eventually evolved into the famous AT-6 Texan. It was satisfactory for its purpose although it did have quirky characteristics in slow-speed flight. Ultimately, the Air Corps added roughly two hundred examples to its inventory before switching procurement to updated variants, most notably the BT-14.

Righetti liked it. "I guess I'll get along OK with my flying, since I'm crazy about the BT-9," he wrote. "It is a very heavy ship compared to the ones I've been accustomed to flying. It weighs over 2 tons [fully loaded] and has 400 horses. It cruises at 140 MPH and I imagine would top around 170. It's really a peach to fly and Pop, it would make you feel safe on account it doesn't bob around quite so bad as the Aeronca K—I'll take you up sometime."

The schedule that dictated Righetti's daily life was structured and demanding, but not harsh by any measure. He described his typical day as a "real snap." Reveille came at 5:30 followed by breakfast at 6:15. The two hours from 7:30 to 9:30 were spent in the classroom. The cadets then moved to the flight line where they were given a briefing prior to two hours of flying from 10:00 to 12:00. An hour of rest and lunch took up the period from 12:00 to 14:00, followed by a one-hour class on Morse code.

The afternoon was rounded off with physical education from 15:00 to 16:00, followed by a rest period that lasted until the evening meal which ran from 17:30 to 18:00. The rest of the night was free for rest and study until 21:00 when the cadets were expected to see to their ablutions before taps was blown at 21:30. The schedule guaranteed more than eight hours in bed prior to reveille the following morning. Moreover, Wednesday and Saturday afternoons were free, as were Sundays.

Righetti was competitive by nature and was anxious to solo in the BT-9 as soon as possible. "I am at present making out very well," he wrote. "I have logged three-and-a-half hours dual time and I expect to solo perhaps tomorrow. If I do I will have soloed in almost record time, but if I don't," he explained, "I won't feel too awfully bad as average time is six hours. Time of solo depends almost entirely on the instructors as some teach a lot of fundamentals and then solo their students, while others want their students to solo early and learn the fundamentals later. I have one of the former types of instructors but feel that I'll solo early as he tells me that I've made very satisfactory progress on my fundamentals."

As it developed, he had to wait longer than he wanted. "I finally soloed today," he wrote a few days later on February 27, 1940. "I could and should have soloed days ago, but the ceiling [lowest cloud layer] has been 600 feet or less since Sunday. And today is a typical southern summer day—it is *very* hot. And we got our full uniforms yesterday—they're all wool and we have to wear upper and lower underwear. Gawd!"

Although the pace at which the cadets washed out during the basic phase was slower than it had been during the primary phase at San Diego, it still continued. Cadets were eliminated for any number of reasons including poor academic performance, inadequate flying skills or disciplinary breaches—among many others. Sometimes, it took only a single, seemingly minor incident such as a hard landing or a breach of flight rules, to cause a cadet to be sent home.

And Righetti, as did every cadet to a certain degree, worried about failing. "I feel that my chances of getting through here are very good although there are plenty of washouts. However, the more washouts I see of the fellows that I know have 'plenty on the ball,' the more convinced I become that he who survives either leads a 'right' life or is a superman."

It was partway through the basic phase of flight training that the students were permitted to use the radio. The experience was new to most of them as the aircraft they had flown during the primary phase had no radios, nor did most small civil aircraft. Righetti enjoyed the experience. "I started my first radio flying on Friday, and boy is it okay," he wrote on March 3, 1940. "We call in, get a clear field and take off. Then, we're supposed to stay tuned to the tower for further directions, but since most of the time they don't give us any, we just tune in some Mexican music and do our lazy eights and chandelles with a 'Mex' rumba accompaniment. What fun! Then, just before we come in, we call in and tell 'em we're coming in so that they won't think we've gotten away with Uncle Sam's $20,000 BT-9."

Notwithstanding his bravado, Righetti appreciated the beauty and sensation of flight. He was particularly taken with night flying. Already established as a top performer among his peers, he was among the first from his class of more than two hundred to start training at night. "It kind of thrills you to just sit up there alone with the stars and moon and the wind that blows against you. I love to fly with the hood [canopy] clear back," he explained, "so as to get the sensation of motion. You can see lights, millions of them, after you get up a bit. San Antonio off a ways, and in between, a bunch of little towns. The field is just a cluster of green, red, orange and white lights—some of them blinking. You've gotta watch them because sometimes they signal to you with them to see if you're minding your business. Most of the time they jabber at you by radio."

Righetti experienced difficulties during mid-March that tempered his usual temerity. He no doubt swallowed some pride when he reported back to the family: "I've run into a little trouble lately with my flying, so to speak. It's the same thing I had almost get me down in San Diego. They tell me I'm dumb and I don't like it so I try too hard to prove otherwise, and as a result, my natural ability suffers."

It came to a head when Righetti flew his twenty-hour check and "sorta messed it up." The chewing out he received included a back-handed compliment. "The flight check lieutenant said, in part, 'Righetti, I feel that you're the best flyer we've got in the outfit, but damn your hide, you don't use your head.' I knew better than he did that my real trouble wasn't that, but rather my old weakness of damfool carelessness."

The lieutenant told Righetti that he was to stay under his tutelage, "for a week or so to see if he can't 'bring out my ability' as he aptly puts it. He didn't say what he'd do if he couldn't, but he made it pretty clear that if I didn't learn to think (get over being careless), that I would be threatened with dire circumstances." Righetti tried to close the matter with a positive note: "I'll let you know just as soon as I see how I'm going to make out. I don't have any serious worries but I'm going to have to change my pace I guess." Despite his declaration that he didn't have "any serious worries," it is certain that Righetti felt otherwise; his entire future hinged on how he performed during the next several months.

As hard as General Hap Arnold pressed to build the Air Corps into a much larger and more capable fighting arm, there was still time during the prewar period to enjoy niceties that not only provided the cadets some needed diversion, but also—in theory—helped to develop them as officers and gentlemen. "We're starting to get excited about our next weekend guests, the five hundred Stephens College gals. We've all been handed a blind date and anticipate quite a time. They call here every three years (the other two they go to Annapolis and West Point). The school is a 'Rich Gal's College' where they go to learn beauty and grace."

Indeed, Stephens College was a private women's school founded in Columbia, Missouri in 1833. It specialized in the liberal arts and on polishing ladies for life in the greater world. No doubt, the school's administrators believed the heavily chaperoned engagements with young, prospective military officers were excellent opportunities to practice the social graces.

Afterward, Righetti indicated that the event was very satisfactory. "The Stephens gals were all that was said about them and more so—they were sure swell kids. We had dates with 470 of them and really had a time. My date was a little large, but she had a big escort too, so we all got along very well."

Aside from structured social occasions such as the Stephens gala, the cadets were allowed off the installation often enough to meet girls from San Antonio and the surrounding area. "The local babes continue to intrigue me—one gal, in particular. Her old man's a prominent lawyer and she's schooled in Louisiana. She's really a beauty, and very Southern. She's twenty-one [he was twenty-five] and has a voice that sorta gets you." Despite his obvious interest in the girl, Righetti soft-pedaled the notion that he had any plans to pursue her. He went on to advise his family that they didn't "need to say too much to *anybody* about anything."

"I'D RATHER FLY THAN EAT"

"Anybody" was Evelyn Shepherd, a bright, articulate and vivacious girl from San Luis Obispo. When Righetti was working toward his certification as a private pilot, she had shared his interest and learned to fly well enough to solo. The two were close and the families knew each other. Although there was never any announcement—and Righetti did not give her an engagement ring—there were varying levels of expectation that they might marry.

Evelyn visited him while he was training in San Diego and was eager to spend time with him in San Antonio as well. Although it seemed that he was anxious to preserve some sort of relationship with her, Elwyn was not as eager to advance their arrangement as she appeared to be. This was entirely understandable. As a cadet in the United States Army Air Corps—assuming he earned his wings and was commissioned as a second lieutenant—the world was his oyster. This was particularly true where women were concerned.

In fact, Righetti noted that he was wary of predatory females. "My local shes [sic] keep me kinda busy. I really have a charmer lined up now but am being very careful that she doesn't get any ideas. Lieutenants in the Air Corps go at a premium here. So I greatly fear that that's my greatest attraction."

The cadets were attractive as potential mates for several reasons. Firstly, the Air Corps had already screened them for their above average intelligence, physical condition and psychological demeanor and adaptability. These factors generally combined to make them interesting, companionable and steady. Additionally, the pay of a military officer, although not extravagant, was quite good. The average yearly wage of a man during 1940 was $956; Righetti's base pay, upon completing flight training and receiving his commission as a second lieutenant, would be double that.[1] He would also receive housing and other allowances, and as a pilot would receive flight pay equal to half of his base pay. So then, at the beginning of his career with nothing but upside remaining, Righetti would be earning three times the salary of the average American man.[2]

When it is considered that the girls maturing into young women at that time had grown up surrounded by the poverty and paucity of the Great Depression, there is little wonder that they were interested in the budding flyers. Aside from their individual attributes and their salaries, the young officers lived a dashing lifestyle as part of a glamorous and tradition-bound organization that promised stability and relative comfort. There was also a sense of community that was difficult to overrate. No matter where a man was stationed, he was bound to find friends from earlier postings, and sure to make new friends he would encounter in later assignments. Those friendships often lasted a lifetime.

In a sense, the officer community in the Air Corps was an exclusive club with both national and international chapters. But it was one with a serious purpose and one that was often deadly. Aside from the dangers the men would face in the event of war, flying was dangerous in its own right. During 1940 the Air Corps suffered forty-six fatal aircraft accidents that killed ninety men.[3] This was during a time when the service counted only 3,500 officers in its ranks.[4] Consequently, everyone lost friends to accidents. In fact, some of them would eventually become the friends that were lost to accidents. More would be killed in the fighting to come.

However, during most of 1940, Righetti's chief concern was simply getting through flight training. And it was a valid one. "This class," he wrote, "has had exceedingly bad luck in washouts, in that 47 have gotten it in the neck out of 249."

Aside from flying and ground school, military discipline also figured into how the cadets were evaluated. At that point, a significant degree of authority was exercised by upperclassmen. Each of the three phases of flight training—primary, basic and advanced—was designed to a nine-week schedule through which two classes matriculated at any one time while logging approximately seventy flight hours. As the upperclassmen graduated, the cadets of the trailing class—halfway through the phase—became the new upperclassmen who were charged with "mentoring" the cadets of the new class just entering the phase.

It was practiced in part because the service was short of the officers and staff needed to closely supervise the growing numbers of cadets. In its worst form it was little more than hazing. Taking examples from the military academy at West Point—but with less oversight—the barely-more-experienced upperclassmen harangued and harried their junior counterparts for offenses that ranged from genuine to groundless. Examples of gaffes that might earn demerits, or "gigs," included sloppy grooming, an ill-kept room, a failure to salute, tardiness, and poor manners in the dining room, among many others. Abuses were common and it was an environment in which bullies sometimes thrived. Upperclassmen sometimes made up offenses simply to harass junior cadets they didn't like. All the cadets had to endure this cycle during each of the three flight training phases.

Righetti survived the hazing in fine fashion; it spoke not only to his fastidiousness and intelligence, but also to the fact that he didn't make enemies. "I'm about as 'gigless' an underclassman that ever hit these parts," he reported. "I've been commended by the captain on my 'eagerness.' I've had two gigs—one, a dusty windowsill and the other an oily cocking piece on my rifle. We're allowed fifty in six weeks."

The hazing created a culture in which cadets in the junior classes were anxious to "give as good as they got" once they became upperclassmen. Righetti showed this same spirit when he wrote home on March 24: "I'm still doing as well as can be expected and am rather tickled at the prospect of being an upperclassman by the time you read this. Our upper class leaves Tuesday and our lower class arrives Wednesday. "Boy, here we'll really work them over."

On the other hand, despite the abuses, the practice was not entirely harmful. First, as intended, it did encourage the junior cadets to behave. It also provided examples of both good and bad leadership that the young men drew from later in their careers. And it revealed their ability to perform under stress. Moreover, it taught the cadets how to exercise peer pressure to influence the behavior of their classmates. In short, the system was an imperfect but practical tool not only for maintaining order and discipline, but also for teaching leadership.

The cadets looked forward to mail each day; letters kept them connected and grounded, and reminded them that, notwithstanding the abuse they endured from their instructors and upperclassmen, they were still loved by someone, somewhere. Righetti was no different and chided his family when they failed to write frequently. It was a theme that was repeated through his career. "Please drop me a line. I'd like to know what's up and you've written one postcard in two weeks. I've even done better than that, and there are six of you."

It wasn't much later that he received a letter from sister Elizabeth that upset him. That upset was likely magnified by the pressure he was already under as a flying cadet. "I've had a swell letter from Betty that sorta told me off," he wrote. "She went over me pretty heavily for ever leaving home. In a way, she's perfectly right, I guess. But she misses pretty badly where she insinuates that I deserted because the going was tough. I'd like to have you all understand that I've gone into this for only two reasons. First, I guess, is that I'd rather fly than eat." Indeed, Righetti's love of flying had always been evident to the family.

The second reason he offered was the fact that there was opportunity— "big dough"—in the aviation industry. "I've always thought of our outfit [family] sticking together and I do plan on using whatever I can get to help out. I hope that you've known this all along, but from the way Betty talked, there was some question in your mind." He closed the letter with an olive branch. "Please write me soon and remember that we Swiss are funny in that though we sometimes don't show it, we *are* loyal to our families, and that it's pretty hard to break the bond that holds us."

Meanwhile, Righetti continued to train, but under a new instructor. The change brought him back to top form. "I did manage to get a very good grade on my forty-hour check, so I'm practically a cinch to graduate [from the basic phase of training]. It's figured here that once we get by that, we are as good as through. I was the second in the class to pass it, so out of two hundred men, that's pretty good."

He also finished his night flying for the phase. "We had landings with the field flood-lighted, with wingtip landing lights and with flares. The first two are cinches, but it's quite a trick to release a parachute flare at two thousand feet in a high wind, and with the 'gun' [engine] cut, get down under it and land before it goes out. It necessitates a pretty steep dive, but once you master it, it's really the berries."

In the meantime, Righetti continued to enjoy the attentions of the local ladies. "These southern Belles continue to intrigue me, so you can't blame me if I attempt to carry out my policy of reciprocity." There was a coed who went to school in Austin and came home on the weekends: "She's an only child, has a new Buick Coupe to go to school with, and I gather is from a moneyed family. She is very attractive, and on top of that, is smart. She's 19, 5'6", weighs 119 and wears *a size 8 shoe.* You can see from this that she is honest."

Then there was the niece of Thomas Gilcrease, the millionaire owner of the Gilcrease Oil Company. "Did I tell you about Betty Gilcrease? She's my best local gal, and is she swell. She's making me a pair of P.J.s out of parachute silk that I furnished." He was also excited about another girl from a more modest background. "I had a *swell* date this weekend with a *swell* kid from down at San Benito, which is along the Rio Grande. She attends Our Lady of the Lake, the exclusive gal's school in San Antonio, and is really a queen. Her dad's a cowman and she's just about the finest person I've encountered as yet. They're not rich—she's making her own way through school. She speaks Spanish as well as English."

At the same time Righetti grew indignant with rumors that he and Evelyn were to wed later that year. "I see no reason why I should abandon the independence of single blessedness in November or any other time in the near future. You can quote me on that, and I'll see that a letter of explanation follows this to the proper sources [Evelyn] in order that we may quell this rumor."

Still, Righetti didn't hold himself blameless. "It's possible that I may have sometime in the past made statements that were perhaps misleading, but surely not a strong enough of one to marry me at any set time." He did declare that he was fond of Evelyn but not at all happy with the talk of imminent marriage. "In short, if it means anything to her, she might find that it was a damn fool play to make so much noise."

Although his flying recovered, he collected more gigs as he progressed through the basic phase. "I got five at one crack for being late to Call to Quarters, Sunday nite. It was worth it though—I was at Betty's [Gilcrease] for dinner. I was only ten minutes late and it won't happen again." A week later he bagged six additional gigs for more pedestrian offenses. "These gigs were two, for unshined shoes in my closet, two, for not getting my rifle in the rack in time, and two, for being in the shower when I should have been in mess formation."

Righetti finished the basic phase at the end of April 1940. "We are now officially through here at Randolph," he wrote on May 3. He was pleased that he completed the phase with strong marks for his instrument flying, "especially so, in view of the fact that I started out kinda weak." He explained that, "you get a canvas hood thrown over your head and must fly by the instruments and not by the seat of your pants which is nearly always wrong when you're blind. Since it is *the* thing in modern and future air work, a great deal of stress is put on our learning it well."

His love life grew messier during this time. "I have a formal invitation to Our Lady of the Lake graduation dance, to be held on Saturday nite. I'd sure like to go—the gal who invited me is probably the sweetest gal in Texas, but Ev kind of cramps my style." The reason that Evelyn was cramping his style was that she was in San Antonio with her mother to visit with him as well as family friends.

"You can see the complications I have to deal with," he continued. "I could pull the often abused but much used 'confinement' gag on Ev, but I'd feel like a skunk, so maybe I'll just tell her the truth, and maybe I'll just not go." Ultimately he noted that the relationship was coming to a close. "I'm just a little afraid that the Righetti-Shepherd nuptials are rather definitely postponed." Still, after her visit he did note, "It's been pretty nice having her [here]—it would have been nice having anyone from home."

The advanced phase of flight training was split between nearby Kelly and Brooks Fields. Righetti was sent to Kelly where his class was put into tents; the infrastructure expansion on the base hadn't caught up with the growing numbers of cadets. "There will be swell new barracks in September, but we'll miss them."

"I have high hopes of getting in the new AT-6 at Kelly which is just off the line," Righetti wrote. "A brand-new ship similar to the BC-1, but much more refined. It's an 'Alclad' [aluminum clad] job, or in other words has an all-metal finish. It has retractable gear, a constant speed prop and cruises at 185—boy, oh boy!"

In fact, although Righetti did fly the BC-1, he also was one of the very first of hundreds of thousands of students worldwide—over many decades—to train on the AT-6, which was an improved variant of the BC-1. Built by North American, the AT-6 was one of the most manufactured aircraft in history and was used by more than sixty different air forces. Ultimately, nearly sixteen thousand examples were produced. The South African Air Force was the last military user, retiring its aircraft in 1995.

Nicknamed "Texan" by the Air Corps, the AT-6 was a rugged, single-engine, monoplane developed as an advanced trainer, but which also saw combat during Korea, Vietnam and a dozen or more small-scale clashes, civil wars and counterinsurgencies. It featured sophisticated characteristics similar to the fighters to which cadets such as Righetti would advance. These attributes included retractable landing gear, a constant-speed propeller, machine guns and a radial engine that produced six hundred horsepower.

On May 16, 1940, just as Righetti was starting the advanced phase, President Roosevelt startled the nation with his call for annual aircraft production to be increased to fifty thousand. It was a ten-fold increase over the previous plan which called for five thousand aircraft per year. Putting Roosevelt's new goal into context was the fact that the Air Corps aircraft inventory—of all types—at the time was only three thousand. In the event, the plan was not ambitious enough and was eventually overtaken by other plans which themselves were made obsolete by more updated plans.

Arnold was certainly gratified to see aircraft production capacity expanded, but he knew that an air force was much more than massive numbers of flying machines. Rather, it was the right numbers of the right types of aircraft. It was the logistical capacity to support those aircraft with material and spare parts. It was mechanics to maintain them. It was airfields from which to operate. It was support personnel—cooks, clerks, doctors, meteorologists and many more—to keep everything running efficiently.

And it was well-trained pilots and crews to operate the aircraft. "At a meeting in the White House, on May 14, 1940," Arnold wrote, "the President agreed that I should get 106 million dollars for a training program, including building costs, gasoline, transportation, and training airplanes of the primary basic and advanced types. Once Congress had okayed this Executive Directive, we had in sight a setup which would permit the training of 6,300 cadets simultaneously. It enabled the Air Corps to start training pilots at the immediate rate of 7,000 a year, and promised me a 12,000-pilot production within a year."[5] In fact, the pilot production rate eventually grew to more than one hundred thousand per year. Righetti was part of the very beginning of the most massive pilot training program in history.

As much as Righetti liked Randolph, and San Diego before it, he absolutely loved his time at Kelly. "This place is without a doubt the swellest place in Texas, and that's a lot of territory," he declared. "I soloed the BC-1 yesterday after an hour's check, and checked out in a new AT-6 this morning. Boy, what ships! The BC-1 is a couple of years old, so is rather antiquated in this game. But all the AT-6s are less than three months 'off the presses.' They both have 600 horses but the AT-6, though bigger, is lighter and cleaner, so cruises 20 or 30 MPH faster."

Near the end of May 1940, Righetti mentioned the war in Europe and what it might mean to his future. His observation was remarkably perceptive: "Just in the event that the hair-pulling across the water makes you wonder about the future security of Army flyers," he wrote, "here's one slant. It's entirely possible, and even probable, that if the mess lasts long enough, and gets dirty enough, the U.S. will be dragged in. But with the newest air force expansion program, before we can fight we have to have flyers, about ten times as many as we have. And before we can have flyers, we have to have instructors, and that's where we who fly a little better than the average come in."

In other words, the best flyers from Righetti's class—40-D—would serve as instructor seed corn for the massive air force Arnold was building. "I guess that unless this thing [America's entry into the war] cuts loose too soon, we'll spend the next few months teaching boys to handle airplanes. That has a lot in its favor, but it may become just a trifle boring in time. It's darn safe though," he continued, "pays a little extra in flight time, gives plenty of hours, and really is rendering a service to old Uncle Sammy. He'll put us where we can do the most good." Righetti additionally noted that, given the choice between fighting and teaching, he might prefer to stay in the States and perform the latter.

His next declaration proved to be as wrong and ignorant as his previous observations on training had been prescient. "Even in the event that I become one of Uncle Sammy's fighting boys, attack or light bombardment [his desired specialty] is almost as safe as a porch swing on a lawn in California. Anti-aircraft is the big threat for the boys off the ground," he declared, "and attack ships fly so low that the dough boys can't swing a gun on them before they're gone. Refer to your war news telling of the German dive bombers for verification." He was dead wrong. In Righetti's defense, he was still a cadet working his way through flight training. Many men of much higher rank were—and would be—much more mistaken about much more important matters.

To this point in his short career, Righetti had assumed that his physical size precluded a career as a pursuit, or fighter, pilot. He learned otherwise while he was in advanced training: "I passed my semiannual physical with a better mark than when I enlisted. Boy am I healthy! I managed to skip a meal and shrink on the measurer so that my dimensions are five feet, ten-and-one-half inches, and 167 pounds. This will allow me to get into pursuit, should I care to, with a half-inch waiver, which is the maximum allowable."

It was at this time that Righetti offered his personal thoughts on the notion of the United States going to war in Europe. "I'd hate to think that this country is dumb enough to fight anyone else's battles for them again. At least, without a lot better excuse than last time." His views were not uncommon, as many Americans were still very wary of getting involved in the fighting. However, with France crumbling under a concerted German onslaught, attitudes were changing.

Indeed, Righetti's own tone changed just a short time later on June 10, 1940—the eve of France's total collapse. "The war progress continues to surprise us. But I don't think we'll be over there for a while yet. Although FDR did sound a little like he thought we might. None of us really worries too much about it, however." On that day, Roosevelt had not outlined a plan for the United States to enter the war, but declared, "we will extend to the opponents of force [the Allies], the material resources of this nation; and, at the same time, we will harness and speed up the use of those resources in order that we ourselves in the Americas may have equipment and training equal to the task of any emergency and every defense."[6] Although he might not have considered it, Righetti was one of "those resources," and he was definitely in the "harness."

Notwithstanding the stress of flight training, the shadow of the war in Europe, and the girl-trouble he had created for himself, Righetti still found time to let his family know that he missed and appreciated them. He sent a note to Pop: "I do think of you all the time, especially so when the going gets a little tough. I don't know who could be a better example of 'stick-to-it-ivness' than you are. And whenever I get a little griped at what might be termed Army highhandedness, I always remember your invaluable advice: 'Anything worth having is worth working for.' It's surely been worth it though," he continued, "The chances are better than even that I'll get an instructor's job, since I'm still comfortably among the top ten fellows here."

Righetti's relationship with Evelyn continued its long-distance deterioration. "Ev called last nite and did a little raving, but cooled down okay, finally. If that dame isn't darn careful, she's going to make herself darn unpopular with a big Swiss pal, I know." The bond they had presumably shared in San Luis Obispo would have been difficult to preserve in such circumstances even if Righetti had been fully committed to it. Without that commitment, it stood little chance of surviving.

It seemed that his liaisons with one or more of his local ladies might also have reached low ebb during this time. "Texas has some swell and some awfully attractive people," he wrote. "But they drawl, and so many people who drawl are easygoing, and easygoing people are too much like I am, to tie up with—figure that out!"

It was apparent that the pressure of the actual flying instruction during the advanced phase was not as great as it had been during the previous two phases. In fact, the cadets were paired together for many of their instrument training flights; this freed instructors for other duties while giving the students additional confidence. "We have a plenty swell time with instrument instruction, hauling each other around," Righetti wrote on June 10, 1940. "This A.M., my student Roberts [Fred] wrote a five-page letter while I flew him around. He's pretty good, so I didn't insist he stay under the hood the whole 1½ hours he had scheduled."

Formation flying was also introduced during the advanced phase. "Everything's well by me," Righetti reported. "We're flying enough to log 3½ hours daily, which is a lot of time in the air. The formation *work* is just that. Holding one of these babies just off of two other guys' tails is a real job. It's dang interesting, but you do have to keep on the ball."

On the other hand, Righetti failed a ground school test for the first time. "I'm rather disgusted with myself," he wrote. He was restricted to certain areas of the airfield until he passed the exam, but wasn't particularly bothered by that aspect. "It's okay though—I didn't have any money anyhow."

Still, failures in the classroom were preferable to failures in the cockpit. "Jake Hanna had a little trouble the other day when he taxied into a ship [aircraft] on the ground," wrote Righetti. "This is especially tough since taxi accidents are branded as just plain dumb." Indeed, lapses in judgment or periods of inattention were considered more problematic than lack of proficiency. Training could overcome many problems, but it was difficult to train a person out of the tendency to make stupid mistakes. "So, he took a pretty heavy razzing and worse, a darn good bawling out. He cut the other ship up pretty badly with his prop."

Ultimately, Hanna was not washed out. No doubt, his performance to that point was carefully reviewed and it was determined that keeping him was still likely to benefit the Air Corps. It is also likely that after having invested so much time and effort in him, it was felt that sending him home at that point would have been a waste.

Moreover, it wasn't just students who had mishaps. "We had a pretty good laugh on my instructor, Lieutenant Van Allen," Righetti wrote. "He was on a cross country [flight] to Miami over the weekend and, in coming into a field bounded by the gulf on the upwind side, he let his motor cool a little too much. Then, because he was a little too high he decided to go around. When he poured the coal to her she just cut out over thirty feet of water. Result: They're still fishing for the ship (BC-1), and he and his passenger had to swim in."

As the end of his training edged closer, Righetti's letters switched focus from his flying to other matters. He wanted his family to make the trip from California to Texas to help him celebrate his graduation. It was a notion he had periodically raised for several months. In mid-June he wrote, "I sure hope you can see coming down." On July 4, he was more pointed: "I sure do want you all to come down if you possibly can. I'll be able to help out on the expenses, but stand by for further information. We graduate three weeks from tomorrow—that's pretty sudden-like." When he asked again on July 15, his note carried an exasperated edge. "I would like to have you down, regardless, but I realize that it's a plenty tough trip and might be kinda expensive. And I wish you'd let me hear your views once in a while. I don't know if you even want to come."

In the same letter he described his final fitting for the uniforms that were required to be commissioned as a second lieutenant. It shed additional light on his long-term plans. "Beside the uniform, we must buy either dress blues or a tux. I'll get the tux because dress blues cost $115 and the tux only about $50 for both summer and winter outfits. Since I don't expect to stay in the service, the dress blues would be out in civil life."

United Press carried the story of Class 40-D's graduation. "Kelly Field was moving along Thursday with its part of the Army Air Corps expansion program as officers of the air training school here prepared to graduate over 200 cadets Friday [July 26, 1940]. The graduating class will be the fourth group of over 200 that has been sent forth with 'wings' since last March 23. The present program calls for training 7,000 Army pilots a year."[7]

Ultimately Mom and Pop did travel to Kelly Field for their son's graduation and his commissioning as an Air Corps officer. And so did Evelyn. "I tried to talk her out of it, but she kind of insisted," Righetti noted. As he hoped, the ceremony and subsequent celebrations were suitably grand and both Mom and Pop were well pleased. Moreover, he was happy to learn that he had been ordered to duty as a flight instructor.

"I'M REALLY ENJOYING THIS ALL"

"Shepherd called me today," Righetti wrote shortly after his graduation, "to reassure me that she had nothing to do with an article that recently appeared in the local paper. Boy, if I was ever fed up with anything, this is sure it. Good gosh, why doesn't someone get smart? I suppose it's mostly my fault, but this marrying business—well, you know how I stand on that."

Notwithstanding his girl problems, Righetti settled into the role of newly minted officer quickly and easily. "I'm really enjoying this all, and still am really tickled to be an instructor." While he waited to be assigned his first set of students, he set up house in town with two other instructors. They rented an apartment with a phone, kitchen, laundry, and maid service for thirteen dollars apiece, per month. "And the little place is really nice. We get our own breakfast at a cost of about fifteen cents per day, each. Our lunches and dinners are good. Lunches at the officers mess at Randolph for thirty to fifty cents, and dinner downtown for about the same. We can live well on forty-five dollars per month, room and board. The people here are swell."

Without any students during his first few days as an instructor, Righetti was tasked to fly one of the airfield's flight surgeons, "a wop from Chicago named Brancato," so that the doctor could collect flight pay. The USAAC's official line was that its flight surgeons needed to experience flying firsthand to better understand what their patients endured. Brancato had never been in an aircraft. "It took me three hours to stop him from shaking," Righetti reported, "and by the end of five now, he will rather gingerly touch the stick, but not for more than a few seconds at a time. Boy what fun. He's rather frank about it though. He admits he flies only because he wants the flight pay."

Righetti was assigned to instruct in the basic phase flying BT-14s—an upgraded version of the BT-9. He welcomed his first students during mid-August 1940. "I now have a full-fledged class of cadets: Cobeaga, Hayes, Stockett and Pound—two of them poor, and two of them worse. I had hoped for a little natural talent to start out with, but no such luck. These mugs will give me something to work on, however, and since my captain knows they're punk, if I can do something with them, it will be very much to my credit."

The cadets were evidently not totally devoid of talent. "I soloed them all yesterday and today, but I'm scared every time they go out that someone will bring me back a little, old, orange piece of aluminum and say, 'Sorry sir, this was all we could find.'"

While Righetti grappled with relationships, roommates and a new job, the Battle of Britain—more than four thousand miles away—escalated toward a furious climax. Hitler planned to complete his subjugation of Europe with an invasion of the British Isles but before his forces could cross the English Channel, the Royal Air Force, or RAF, had to be neutralized; an amphibious assault could never succeed without air superiority. To achieve it, the Luftwaffe launched a concerted bombing campaign against England during July 1940, only weeks after the Fall of France.

It grew to be one of the fiercest air battles in history. The Germans struggled to adapt their tactical air force to a strategic mission for which it was ill-suited. The Luftwaffe's bombers could not carry bomb loads that were big enough, and its fighters did not have the range and endurance necessary to provide the coverage the bombers needed. Moreover, informed by poor intelligence and hampered by ignorance and ego, the Luftwaffe's leadership performed poorly.

But just as the RAF started to crumble under the weight of German attacks on its airfields, the Luftwaffe shifted the focus of its efforts against London. The great, old city—and its resilient citizens—absorbed the onslaught while the RAF caught its breath. Ultimately, the RAF recovered and dealt the Luftwaffe a battering that stunned the Nazi leadership. By the end of October the British had prevailed and an invasion was out of the question. The island nation from which the American air forces would eventually launch their greatest strikes against Germany was saved.

Arnold was impressed. "At the peak of its triumph, Göring's Luftwaffe was suddenly demoralized—not merely outfought, but out-thought. By the end of the battle, both air forces had scraped the bottom of the barrel; both British and German pilots and planes were nearly gone. But in the mutual exhaustion, the English victory was complete—not only on a ratio of two enemy planes shot down for every RAF fighter lost—but because the Anglo-Saxon world still stood intact."[1]

Meanwhile, Righetti continued to learn the flight instructor trade.

"I know that by now we're rather soundly condemned for not writing sooner, Righetti wrote home after the turn of the new year, on January 21, 1941. "But you know darn well there's a great deal to keep the newly-married busy."

He had wed.

Her name was, or had been, Edith Cathryn Davis. But she went by Cathryn; no one called her Edith. In truth, she was a young lady of many names: Cathryn, Kate, Katie, Katy, Kay, Kathy, Katydid and most especially, Kakie or Kaki. The origins of the latter appellations were lost somewhere in her childhood, but it was the name most often used by her family and close friends.

That Righetti chose Cathryn from among so many other attractive and intelligent young women said much about her attributes. Firstly, she was beautiful. Large, bright eyes dominated a symmetrical, heart-shaped face. Her smile was lively and ready, and it showed pretty, white teeth. It was all framed by thick brown hair, streaked through with flashes of auburn.

Cathryn was petite—only five feet two inches and just more than a hundred pounds. In fact, she was only eighteen and had probably stopped growing just a year or two earlier. Still, despite her age, she was intelligent and witty and always had a book at hand. And she appreciated education even though she was too young to have matriculated beyond high school. Whereas a vapid mind could quickly turn a trim figure and pretty face into thin gruel, such was obviously not the case with Cathryn. Physical attractiveness aside, it was likely her sharp—if not fully developed—intellect that compelled Righetti to overlook the difference in their years.

Unlike several of the women that Righetti had dated, Cathryn did not come from a well-to-do family. Her father, James Earl Davis, worked at a lumber mill in the "Big Thicket" of east Texas during the years following World War I. He was made a widower when his first wife died after bearing two children. He then married Cathryn's mother, Roberta Evans, who gave him three more children, including Cathryn. The family moved to San Antonio when she was still young, and lived a working-class life.

Aside from dates in town and at the officers' mess, Righetti took Cathryn to the airfield and parked his car near the end of the runway where he could watch his students take off and land. This not only fulfilled his instructor duties but also, presumably, impressed Cathryn. In turn, there is little doubt that Cathryn—with her good looks and syrupy south Texas accent—made quite a favorable impression on Righetti's students and the other instructors.

What imperative there was for them to marry so hurriedly is not known. Cathryn was not pregnant. It is quite possible that they were simply excited at the idea of marriage and by their feelings for each other. Certainly there was no reason why they should not have wed as both of them were of age and had no entanglements to preclude it. Moreover, it made no sense to wait until an elaborate wedding could be planned; neither of them could afford such a thing.

Regardless of the motivations for their rushed nuptials, they were happy. In her first letter to Mom—her new mother-in-law—Cathryn described the small ceremony in cursive script that was neat and confident. "We received your wire and were very happy to know that we have your blessings even though we did surprise you. We were married Saturday [January 18, 1941] at six o'clock in the home of our minister. My brother and youngest sister attended, and Elwyn's buddy [William] Markland was the only 'outsider' present."

Still, as happy as Cathryn and Elwyn were, it was evident as she closed the letter that she was fretful about being accepted by his family. "Please write us soon, for I am anxious to know just how great the shock really was." She signed off as, "Kakie."

"We're both very well and very happy," Righetti wrote a few days later. The two of them had just moved into a small house east of the airfield. "I absolutely cannot see now why I have been ducking matrimony so long. Perhaps it's because I've been waiting for Cathryn. She's just naturally a queen and tops as far as 'the gal for me' is concerned."

"Everything's okay with my class," he continued, "but I sure got handed a mean mess for students this time. It was necessary for me to wash my first boy out the other day, thereby ruining a darn good reputation that I was enjoying of never having lost a student. He was really rank however, and I'm sure that it's all for the best since he was bad enough to scare me. I had to talk him out of the controls twice when he attempted to freeze on them. This way, with him back on the farm, we'll probably both live longer."

His woes with the "mean mess" continued as he noted the following week. "Everything is still perfect, outside of the fact that my class turned out awfully rank. I washed [out] two and one resigned, so I just have one of the originals left." It was obvious that he was hurt that his small class turned out so badly. "I was kinda put out at losing these boys, but I got swell support, both from the flight and stage commanders. The washed out cadets have long since departed for home and safety, so I have gotten over the heel feeling."

Righetti's experience with this particular set of students might have been due to one or more of several factors. Firstly, it might have been attributable to poor luck. That is, the students might simply have been chronically substandard, and had somehow slipped through the training machine until they were assigned to him. Or, it is possible that the chemistry between him and them was a gross mismatch that made it difficult for him to teach or them to learn. There is also the possibility that, in its haste to get greater numbers of bodies into the flight training "hopper," the recruitment offices relaxed their screening to such a degree that unqualified candidates were admitted into training.

Indeed, after the fact, the service noted: "Not only were the numbers to be trained greatly increased after 1939, but the raw material itself was basically different. Though for some time yet the Air Corps was in position to depend upon volunteers and was fortunate in drawing perhaps more than its share of the more promising recruits, the motivation of the new volunteer was quite unlike that of the old. Under the pressures of a national emergency [impending war], he had chosen the Air Corps in preference to service in the Army or the Navy, and not because of the appeal to him of a career in the air service."[2]

Righetti and Cathryn gradually settled into real life. "Right now, I've got a dinger of a boil on my chin, which is really giving me a workout," he wrote. "If it's meanness coming out, I sure ought to be an angel from now on." Indeed, if that were the case, he should have been a saint by the time the massive sore finally healed. Penicillin was not yet available and the infection worsened as he reported a short time later. "I kinda got in trouble with my boil, so landed in the hospital for a few days. However, I'm out now and back on flying status, so everything's okay. It was right on the corner of my chin and jawbone so I was really horrible to see."

As horrible as he might have been to look at, it seemed to have made no difference to his new wife. "Cathryn, with a little of the novelty worn off, now turns out to be even better than I thought. Her cooking is excellent and this little old shack has sure turned into a home under her dang capable supervision. We are going to do something this month we've never done before—start a savings account. So, who sez that two can't live cheaper than one?"

Although his military career was just getting underway, Righetti saw it as only an early step for bigger and better things. He had already enrolled in a service-sponsored correspondence course for a law degree, and was additionally contemplating a business management course. He declared that once he had a few years of flying under his belt, "I should be lined up for a pretty fair airline executive position at age 35 or 40 when the docs start quirking their eyebrows at my blood pressure and eye reports." Such conjecture made it apparent to Mom and Pop that their son had no desire to return to the ranch.

As a married officer, Righetti was eligible to move into officers' quarters on Randolph. "We're at present rather tickled at the prospect of moving on to the post," he wrote during February. "We should be there within a week or ten days. The post homes are very nice as you must have noticed when you were here. Three bedrooms and two baths upstairs, maid's quarters, a keen big living room, dining room and kitchen downstairs. A big fireplace and air conditioning throughout." So, at the very time that Mom and Pop were finally getting electricity to the ranch house, their son was moving into an equally large residence with much more modern amenities, to include air conditioning. It had been recently occupied by a colonel and was located, "three doors from the officers' mess and pool, and surrounded by rank."

"Except for the fact that moving out there will necessitate our buying furniture for the bedrooms and living room, we'll save at least $13.75 per month by being post residents. And the $13.75 per month will buy our furniture. We'll also save the car and gas by not having to drive to work." That Righetti bothered to note cents reinforces the fact that fractions of dollars were meaningful during that time—at least to him and his family. Indeed, he bemoaned the fact that he was being "nicked" for $21.76 for federal income tax, and $13.40 in license fees for his car.

"Cathryn has been putting every cent she could wangle out of me into material to fix things up nice for when the folks come down. She's a junk-shop maniac but has really turned out some attractive furniture. She buys chairs, has me tighten them up a bit, paints them, reupholsters them, then slaps a slipcover over 'em and they do look pretty swell."

Righetti and his new wife scrimped and saved, as did most newlyweds. However, worries about dollars and cents were less important to Arnold and his staff as they scrambled to grow the Army Air Corps. It was in March 1941 that the plan to train seven thousand pilots per year was scrapped and replaced with a plan to produce thirty thousand pilots per year. At the same time, the number of air groups the service was racing to field was raised from 41 to 84.[3] And this was well before the former number was even close to being met.

Operating such a force would require infrastructure and support personnel that were additionally costly. Yet, with most of Europe under the thrall of the Nazis, Congress had long since stopped asking what the money was for. Rather, the nation's lawmakers were interested in funding even more. Indeed, if money was to be spent, congressmen were anxious to ensure that a fair share of it was spent in ways that benefitted their constituencies.

Righetti took Cathryn to San Luis Obispo to meet the folks during May 1941. She was understandably nervous about how she might be welcomed into the large, tight-knit family that Righetti had described to her, but she apparently was easy to like. She wrote Mom and Pop after the visit. "I certainly do appreciate you folks being so very nice to me and making me feel like I 'belonged.' That had worried me a long time and when you all were so very kind, I wonder now why it ever bothered me at all." Righetti confirmed Cathryn's feelings: "I don't guess I've said thanks to every one of you for being so swell to Cathryn. Kaki was worried to death over meeting you all, but has since not stopped raving over how much she loves each one of you."

"Our trip back was pretty swell. I was rather pleased when Cathryn said at Boulder Dam, while we were going through its innards, 'You know, when I see all this and stop and think just a moment, it doesn't make me scared of Hitler at all.' Pretty well put, wasn't it?"

Notwithstanding Cathryn's declaration that she was not frightened of Hitler, the dynamic at American military installations across the globe began to reflect the realities of the growing conflict. "Randolph is now a closed post," Righetti reported, "and no one can come on the field without darn well defined business. Everything (hangars, airplanes, gas supply, buildings, etc.) posts a 24-hour guard, so we feel like war is already here. We can't even get back on the base without positive identification."

The increase in security followed President Roosevelt's declaration of May 27, 1941, in which he stated, "that an unlimited national emergency confronts this country, which requires that its military, naval, air and civilian defences [sic] be put on the basis of readiness to repel any and all acts or threats of aggression directed toward any part of the Western Hemisphere."[4] At that point Great Britain, virtually alone, struggled not just to contain Hitler's forces, but simply to survive. Indeed, on that very day, British troops fought unsuccessfully to repel the German invasion of Crete. London and other cities in Britain were still being bombed. And the U-boat scourge was choking the island nation's lifelines to the rest of the world. On the bright side, the seemingly invincible German battleship *Bismarck* was sunk that day by the Royal Navy.

Roosevelt's pronouncement served several purposes. Firstly, it gave Hitler notice that the United States would not tolerate Nazi incursions into the Western Hemisphere. Moreover, it underscored the fact that the United States would defend shipping in the Atlantic and continue to send aid to Great Britain. Further, the declaration gave him executive powers over virtually everything related to the nation's security. This included not only military forces and bases, but also national infrastructure such as highways, ports, power plants and even radio stations and securities exchanges. And perhaps most important, it was an unequivocal message to the American people to prepare for war.

It was during this summer, following the declaration of the National Emergency, that Righetti first mentioned his weariness with flight instructor duties. "Everything's still Randolph and this place is getting monotonous. I know now that I can stay here as long as I want, so I've definitely decided to ask for a change—I don't want to fly these tubs until I'm too old to appreciate a hot airplane."

He wasn't alone in his desire for some sort of excitement beyond that provided by flight instruction. "Two of my better friends left yesterday for China with about 100 Air Corps men who are under contract to keep the Burma Road open. They'll clear $600 per month plus expenses and get a $500 bonus for each enemy [Japanese] aircraft shot down. Whyinell [sic] am I married and forced to be responsible? I could make $20,000 in two years if I lasted." Although he had no way of knowing it, the program he described was organized as the American Volunteer Group, which later became more popularly known as the Flying Tigers.

Although Righetti's brother Ernie loved and admired him, military service was out of the question because of the limp that polio had given him. On the other hand, his youngest brother Maurice was seventeen at the time and very keen to follow Elwyn's example. "Maurice, I realize that I've never actually given you my opinion on what I think you ought to do regarding your education," Righetti wrote. "I'm not going to now—it is, after all, very much just up to you. But I can speak from my own experience and considerable from the boys I know when I say, *get a college degree* if you possibly can. Above all else, don't let a lousy CAA [Civil Aeronautics Authority] program and a few hours in a beat-up [Piper] Cub turn your head. I frankly believe I can teach you more and better stuff in two weekends than they will in 35 flying hours."

The CAA program that Righetti viewed with such disdain was the Civilian Pilot Training Program—the CPTP. Started in 1939, it was designed to give no-cost initial flight training to as many qualified persons as were interested. Although chief among the publicly stated objectives was the expansion of aviation in the United States, its military value was apparent. It included basic flying and ground instruction and ultimately gave training to nearly half-a-million individuals. Righetti, like most military flyers of his vintage, considered it a second-rate program headed by civilian amateurs. Nevertheless, some of the most successful pilots in the coming war received their first flight training through the CPTP.

There was big news for the family in November. "We finally got the lowdown from the doc," Righetti wrote, "and he tells us it should be around June 1, but we're holding out for June 3, so Pop's first Righetti grandson will be born on his birthday." Cathryn was pregnant. "Cathryn feels swell except she's kinda excited—I guess she'll get used to it."

The news of the baby was accompanied by more welcome news when Righetti was promoted to first lieutenant on November 1, 1941. With greater rank came greater opportunities and rumors of imminent reassignment were upended on an almost daily basis by fresh rumors of imminent re-reassignment. New training bases were being made operational at an unprecedented rate and Righetti, only just more than a year removed from flight training, was now one of the most experienced instructors in the United States Army Air Forces, or USAAF; the Air Corps had been renamed on June 20, 1941.

With his experience—as thin as it was—Righetti was an obvious choice for taking a leadership position at one of the newly opened training airfields. "We're expecting to transfer soon and are hoping it will be while Kay is still feeling okay. Our new post will definitely be Mission and I think we'll like it." Righetti was likely trying to put some shine on an undesirable assignment that would take them to the hot, scrubby hinterlands of the Rio Grande Valley. Mission was the more commonly used name for Moore Field which was located about fifteen miles northwest of the town of Mission in south Texas. It was remote and offered few large town amenities.

"THE CHANCE OF A SKUNK
PICKING ON A LION"

The Japanese sneak attack on Pearl Harbor on December 7, 1941, brought the United States into World War II.

"Dearest Family," wrote Righetti the following day from his post as Randolph's airdrome officer. "Well, I guess everybody is a little astounded by the rather unexpected turn of events. I don't guess it'll be so bad, however, since the consensus seems to be that there's nobody we all would rather shoot than the Japs. Naturally, I couldn't say all I'd like to about our chances, etc., on account of military stuff and such, but let it suffice that the little brown brothers stand about the chance of a skunk picking on a lion. There'll be some smell, but I feel the final count will be about the same."

"I'd sure like to be in a fighting outfit," he declared. "The first casualty reports say I lost one of my students who was also an especial friend. I imagine there are strong feelings on the coast. Please tell me about it." Righetti went on to describe that the base had been understandably busy and that all leave had been cancelled. There was little hope that he and Cathryn would make it home during the Christmas holidays.

Then, with a baby on the way, he highlighted his new wife's practical nature now that the nation was at war. "Cathryn's planning on buying three-cornered cloths [diapers] right after next payday before cotton goods get too expensive." But he also brought up a more serious topic. "There's some little possibility that I may draw an assignment one of these days where Cathryn couldn't go, and in such a case I'd certainly like to have her with you all. I could afford about $250 per month board after making the car payment—now practically our only bill. I know you all and she would use the dough a lot more wisely than would her family, and she has expressed her preference of living with the Righettis. Maybe it would help you a little."

The war became very real, very soon. It was only about a week later when Righetti wrote the family: "We got this Xmas card from Chris 10 days after he was killed at Pearl Harbor. It was rough because he was a kind of fixture around the house when he was here. He was my favorite student."

As anticipated, Righetti was transferred to Moore Field during early 1942. He took Cathryn with him rather than leaving her with her mother in San Antonio where she might have been more comfortable. It was the third house she had set up in a year. She was weary not only from the move, but also from her pregnancy. "I can't use any clothes until July. I have been feeling fine lately. The only thing that bothers me is that I am getting too fat. My top weight should not be over 117 and I weigh 115 now."

"By the way, I think I will name Miss Righetti, Elizabeth Kyle. Kyle is a family name." She meant the name as a tribute to the Righettis as Elizabeth was Mom's name as well as the name of Elwyn's older sister. "But if it is a boy, I don't know what we will name it since Elwyn is going to choose the name."

Choosing a boy's name never became an issue. Elizabeth Kyle Righetti was born on May 30, 1942, in nearby McAllen, Texas. She was healthy and beautiful and had a lustrous head of dark red hair. Mom Righetti and Cathryn's mother came to help with the newborn, and both mother and baby thrived while Elwyn toiled at the flight instruction business, flying AT-6s.

With the USAAF expanding at a seemingly impossible rate, Righetti and Cathryn and the new baby spent only part of a single hot summer in the Rio Grande Valley before he was transferred back to San Antonio. The service was still trying to sort out its pilot training concepts and it shuttled personnel from one base to another until they fell into a niche or were overlooked and forgotten in the chaos. On October 7, 1942, Cathryn noted—without complaining—"You know we spend most of our time moving. We have moved three times since August 24."

Righetti was assigned to the 1030th Basic Flying Training Squadron at Kelly Field. They were given quarters about which Cathryn was judicious with her praise. "Our quarters here on the post are pretty good for Kelly Field. However, everything here is so old that it is about to fall to pieces. That is, everything but the flying line, and that is in very good condition. The other day [September 27] when Mr. President [Roosevelt] was here, they didn't give him a chance to see anything but the line. They whisked him by the quarters so fast it would have made your head spin."

At that point, Righetti had already been promoted to the rank of major. Before the war it would have taken him more than ten years—if ever—to achieve the same rank. However, by the start of 1943 the USAAF's officer cadre had already expanded nearly forty-fold from 3,500 when he was commissioned in 1940, to 140,000. Overall, the service had grown from 45,000 to 1.7 million men during the same period.[1] Indeed, only one in 36 personnel had been on the job for more than three years. In essence, virtually everyone in the USAAF was an amateur.

Nevertheless, the quality of the new men was generally excellent and proven performers were promoted quickly. Moreover, the relatively few prewar men who led them proved up to the task. Together, in combination with reasonably well-considered doctrines and plans—that admittedly changed too often—they were evolving into the world's most powerful air force.

Righetti was put in command of the 1030th and had the mission of preparing instructors to teach the basic phase of flight training. "Things are going well now," he wrote in early 1943, "but it's sure work, work, work. I have my school well set up and we're milling out instructors. I just finished writing the instructor's manual and guess I did a good job since it's to be used in all of the training centers, starting next class."

The pace never let up. "If I was busy before, I'm a hundred times that now," he wrote a short time later. "Honest, I didn't know there was so much work in the world." There was an upside; Righetti was making more money than he could have ever reasonably expected to earn at that point in his career. "Our financial setup is really improved and we're awfully proud of it. Each month I write $250 off my checking account and forget I had it. This will mean $1,000 each four months, and 3 Gs [$3,000] per year." He was on pace to save well more in a year than most men received in their paychecks during the same period. And he occasionally supplemented his military pay by other means: "On top of that, I've taken in $136 in poker lessons the boys have given me this month."

By this time, flight instruction, together with the administrative duties for which he was responsible as he rose in rank, no longer excited Righetti as they once had. More and more he wanted a combat posting. However, as a proven flight instruction expert he was needed where he was. Any of the men that he and his staff trained could be sent into combat. But none of them could step into his position and perform nearly so well; he was an important component of the USAAF's training machine. Pulling him from that machine would reduce its effectiveness. In short, the USAAF saw little upside to sending Righetti into combat.

Nevertheless, he found ways to divert himself. For instance, he was constantly "on the road." That is, both for training purposes and for official business, he flew across much of the nation. These trips afforded him paid opportunities to visit with far-flung family and friends, or simply to explore new places and meet new people, to include major and minor celebrities.

For instance, a conference took him to New York. "I started out very well by having a letter of introduction to Joan Roberts—star in *Oklahoma*, the play of the year. It was really some show. Being a stage door Johnnie was quite an experience, and Joan really showed me the town. She's just a kid but is really going places. She leaves for Hollywood in June with a seven-year contract at Selznick's. Watch for her—she'll be one of the big singing stars in a little while."

On another trip he lunched with actor Jimmy Stewart at Hobbs Army Airfield, New Mexico. Stewart, who became a genuinely skilled and respected combat bomber leader, was the student of one of Righetti's friends from flight school, Mark Richards. "Jimmy Stewart is stationed there and we had lunch with him. He's quite a chap."

As a more senior officer he was able to cherry-pick some of the better assignments. For instance, he might have served in some capacity in the making of the film, *A Guy Named Joe*, either participating in flying scenes or serving as a technical advisor, or both. A photograph shows Elwyn Righetti, smiling and in uniform, standing with Irene Dunne and James Cagney.

Another assignment had him spend a day with renowned photographer Ivan Dmitri, who was equally famous for his watercolor paintings and etchings under a different name: Levon West. "I spent today with Ivan Dmitri who is supposedly the foremost color photographer in the U.S. He's on the *Saturday Evening Post* payroll and makes much of their stuff. Watch for his story in about three months—it's on airfield mascots and should be interesting. I flew him to Brooks and Hondo. In return, he took about ten pictures of Kyle and thinks she's so pretty that they'll make magazines. He's sending us the proofs in a week or ten days and we'll pass them on to you all. He said to expect her on a magazine cover."

Sometimes Righetti simply visited with friends. "I spent Tuesday nite with Dick Ellis at Montgomery [Alabama] and we recreated ourselves by spot-lite hunting rats in the city dump. Got about ten apiece as big as squirrels."

He also flew home to visit Mom and Pop. Sometimes he flew directly from Texas, and at other times he picked up new training aircraft from the southern California factories and made the short flight north to San Luis Obispo where he spent a night or two before heading back to San Antonio. He often announced his arrival by flying low, fast and loud over the ranch house. "So, if a red-nosed AT-6 buzzes the house, please stand by the phone." His impromptu one-aircraft air shows were impressive. He once terrified sister Betty's young twin boys so badly that they hid in a box of laundry.

Betty remembered that he was quite taken with the musical *Oklahoma!* "He used to come home for a visit and he'd sing, "I've got a wonderful feeling, everything's going my way."[2] There were other diversions. He spoke Spanish well enough that he was sometimes used by his superiors to translate for visiting dignitaries. Moreover, he still loved to hunt and regularly took a shotgun on flights to the Midwest where he gunned for pheasant.

He also hunted at home in Texas—not always to Cathryn's pleasure. "Elwyn has gone hunting this afternoon again. He has been out several times and gotten so many doves that I told him not to bring any more home. So, he said he would take them down to Mother's. We have had doves almost every day since the season opened, and I think he is sort of tired of eating them too." Righetti's bird-hunting skills transferred well to competitive shooting and he was frequently sent to compete at skeet and trap matches at the national level.

Cathryn, busy at motherhood, tolerated her husband's frequent absences well enough. At least—unlike many wives—her husband was safe at home most nights. Other husbands, some of them trained by hers, were dying over Europe and the Pacific. And she and Righetti both adored the new baby that took so much of her time and attention. "She is really quite a girl now," she wrote. "She still looks very much like Elwyn, but is much more beautiful. Her hair gets lovelier every day—it is a rich golden auburn now and her eyes are still sort of 'no color,' like mine."

"At last she has two beautiful teeth and she is so proud of them that she shows them to everyone. Mom [Righetti], she still has that marvelous disposition—she is always laughing and never becomes sulky around strangers. Matter of fact, as the old saying goes, 'she never met a stranger.' Everyone here is completely captivated by her sunny disposition." Righetti was somewhat less loquacious, but it is evident that he loved Kyle very much: "The baby's fine and healthier and prettier each day—what a gal."

Cathryn, like many women of the day, was a smoker. Camel was her brand. Righetti didn't smoke, and wanted her to give it up. Indeed, he tried cajolery, persuasion and everything short of begging. Finally, he offered her one hundred dollars to stop. It was a considerable sum for the day but she ultimately declined.

Notwithstanding his wife's smoking habit, Righetti was blessed with all he could reasonably expect, or even want. He had an engaging, professional and well-paid career at which he excelled, as well as a beautiful wife and daughter. He was as active and occupied as he could hope to be. But more and more he chafed to get to a combat unit. Instead, he was kept in the training machine and given bigger assignments with greater responsibilities.

Meeting those responsibilities was an imperative. Even mid-war, the standardization of both ground and flight instruction was poor. Although the service had never put a great deal of emphasis on consistency in methods, the problem was exacerbated as it hurried to multiply itself many times over. That growth is illustrated by the fact that when Righetti graduated from flight training he was one of 1,849 student pilots under instruction. By mid-1943, the USAAF had 114,448 student pilots under instruction.[3] Understandably, in its rush to assimilate as many men as possible, the USAAF made missteps.

The experience of an instructor who taught college-level German before joining the USAAF offers a good example. Perversely, he was assigned to teach navigation. It was a mathematically intensive subject that had nothing to do with the language arts. "I don't suppose I knew much more than the kids I was teaching," he said. Implying that such mismatches were not uncommon in the USAAF's training organization, he declared. "I've never understood how we won the war."[4]

A key tenet of General Arnold's leadership style was that he told his subordinates what he wanted done, but not how to do it. He believed in giving them the freedom to perform their duties however they saw fit. This lack of direction resulted in shortcomings in the training environment. Flight instruction varied from one airfield to another, even among the same phases and among the instructors in the same phases at the same base. The results were predictable as, worldwide, the number of aircraft destroyed in flying accidents was double the number lost to enemy fire.

Recognizing that something had to be done to standardize training, and consequently improve effectiveness and safety, the USAAF instituted the Central Instructor School concept during March 1943.

The notion was for one school—the controlling authority for a specific discipline—to train, standardize, and qualify each instructor prior to turning him loose with students. So prepared, the new instructors would at least be teaching from the same syllabus. Central Instructor Schools were created at different bases for single-engine pilots, bomber pilots, navigators, bombardiers, aerial gunners, and so on. It meant big changes for Randolph Field; aviation cadet training was moved to other bases and several Central Instructor Schools were formed.

Righetti was part of the change as Cathryn noted during early February 1943. "Elwyn is going over to Randolph [from Kelly]. He has a good job over there. He is so modest he won't say much about it. All I know is that that he is going to be one of the Big Shots in the big school. We certainly have reason to be very proud of him."

Righetti didn't beat his chest about the new position. "My job isn't quite as big as it could be yet. Since we're training all of the pursuit [fighter] instructors in the country, the position is actually three times as large [as his job at Kelly Field]. So, my story in short is simply that I will be responsible for half the men trained for pursuit instructor in the U.S. (there will be two squadrons)." He additionally noted that his new boss, Lieutenant Colonel Fred Gray, was "a wonderful guy to work for and lets me do things pretty much as I please."

A public relations photo dated March 27, 1943, showed him leaning over a pilot seated in the cockpit of an AT-6. Righetti pointed into the distance. The caption read: "Major Elwin G. Righetti, 27, commanding officer of the 46th Squadron of single-engine advanced trainers, outlines a formation to Captain W. J. O'Donnell, at the new Central Instructors School at Randolph Field, Texas. Major Righetti, who received his commission as major last November after three years in the U.S. Army Air Forces, is in charge of one-half of the pursuit pilot instructors in training at the 'War College of the Air.'"

The Associated Press wrote a four-part series that highlighted Righetti's organization. It outlined the various fighter tactics that instructors were taught, to include aerobatics, formation flying, precision navigation and air combat maneuvers—among others. It additionally noted that the school taught the instructors how to get the best possible performance from their aircraft. "Flying is 90 percent headwork and ten percent hand and footwork. The ultimate point is that maximum performance of a plane in the air is the sum total of the plane's capacity and the pilot's ability, welded together in a single unit."[5]

The series ended by "emphasizing two of the most important qualities implanted in American pilots by AAF training—first, teamwork, the insoluble factor in flying success; second, complete confidence in the plane and in himself, a consideration of paramount importance to a flier whose future job will be to survive and kill in aerial combat." Indeed, these were qualities that would play a critical role in Righetti's future.

Despite his new billet, Righetti still worked to get a combat posting. He wrote confidently of being on his way overseas by August or September of 1943. It is not evident whether he preferred to serve in the Pacific or Europe. By this time, the Germans and Italians had been pushed from North Africa. Fighting in the Mediterranean and over Italy was still intensive and the enormous weight of Allied airpower—much of it American—was making itself felt as great numbers of superbly maintained, supported and flown aircraft pressed the Luftwaffe hard.

On the other hand, USAAF fighter operations from England only got underway during the spring of 1943. Moreover, the early-model P-47s in service at that time didn't have the range to take the bombers to the most important targets. Consequently, unescorted along much of their routes, the bombers were regularly savaged by German fighters. On the other side of the world, combat action in China and the South Pacific was red hot, but the Japanese were increasingly spread thin—unable to match the United States in men and material.

It is likely that Righetti would have welcomed any assignment that put him in harm's way. Hoping to follow his lead was youngest brother Maurice, who started training at about the same time Righetti moved to the Central Instructor School. "I imagine it is pretty tough with the kid away," Righetti wrote to Mom and Pop. "I rather think he'll make a big go of things and you all will be pretty proud of him—he's too smart to get hurt. I now have contact with him and I'll soon know just how big a man I am when I try to get him where I want him. I just guess he'll be an instructor one of these days to get some seasoning, then the two of us, with a little help, ought to be able to put this war on ice."

Righetti kept a close watch on Maurice and flew to Omaha where he was part of the College Training Program—a USAAF scheme that pooled aviation cadets until training backlogs were cleared. "I managed to get to Omaha Saturday evening so spent a very enjoyable time with the kid. He's well situated, happy and doing fine. I expect that Maurice will come to San Antonio Aviation Cadet Center about the last of July, so I'll really have him under my thumb." Whether or not Righetti's little brother appreciated such close attention is not clear.

However, as he approached the end of his training, it was apparent that Maurice's plans did not align with his brother's. Elwyn reported home: "After some discussion and considerable figuring, we find that he is destined to become another of Uncle Sam's fighting instructors. Maurice doesn't think so very much of it all, but I rather feel that the seasoning to be derived from it will make the assignment well worth his time." Ultimately, Maurice did enter instructor school following his graduation and actually flew with Righetti on a few occasions.

Elwyn and Maurice were not the only Righettis who served in uniform. Sister Lorraine enlisted into the Women's Army Corps, or WAC, during July 1944. The nation was anxious to get women into service in order to "free a man to fight," and Lorraine answered the call. It was a bold move as, notwithstanding the war, many citizens held conservative views against the notion of women in uniform. The coarsest and meanest factions tried to characterize these women as prostitutes or lesbians, and the wives of some servicemen worried about the temptations they might present.

But the family was proud of Lorraine. For his part, Elwyn was especially delighted by her service and maintained a steady correspondence with her. "Glad to hear that you're happy and surely nominate you for my heroine—you're quite a gal." As it developed, Lorraine did well and advanced quickly in rank as a clerk-typist and was ultimately assigned to work in the Pentagon.

While Righetti headed training efforts that would ultimately prepare men for the combat he so desperately craved, life at home offered its own mundane scares. "We had a little trouble the other morning," he wrote, "when Kyle swallowed a coke bottle cap. But, luckily it went down sideways so she could still breathe. And although it was nearly a half-hour before the doc got it out, she suffered no ill effects outside of a slightly cut throat. She's okay now."

"I'M GOING OFF TO WAR NOW, MOM"

Righetti's aspirations for a combat posting during 1943 went unrealized. Indeed, approximately half the American men who served in uniform during World War II never went overseas. Righetti didn't want to be one of them and ultimately received orders overseas in 1944. He tried to explain his motivations in a Mother's Day letter to Mom.

> I'm going off to war now, Mom. Not because I have to from the Army's angle—they'd prefer that I stay here—but because I have to from my angle. I'm terribly tired of this war and feel very strongly that I can do a great deal more toward ending it where the shooting's going on. I realize that you'll probably fret a bit over me, but you needn't, mom. If you had played this game even just [a small portion] of the 2,000 [flight] hours that I have, you'd know that you don't get knocked off until your number comes up. And when that time comes, there's nothing you can do.

His bravado continued: "I expect to get back from my overseas tour, but if I don't, remember that I kept a whole bunch of other guys from getting home too, and that I was working on my interpretation of being a good American." This declaration to his mother that he expected to kill the sons of many other mothers almost certainly did not comfort her. However, notwithstanding its callousness, it was a realistic assessment of the nature of his future assignment.

It is true that Righetti could have stayed at Randolph Field for the duration of the war. His unit—largely due to the energy he put into it—was doing very well. Indeed, the confidence that his superiors showed in him when they promoted him into the job proved to be well-founded. To their minds, there was no reason to send him anywhere.

However, Righetti still wanted a combat posting. Although it was clear, as he told his mother, that he believed he could "do a great deal more toward ending it," and that he felt a sense of duty as "a good American," those weren't the only considerations. Probably the most important motivation behind his desire to get overseas was that he judged he wasn't doing his part from both a professional and a personal perspective.

Professionally, many of his peers, friends and students had already completed combat tours, or had been shot down and captured, or killed. For instance, Fred Roberts escaped the hellish Japanese invasion of the Philippines and later spent a week at Randolph with Righetti and Cathryn. Righetti recalled Roberts's decorations in detail: "He got out of the Philippines with 2 [aerial] victories and a few scars—also the DFC [Distinguished Flying Cross], the Air Medal, the Silver Star and the Purple Heart." Righetti understood that the awards meant something, and would continue to mean something, through the war and beyond. And more and more, wherever he turned, there were uniformed men with decorations that reminded him that he had never even seen a shot fired in anger.

He jokingly referred to the trainer-choked skies around Randolph as a never-ending "Battle of San Antonio," but he itched for action. It was true that he was a critical contributor to the war effort, but his combat accomplishments—or lack of them—would be a factor in future promotions. As it was, many of the instructors working for him had considerable combat experience flying the same sorts of operations that his group was responsible for teaching. Notwithstanding his superior rank, he certainly must have felt his credibility was thin in comparison.

Moreover, despite the fact that his job kept him busy, Righetti was bored. In the entire USAAF, there were very few men with as much instructing experience. Additionally, with more than two thousand hours of flight time, he was as "stick-and-rudder" skilled as he would ever be. At Randolph, there was little more for him to learn or do.

Still, it is certain that Righetti had misgivings about going to war, as would anyone in his situation. He adored his beautiful wife, and Cathryn reciprocated with an obvious love for him and his parents and siblings. And she had borne him a treasure in the form of Kyle. He was a doting father: "Cathryn is 100% and you ought to see our beautiful dotter. I mean, that gal's a queen."

Righetti was also concerned about how and where Cathryn and Kyle would live when he left for combat. "Katy still hasn't decided definitely where she will spend her time while I'm across," he wrote. "So any suggestions along this line would be more than appreciated. It's high time we made our minds up." He wanted her to go to San Luis Obispo to live with his family and she had earlier said that she also wanted to do so. However, her mother lived only a few miles away in San Antonio and Cathryn might have dithered simply because she wanted to put off a decision that was certain to hurt her mother's feelings.

As much as he worshipped Cathryn, Righetti was still worried about her ability to take care of herself and Kyle if something happened to him. In fact, not long after they were married he had sent instructions to Ernie advising him that he would remain as the beneficiary of his life insurance. "It's not absolutely impossible for me to get bumped. And when and if I do, Cathryn would be a damned attractive widow [and] with ten G's [$10,000] besides, for some bird dog to chase." In the event that he was killed, Righetti asked Ernie to help take care of Cathryn, and to invest the life insurance payout.

Righetti's departure for combat became more real during early June 1944 when he was sent to Aloe Army Airfield near Victoria, Texas. There, he flew P-40s as part of a fighter conversion syllabus that emphasized aerial gunnery and strafing. With plenty of experience flying the P-40, and more flying time than virtually anyone at the field, he did very well. "I got a lot of good out of the 40s at Aloe," he wrote, "and my gunnery was excellent. I'm very pleased with my fighter pilot ability at this stage, so I shouldn't have too much trouble making a top hand on the other side."

But there were administrative delays in getting him to "the other side" and Righetti spent all of July waiting. By the end of the month the Allied armies were breaking out of Normandy and he wondered at the possibility of a sudden German collapse; Cathryn no doubt hoped for just such an event. He wrote home that both Cathryn and Kyle were, "Swell, but puzzled by it all." Certainly Cathryn, like millions of wives, was anxious at the notion of her husband traveling across the globe to be shot at. Righetti spent considerable time at the airfield rather than tip-toeing around a house that was charged with anxiety at his imminent departure. There, he took advantage of his unit's fighters to get ready for combat. "I've been beating our own P-51 and P-47 around considerable—getting pretty sharp too."

And then, on August 2, 1944, he was on his way. Before he left the States he was required to pass through the Overseas Replacement Depot at Greensboro, North Carolina, in preparation for travel to, and operations from, an undefined destination characterized as "cold, wet and windy." This was understood to be England.

The depot at Greensboro was one of the mobilization miracles that were so representative of the resources the nation put into winning the war. Built in less than a year, it featured nearly a thousand prefabricated buildings, including more than a dozen mess halls, five chapels, three libraries, a host of gyms and movie theaters, and a hospital. There, the men—up to forty thousand at any one time—underwent final medical processing, were issued destination-specific clothing, received lectures about a wide-ranging series of topics, and were matched to transportation overseas.

Righetti expected to pass through Greensboro quickly. "Finally got here and situated and like the place fine since I'll only stay ten days or so," he wrote on August 7. A week later he declared, "This place has become very monotonous by now." He was still stuck in Greensboro when he wrote the family on August 21, more than two weeks after arriving: "Goddam this place anyhow. The way the war is going I'll miss the whole European show if some knucklehead doesn't move me soon." In fact, during this period Allied aircraft gutted a group of German armies in the Falaise Pocket in eastern Normandy that numbered nearly half-a-million men. The stench of so many rotting corpses permeated the cockpits of aircraft over the battlefield.

During this time Righetti became aware—even self-conscious—of how young he was relative to his rank as a lieutenant colonel. "This is quite a barracks I live in," he wrote. "It's called 'Brass Row' with a capital 'A.' Restricted to colonels, it houses some 10 lieutenant colonels and 4 eagle jobs [colonels]. All pretty regular guys, but most with very impressive records. I sometimes feel I have no business here since I'm the youngest guy by at least 6 years."

He was obviously heartsick three weeks later when he wrote Cathryn on her birthday, September 11. By that time she and Kyle were living at the ranch in San Luis Obispo. Nowhere in the letter did Righetti mention his frustration at being held for more than a month at Greensboro. Rather, he seemed simply deflated. "Today, your birthday, and I've thought of you constantly. It's hell, no less, to be away from you." After some newsy bits, he chided her gently as he had received very few letters from her since he had left Randolph. He closed by reminding her how much he missed and wanted her: "I love you more than I ever have before, and would give everything I own to be with you now. Please write soon."

He finally arrived in England at the start of October; he described the weather as "wintery but not uncomfortable," and was assigned to the Eighth Air Force, commanded by famed air racer James "Jimmy" Doolittle, who became additionally renowned after leading a daring bombing mission against Tokyo during 1942. Righetti went to Fowlmere where he flew a couple of transition sorties in the P-51, and also to Duxford where he flew one of the 78th Fighter Group's P-47s. Although he had been on the island only a very short time, the English had already made a favorable impression. "British people marvelous, friendly, sincere and interested in our welfare—truly a wonderful ally. All of them have been through so much, too."

Righetti connected with a great many of the friends and associates he had made since entering the service five years earlier. His friend, mentor and former boss at Randolph, Fred Gray, was the commander of the 78th Fighter Group, part of the 66th Fighter Wing. Gray, who Righetti had described to his folks in 1943 as a "wonderful guy," shopped him around the 66th's headquarters where he himself had spent time before assuming command of the 78th the previous May. During these rounds Righetti made a good impression and was ecstatic when he was assigned to one of the 66th's fighter groups, the 55th, on October 24, 1944.

Righetti arrived at Station F-159, Wormingford, the following day. Wormingford, located, about sixty miles northeast of London, was the home of the 55th Fighter Group. He made his way to the pilot lounge of the 338th Fighter Squadron, one of the 55th's three squadrons. There, men chatted, or played cards, or read or otherwise occupied themselves. He found no peers there. Nor would there have been any peers in the 55th Fighter Group's other two squadrons, the 38th and the 343rd. When he started training in 1939 he was one of fewer than twenty-five thousand men in the United States Army Air Corps. Now, in October 1944, the service numbered well more than two million men. Consequently, of the nearly two thousand men at Wormingford, only Righetti and a few others had been on the job more than five years.

Among the pilots in the room, none of them had nearly as much flying experience. In fact, he had logged more than two thousand flight hours since 1939. But that time had been flown as an instructor at various bases in Texas. In those crowded skies he had trained the instructors of the pilots who now lounged around him. In fact, he had trained the instructors of their instructors. And even a few of *their* instructors.

The men in the 338th's hut—mostly lieutenants and captains—shot sidelong glances at Righetti. One of them remembered him as "tall, dark and muscular—not a bad looking guy."[1] They had no idea who he was, although they probably guessed that he was a staff officer from higher headquarters, or someone's friend or relative stopping by to visit.

Most of them would not have guessed that he was newly assigned to their unit. Fighter groups in the Eighth Air Force were typically commanded by a colonel, and sometimes a lieutenant colonel. The three squadrons that comprised a fighter group were usually led by a major or lieutenant colonel. These were leadership positions, and leadership at that time and place demanded combat experience. The awards, or rather the lack of them, on Righetti's uniform belied the fact that he did not have that experience; he had no idea what it was like to shoot at someone who was shooting back.

However, his skills as a leader and administrator were already proven. He had worked wonders during the time he worked in the training command—his advanced rank was proof of that. And he was gregarious. He genuinely liked people, liked to socialize and liked to learn. He only needed seasoning in combat before assuming a leadership billet in a combat unit.

None of these men knew any of that. And it is likely that they didn't particularly care. Most of them felt that after a year of combat operations the 55th was muddling along well enough. The 55th had originally started flying combat missions out of Nuthampstead, about 30 miles west of Wormingford, in October 1943. The aircraft they flew at that time was the twin-engine P-38. The USAAF's leadership had high hopes for the P-38. It had the range to escort the Eighth Air Force's heavy bombers deep into enemy territory, as well as the performance—at least on paper—to match the best German fighters.

In the event, expectations for the P-38 were never fully realized during its early service from England. Firstly, it was not an easy aircraft to fly and engine failures on takeoff or landing could be fatal. And upon encountering the enemy, the transition from cruise flight to combat involved so many steps that some men were shot down before they could even get their aircraft properly configured. Further, due to compressibility issues leading to loss of control—especially in the early models—German aircraft had only to dive away from high altitude to escape the P-38.

Nor was it an easy aircraft to maintain for the simple reason that it had two engines rather than one. Worst of all was the poor reliability of those engines. For a number of reasons, although they performed well in the Pacific and North Africa, they could not be made to work as well in the cold and wet of Northern Europe. Lives were lost because of it.

Many men hated it. Russell Haworth trained in P-38s and arrived at the 55th just as it was transitioning to the P-51. "Whoever made the decision to buy the P-38 as a fighter plane," he said, "should have been shot for treason!"[2] Haworth's contempt for the P-38, if not shared by all the type's pilots, was perhaps warranted by the 55th's experience, to include its first loss on October 15, 1943, when Hugh Gillette's aircraft simply caught fire. He bailed out over the English Channel and was never found.[3]

Another example was the experience of Victor LaBella who went down over Germany on March 22, 1944. "About twenty minutes into Germany my right engine began to lose power. I turned towards home and my good engine began to lose power too and I started a descent. I descended to the tops of the cloud cover at about 1,500 feet and decided to leave the airplane." LaBella rolled his ship upside down and bailed out. He was immediately captured and made a POW.[4] These are two among many examples that illustrate how the P-38 failed its pilots over Europe. In fact, Jimmy Doolittle wrote Henry Arnold that the P-38 was "second-rate" compared to the P-47 and P-51.[5]

Frank Birtciel was one of the 55th's old hands—part of the initial cadre of pilots that arrived in England in September 1943. He flew 72 missions in the P-38 and signed on for a second tour as the group was transitioning to the P-51 during July 1944. "At the time we wore British flying helmets [C-type] with earphones that stuck out quite a bit. When they brought a P-51B to the base for us to try, I had a hard time moving my head around inside that narrow birdcage canopy; I really didn't like it. But when I got a chance to fly the P-51D with the bubble canopy I found that I could look around with no problem. I was sold."[6]

"As it developed, I much preferred the P-51 to the P-38," said Birtciel. "It was far simpler to fly which made a real difference during combat. And I could stay warm in the P-51 which was something I could never do in the P-38. In fact, if we hadn't transitioned to the P-51, I wouldn't have volunteered for another combat tour because the P-38 was so miserably cold."

When compared to the P-51, the P-38's two engines were a double-edged sword. Although they provided a degree of insurance if one engine failed, they also doubled the odds that a pilot *would* experience engine trouble—two engines provided twice as much opportunity for something to go wrong. And a P-38 with a bad engine was a magnet for enemy fighter pilots. Indeed, the cockpit of a P-38 on one engine was a place no pilot wanted to be, although it was inarguably a better place than the cockpit of a P-51 with a dead engine, or one that was afire.

At any rate, certainly due in part to the shortcomings of the P-38, the 55th Fighter group had a combat record that was only passable. Relative to some of the other fighter groups in the Eighth Air Force's fighter component—VIII Fighter Command—it was not a high scorer, nor did it produce many aces. Following the move from Nuthampstead to Wormingford during April 1944, the 55th continued to fly its P-38s until July when it transitioned to the P-51. That transition was completed on July 18 and was regretted by virtually no one. The P-51 had better range than the P-38, was much easier to fly and maintain, and was faster. Most important to many men was the fact that the cockpit was comparatively warm and comfortable.

However, regardless of what aircraft a unit might fly, its effectiveness hinged at least as much on its leadership. When Righetti arrived, the group was commanded by George Crowell. He had been with the 55th since the early P-38 days and was generally considered to be a competent officer and administrator. However, his leadership in the air was described by some as indifferent. He was not aggressive and preferred to stay close to the bombers rather than to chase after enemy fighters.

Tellingly, Crowell had never been credited with any aerial victories. This was unusual as group commanders had more opportunities for air combat than anyone else. "He was very good at turning around," recalled one of his pilots. Another recalled that, "It was a big joke around the group that if the mission was expected to be a rough one, he would have 'engine trouble' and turn back."

Others had different recollections of Crowell. Herman Schonenberg, one of the 338th's young lieutenants, was one of those. "He knew what our priorities were and conducted himself accordingly. This may be why some would call him cautious. I personally had great respect for him and felt very comfortable having him as a leader."[7]

Captain Darrell "Pops" Cramer, the 338th's operations officer, approached Righetti and introduced himself. Of all the men in the room, aside from

Righetti, he had been in the service the longest. He was an ace and had combat experience dating back to the early fighting in the Pacific on Guadalcanal where he was credited with downing two Japanese aircraft. At only 21 years old, his hair was already starting to gray. Cramer recalled when he first heard of Righetti: "Shortly before the end of October 1944, my squadron commander told me there was a new guy coming into our squadron to get some combat experience. He told me I was to be the new guy's instructor pilot and [would] take him through the first few sorties. The new guy was Lieutenant Colonel Righetti."[8]

"After introductions were made," said Cramer, "it was obvious that he was anxious to get started, so talk immediately turned to combat flying." Cramer's recollections of Righetti were favorable. "True, he was older than most of us, but he did not look or act older. He had a boyish grin and a pleasing personality, and he was a pleasure to have around. He had a very good sense of humor, and he could laugh and joke with the best of them."

The plan to integrate Righetti into the 55th was largely his own, and was methodical and practical. Initially, he wanted to fly combat as a wingman. "If I'm going to make a good fighter [group] commanding officer," he wrote, "I do want to know how my boys operate."

Assuming his progress was satisfactory, he planned to fly as an element leader of a two-ship formation, and then as the flight leader of a four-ship formation. Squadron and group leader assignments—again, assuming he proved himself capable—would follow at the appropriate time. Considering his experience, none of this should have been particularly difficult for Righetti except for the mental stress of knowing that people would live or die based on his decisions.

Although Cramer was in line to take command of the 338th, he didn't see Righetti as a threat despite the fact that Righetti was senior to him. "He understood what was going on in our group and he was honest and straightforward in his comments and actions. For example, he told me up front that he was scheduled to go to another group as soon as he had gained enough combat experience to command the respect of the pilots in the [new] group to which he was to be assigned." In other words, Righetti's time in the 55th was expected to be only long enough for him to get the combat time he needed to take command of another fighter group.

Edward Giller was the commander of the 55th's 343rd Fighter Squadron. Like Cramer, he shared his experience with Righetti. "He approached me to learn as much as he could. I liked him—he was aggressive and eager to fly combat. He also talked with a lot of the junior pilots. This willingness to absorb information from everyone was not particularly unusual among the most successful pilots."[9]

Giller mentioned that Righetti was "eager." This was a trait with which he had been closely identified since his early days as an aviation cadet. And it was the basis of a nickname that followed him through the rest of his life; to many of his friends he was known as "Eager El."

As Giller noted, Righetti was happy to mix with the youngsters—the lieutenants. He liked socializing, joking and horseplay, and he knew that notwithstanding their junior rank, every one of the lieutenants had more combat time than he did. Consequently, he understood that there were things they could teach him. Russell Haworth recalled that he and his peers discussed fighter tactics with Righetti "extensively," and that he "didn't miss a thing." John Cunnick, another lieutenant, was likewise impressed. "I liked him. He was friendly and he listened to what you had to say."[10]

However, Righetti's somewhat egalitarian approach toward assimilating himself into the 55th was not without a bump or two. Anxious to ensure that he understood how the group's rank-and-file pilots lived, he decided to move into one of the open-bay barracks with a dozen or so lieutenants. He was keen to fit in and asked the lieutenants about housekeeping duties. Ray Sharp, a chubby young pilot who had been flying combat since that summer, told him to go outside and get coal for the stove. It was an impolitic order. No matter the arrangement, junior officers definitely did not tell lieutenant colonels to haul coal.

Righetti subsequently shared some well-considered words with Sharp. That he did not more demonstratively upbraid him was probably due to a desire to understand the unit's dynamics before making waves. The incident evidently had no lasting effect as he noted in a letter to Lorraine, "I live in a barracks now with my flight and never knew quite as swell a bunch of fellows."

All-in-all, his enthusiasm at having finally arrived at a combat unit never wavered. "I am so very happy with my assignment that I gotta tell someone about it," he wrote home. "If I had picked over all the jobs in [the] E.T.O. [European Theater of Operations], I'm sure that this would have been my first choice. Am flying the pilot's dream airplane [the P-51 Mustang] which really means a lot. If I don't get to the top of the heap in a few months it won't be because of a bad starting break."

As excited as Righetti was about the P-51—and he was very excited—every fighter group in the Eighth Air Force except the 56th flew it by this point in the war. The P-51 had a unique history. Rather than license manufacturing the Curtiss P-40 for the RAF as requested by the British Purchasing Commission, North American Aviation offered to build a completely different fighter. The British agreed and North American produced the first prototype, the NA-73, in less than four months. It was an astoundingly short period that reflected the urgencies of the time; the Battle of Britain was in full swing and Righetti was training his first class of students. Since then, the Mustang had evolved into the finest escort fighter of the war.

The type was given the P-51 designation by the USAAF. The British name, Mustang, was adopted by the Americans. Early models were powered by the inline Allison V-1710 engine which proved to be very smooth and reliable. However, it had only a single-speed, single-stage supercharger and consequently suffered from poor performance at high altitude. That real shortcoming aside, the early Mustang was still well-loved by its pilots as it was fast, especially long-legged, easy to fly and good looking.

During early 1942, the RAF's Army Cooperation Command was the first to use the Mustang operationally. After several months of operations the type's exceptionally long range was exploited when it was flown on a daring long-range photoreconnaissance raid against the Dortmund-Ems Canal in Germany on July 27, 1942. Still, despite its exceptionally long reach, the Mustang's poor performance at high altitude meant that it was destined to be little more than a bit player in the strategic air campaign against Germany.

That changed when the airframe was mated with the license-built, Packard Merlin V-1650 engine which had a two-stage, two-speed super-charger. It was an American-produced version of the same, excellent Rolls Royce engine that powered the Spitfire and other British types. In the event, the combination produced an aircraft that was nothing short of remarkable. The new aircraft, manufactured as the P-51B, pre-served the excellent qualities of the original Mustang while also giving it superlative high-altitude performance. Most importantly, equipped with external fuel tanks, it possessed the range necessary to take the Eighth Air Force's bombers wherever they needed to go.

And it started doing so during December 1943. Its appearance startled the Germans and its performance alarmed them. Moreover, unequaled range aside, it could meet the two main German Air Force fighters, the Me-109 and FW-190 on equal or better terms. And it was flown by well-trained pilots. Accomplished Luftwaffe ace Walter Wolfrum recalled that, "It was an awful antagonist in the truest sense of that word, and we hated it. It could do everything we could do and do it much better."[11]

Like its contemporaries, the P-51 was modified over time. Beginning during the spring of 1944, the P-51B (which differed from the P-51C only in where it was manufactured—Inglewood, California, rather than Fort Worth, Texas) was gradually replaced by the P-51D which had a bubble canopy as opposed to the more traditional greenhouse type. Its wings were also fitted with six .50 caliber machine guns, three in each slightly modified wing. This was a significant improvement over the two, jam-prone guns that the earlier models carried in each wing. The P-51D was the model that Righetti so loved to fly. "Don't guess I'll ever be satisfied in anything but the 'five one' again. What a dream airplane!"

From a career perspective, it is possible that Righetti was so thrilled about his assignment to the 55th because he saw an opportunity to improve a unit that had everything it needed excepting inspired leadership. But for their part, many of the 55th's men were wary of him; he was unproven and had been dropped into their laps seemingly out of nowhere. For all they knew he was there because he had powerful friends who were giving him a shot at combat at their expense.

Righetti's first day in combat came at the end of October 1944. It had been five years since his enlistment as an aviation cadet. "Tomorrow is my big day," he wrote on October 28. "Long mission over rough country—imagine seeing Berlin before London. Am definitely settled in the 51 and love it more each day." Righetti's letter underscored his genuine conviction to learn from whomever he could, however he could. "I'm flying wing for a Captain Cramer who has 8 kills to his credit—2 Japs and 6 Huns. He's really the boy to learn from and I'll say 'yes sir' to him any time they want me to."

As it developed, weather caused the mission to be scrubbed and it wasn't until October 30, that Righetti flew his first combat mission. The group rendezvoused with B-17s from the Eighth Air Force's 3d Air Division, but poor weather forced the mission to be recalled before the target at Merseburg was reached. No enemy fighters were encountered. Although Righetti saw no action, the mission was a good introduction to the procedural aspects of high-altitude bomber escort operations.

"HAVE MY OWN SQUADRON NOW"

Early during the war the Allies understood that before they could send an invasion force across the English Channel they first had to neutralize the Luftwaffe. That is, the German air force had to be degraded to such a degree that it could not stop the Allies from establishing a beachhead. Ultimately, this was done at tremendous cost during 1943 and the first half of 1944 while Righetti was training pilots. Indeed, that cost undoubtedly included the lives of some of the pilots that Righetti had trained. Still, the return on investment was the fact that the Allies in France and the shipping that supported them were seldom threatened by the Luftwaffe to any substantial degree during the months that followed the D-Day invasion of June 6, 1944.

But the Luftwaffe, although it was steadily worn down through the summer and fall of 1944, was not completely moribund. In fact, despite the tremendous bombing pressure, Germany increased its production of aircraft during this period. A chief factor in this accomplishment was the dispersal of much of its aircraft industry from massive factories to small, difficult-to-target shops located in tunnels or forests, or hidden in plain sight in isolated towns and villages. The aircraft components these little factories fabricated were subsequently transported to assembly sites where they were quickly fashioned into finished aircraft and delivered to operational units.

Actually, the primary problem for the German air force was not the availability of aircraft, but rather a shortage of skilled pilots to fly them.

The Luftwaffe's leadership had never foreseen the sort of air war it ended up fighting and consequently failed to train the huge numbers of pilots it needed. It struggled to make up the shortfall, but the shift of the Allied bombing focus to petroleum targets choked off the fuel it needed. This scarcity, together with a lack of skilled instructors and qualified students, made the task impossible. Essentially, by the time Righetti started flying combat, the Luftwaffe's training machine was an utterly inadequate dilapidation.

Nevertheless, Adolf Galland, the head of the German fighter forces, had a plan to disrupt the American daylight bombing campaign. To that point in the air war the Luftwaffe had maintained a certain percentage of its fighter units in operational readiness, while others were held back to refit or train. But since early 1944, as the number of American fighter escort groups approached its peak, the Germans were typically out-numbered at any given time and place—despite the fact they operated over their own bases. To counter the American numerical superiority, the Luftwaffe massed its fighters in great formations and vectored them against unprotected segments of the bomber stream.

But the tactic was imperfect and the unwieldy formations were inter-cepted and savaged by the American fighters as often as not. The prob-lem was exacerbated by an inane order from Reichsmarschall Hermann Göring, the head of the German air force, which prohibited his pilots from engaging the American fighters: they were allowed only to attack the bombers. Of course when under attack themselves, this mandate was impossible to obey—and to enforce—but it was demoralizing non-etheless. This was especially so when the German fighter pilots found themselves in an advantageous position against their American coun-terparts and were compelled to give it up and press after the bombers.

Galland bemoaned the lopsided advantage of the Americans and the stupidity of Göring's directive. "Wherever our fighters appeared, the Americans threw themselves at them," he said. "During takeoff, assembling, climbing, approaching the bombers, once in contact with the bombers, on our way back, during landing and even after that the Americans attacked with an overwhelming superiority. Yet, even this did not change our orders: 'Only the bombers are to be attacked!'"[1]

Indeed, through his career Galland was handicapped by the arrogant incompetence of his boss, Hermann Göring. One of the most cruel and sycophantic of Hitler's many sycophants, Göring had wormed his way into the Fuehrer's confidence during the early years of the Nazi party's expansion, and aside from being made the head of the Luftwaffe, was given a dizzying collection of titles and responsibilities, from the Prime Minister of Prussia to the Marshal of the Greater German Reich, to the Master of the German Forests—among others.

A competent pilot and an ace during World War I, Göring was put in command of Manfred von Richthofen's Jagdgeschwader 1 late in that war. Nevertheless, his was not an intellect or a personality that was suited for the responsibilities with which Hitler entrusted him. In fact, from early during the war—in dramatic contrast to Arnold and the USAAF's leadership—he was more interested in pleasuring himself, than in his official duties. In guiding the German air force he was grossly overmatched by his USAAF and RAF counterparts in every respect.

And the Luftwaffe paid dearly for that massive deficit in leadership. To say that the fighting was lopsided is one thing, but putting numbers against that declaration underscores how horrific it was for the Germans. During the spring of 1944, the Luftwaffe fighter units assigned to the defense of the Reich lost more than 80 percent of their aircraft each month. On average, a German pilot survived being shot down two or three times before he was killed or wounded so badly that he could not return to service. Accordingly, the American fighter escorts encountered very few opponents with more than three months of fighting under their belts.

However, Galland planned to create an attacking force so immense as to be impervious to the USAAF's escort fighters. Nothing else had been able to stop the seemingly endless streams of bombers and he was anxious to test the notion that sheer numbers could achieve what tactics, guile, and technology had not. His plan was simple. By holding back the bulk of his fighters for a period of weeks, he hoped to marshal more than two thousand—and perhaps three thousand—aircraft. Then, on a clear weather day, he would send his colossus after the Americans. Galland hoped that this *Großer Schlag*, or "Big Blow," would knock down perhaps five hundred bombers and he was prepared to lose an equal number of fighters as well as one hundred pilots, perhaps a few more. Such a blow could not help but cause the Americans to pause their campaign and thus give the Luftwaffe—and German industry—time to refit and regroup. What would follow was unknown, but it could surely be no worse than the pounding that Germany was then enduring.

The problem with Galland's plan was that, as his force of fighters grew, his superiors—desperate to protect Germany's most important war-making infrastructure—lacked the discipline necessary to keep the carefully husbanded fighters on the ground and out of harm's way. Certainly the Americans did not alter their bombing schemes to accommodate Galland's preparations, and as their aircraft motored toward Germany's most vital targets, Göring and Hitler could not resist ordering Galland's carefully conserved forces airborne. One of these breaches occurred on November 2, 1944. It was the day of Righetti's second mission.

On that day the Eighth Air Force scheduled 1,100 bombers and nearly 900 fighters for a raid against the Leuna synthetic fuel refinery at Merseburg, near Leipzig. The 55th Fighter Group was tasked to provide close escort to B-17s of the 3d Air Division. Righetti was assigned once more to fly as wingman to Darrell Cramer as part of the 338th Fighter Squadron's White Flight. "The mission was just another in a long string of missions," Cramer recalled. "I don't remember anything in particular I said to Righetti in my briefing before this mission. He was a member of my flight and I briefed the flight as a whole and not Righetti singularly."

The 55th launched 69 aircraft at 9:58 that morning. The takeoff and climb were uneventful and the group rendezvoused with their assigned B-17s over the English Channel an hour later. No enemy aircraft were spotted on the way to Merseburg but the antiaircraft fire was heavy and accurate and the group counted seven bombers shot down over the target.

It was only after the bombers turned for home that the 55th encountered the enemy as recounted by the group's mission summary report. "While proceeding at 32,000 feet on [a] SW course from Merseburg, 100 single-engine enemy aircraft were sighted at 1220, flying on about the same level and heading NW toward the bomber track."

None of the 55th's flyers had ever seen so many German fighters—a mix of Me-109s and FW-190s—all at once. "They were in three separate gaggles of about 30-plus aircraft each, about 4,000 yards between gaggles, and the last bunch some 500 feet higher than the others, but with no umbrella force above."

The 55th's three squadrons—outnumbered for the first time in recent memory—turned directly at the Germans, who started to climb. The enemy formation was "immediately routed as our lead flights passed through their formation." In fact both sides broke up into groups of twos and threes and fours as the fighting began. At that point, Göring's mandate against engaging American fighters was obviously ignored by many of the enemy pilots who were "fighting aggressively and attempting to beat off our attack." Others dived for the protective cover of a layer of clouds while a handful, "were seen to pussyfoot in on the bomber formation from 5–6 o'clock on exactly the same level, the attention of the [bomber] gunners apparently being drawn away by the dog fight."

Darrel Cramer, with Righetti and two other pilots on his wing, considered the whirling fight around him. He quickly decided that the odds of bagging a German were better below the clouds where many of them had already fled. Nevertheless, after leading the flight down through the murk, he found the sky empty. However, it wasn't long before Cramer spotted a train and he and the rest of the flight made quick work of the locomotive while also shooting up several rail cars.

After leading the flight away from the shot-up train and taking a southwesterly heading, Cramer sighted an enemy aircraft approaching head-on. "The bandit was called by Captain Cramer," recounted Righetti, "who immediately pulled up toward the enemy aircraft. The Me-109 started a turn to the right, and Captain Cramer fired one burst, getting strikes."[2] The enemy pilot, desperate to escape, dived for the ground and rolled out of his turn directly in front of Righetti. "Since I had outrun Captain Cramer on his pull up, and had turned sharply left, I became positioned in between my leader [Cramer] and the 109."

It was the moment of truth. All of Righetti's years of experience, all of his training, all of his requests for a combat posting would—or would not—be validated during the next few seconds. His heart pounding, he nudged the aircraft's control stick and leaned forward. Through the gunsight he framed the German fighter underneath the gently moving illuminated reticle and checked that his guns were armed. "At 200 yards," he said, "I fired one short burst and observed several strikes back of the cockpit. The enemy aircraft attempted very little evasive action but headed for a flak nest straight ahead. Just before reaching the flak, I fired a three-second burst and observed numerous strikes in the vicinity of the cockpit."

At that point, the German pilot and his pursuers turned sharply away from the antiaircraft position. Out of the turn the enemy plane skidded into the ground where its wingtip caught a hedgerow that knocked it akimbo. The aircraft "was washed out completely." The four, silvery P-51s flashed past and winged for home.

Righetti had scored, but his flight leader, Darrel Cramer, was angry. He recalled the encounter with the Me-109. "When I got into a good stern chase position and closed to firing range, I opened fire. Shortly thereafter I was amazed to see another P-51 converging on me from my left and he too opened fire on the Me-109. My bullets were missing his plane only by a few yards, and I immediately quit firing."

Cramer realized the other P-51 was Righetti. "In the excitement of his first combat, he had ignored his responsibility as a wingman and he did not have any idea where I was," Cramer recalled. "If I had not gained a little altitude as he attempted to get into firing position, I might not have seen him and a midair collision could have resulted."

After landing, Cramer took his turn with the rest of the pilots to debrief with the squadron's intelligence officers. "Righetti was as excited as any new lieutenant would have been after his baptism under fire. I did not want to dampen his excitement with what I had to say to him, so I waited until we were alone." Cramer's discretion indicated his considerable maturity.

"Then I gave him a chewing out like he probably had not had in his military career," Cramer said. "I told Righetti that if he were a new 'dumb John' lieutenant I would have grounded him for at least two weeks and thrown at him all other disciplinary actions I could take. He had violated air discipline and had failed in his responsibility as a wingman. He had left his position as wingman and he didn't have any idea where his leader [Cramer] was when he went after the Me-109. I asked him how he could expect air discipline and enforce it when he became group commander if he violated it when he was a wingman."

Although the justified upbraiding came from a man who was considerably junior in both rank and age, Righetti's response was on the mark. After all, he desired not only to learn as much from Cramer as possible, but also to gain command of the 55th. "Righetti immediately acknowledged that he had goofed up in the excitement of the moment," said Cramer. "And he promised it would never happen again."

Righetti was as good as his word. "On the remaining missions during which Righetti flew under my supervision," Cramer said, "his performance was excellent and there was never another breach of air discipline." Ultimately, the two men shared a half-credit each for the Me-109 they downed on November 2, 1944.

Righetti's rounds found their mark the first time he fired at an enemy aircraft. This was unusual as many men—subject to buck fever if not outright fear—sprayed their machine guns wildly during their first few encounters with the enemy. Righetti had the advantage not only of greater flying experience and skill over the typical young fighter pilot, but he was also an experienced hunter and marksman. There was the additional fact that the enemy flyer he and Cramer knocked down fled in a straight line rather than maneuvering aggressively.

That late in the war, Righetti also had the advantage of the K-14 gyroscope gunsight. The manual for the device, in very simple terms, described its virtues: "As you adjust the K-14 gyroscope gunsight, it automatically gives you the correct lead and shows you the range of the target. In other words, it's the answer to a poor deflection shooter's prayer."[3]

Certainly, this was no exaggeration. Earlier gunsights projected fixed, illuminated circles on a plate of glass. The pilot was required to not only estimate the range to the aircraft at which he was shooting, but also to calculate the deflection. An aircraft heading straight away made an easy target at zero degrees of deflection, while one that crossed in front of the firing aircraft from one side to the other presented 90 degrees of deflection and was very difficult to hit.

During a twisting, turning dogfight a pilot had to not only fly his aircraft against his quarry, and keep an eye on his wingman, and watch for other enemy fighters, but also determine the correct firing solution after solving for range and deflection. Then, he fired his guns. A second or two later—if he had correctly considered all the variables—his rounds arrived at precisely the same point in the sky at the exact same instant as the enemy aircraft.

It didn't work very well. Most pilots fired from too far away and underestimated how much lead (rhymes with seed) was required. That is, they misjudged how far ahead of the enemy aircraft they needed to aim. Indeed, some of the most successful pilots were those who eliminated these difficulties by flying directly behind their intended targets and holding their fire until they felt a collision was imminent. Other pilots simply sprayed bullets in front of their intended target and hoped for the best.

The K-14 greatly eased the task. It was manufactured by Sperry and was actually a licensed version of the British Mk IID gunsight developed by Ferranti. The system's mechanical analog computer used information from its gyroscope to analyze the firing aircraft's motion and calculate the lead required to hit a target.

To use it, the pilot first set the wingspan of the type of aircraft he was most likely to encounter by moving a pointer along a scale mounted on the front of the sight. The wingspan was usually set at 30 feet which worked well for both the FW-190 and the Me-109. When the sight was turned on, six small illuminated diamonds formed a circle on the glass plate that made up the sight. In the center of the circle of diamonds was an illuminated dot, or "pipper." When the gyroscope was "uncaged," or released, the pipper and its circle of diamonds moved around the sight depending on how the aircraft was maneuvering.

On the throttle was a twist grip that was connected to the gunsight via cables and pulleys. As the pilot maneuvered to fire on an enemy aircraft, he twisted the throttle so that the circle of diamonds with the pipper at its center changed size to match the wingspan of his target. "As you maneuver to place and keep the dot on the enemy," explained the manual, "use the twist grip to adjust the reticle of diamonds, so that the inner points surround him. You must keep the sight on the target for one second before firing to give the sight time to do its work. Fire a burst of at least two seconds."

And it was essentially that easy. Herman Schonenberg recalled that after the introduction of the K-14 that, "there was little guesswork in aerial fighting."

Following his first combat mission on October 30, Righetti flew eleven missions through the month of November during which he quickly proved his competence. Although the original plan was for him to gain experience before being sent to take charge of a different group, that plan was changed and he was notified that he would be given command of the 55th's 338th Fighter Squadron, preparatory to being moved up to command the entire group—if things went well.

Darrell Cramer—who had earlier upbraided Righetti for his single-minded aggressiveness when the two had downed an Me-109 together—recalled and appreciated Righetti's forthrightness. "Before it was announced that Righetti was being assigned permanently to the 55th, he came to me and told me what was going on. He told me that he knew I was counting on becoming the next 338th commander. He told me I should not be disappointed he was being assigned to that position, because he would be there only a few weeks, then he would become the new group commander and I would get the 338th at that time."

Righetti led the 338th in combat for the first time on November 21, 1944. It had been only three weeks since his first mission. He was given command of the squadron just a few days later on November 25, 1944. If he celebrated at all it was likely a low-key event as he spent only one sentence in announcing the new assignment to his family: "Have my own squadron now, so am very happy about things."

And there was no question about his readiness as recalled by Darrell Cramer, the 338th's most experienced pilot. "By the time he became a squadron commander," said Cramer, "he had already established himself as a very capable pilot and an aggressive combat leader. He was the kind of leader whose attitude was 'come follow me,' and we were glad to follow him."

Righetti actually seemed more excited about being assigned an aircraft, Serial Number 44-14223, and having it personalized. "My own airplane is finally in the paint shop, getting the *Katydid* and picture inscribed on it—also one swastika." He further described it in a letter to sister Lorraine: "My ship is the *Katydid* with one large sexy green grasshopper painted thereon and it's the sweetest piece of equipment in the world."

He wrote to younger sister Doris on December 2. "Thought I'd drop a note to say happy birthday. Never can tell about these deals. Might not get to say that I wish you a lot more of them." His maudlin comment certainly wasn't intended to take the shine from his birthday wish to Doris, but the fact that he might be killed was something Righetti mentioned regularly in his letters. He didn't need to do so as the family certainly understood that he might perish, and they fretted about it continuously. Indeed, the war came especially close to home during this time when the family learned that James "Buster" Righetti, Elwyn's cousin, had been killed while fighting as part of Patton's 6th Armored Division.

That Righetti actually considered his mortality wasn't unusual. Every airman did so—death was all around them. The loss rate for fighter crews hovered at just under two percent per sortie at that point in the war.[4] This meant that anyone who flew more than about fifty sorties—which wasn't even a complete combat tour of 270 hours—was on borrowed time.

"I do not believe Righetti ever talked to the pilots of the group about being shot down or of being made a POW," said Darrell Cramer, "[But] on one occasion he did tell me that, considering the types of mission we were flying and the heavy flak that we encountered, he did not expect he would finish his combat tour—he expected he would be shot down some day." Likewise, Righetti's crew chief, Millard "Doak" Easton, remembered that *Katydid*'s tailwheel was hit on one sortie, and that a 20-millimeter cannon shell had punched through the ship's cowling on another. "He told me the next one would be in the cockpit."[5]

Righetti's apparent fatalism was not unusual. In fact, some of the pilots fully believed that they would not survive their combat tours. One of these was Russell Haworth who had arrived at the 55th a few months before Righetti. His tendency to leave the group to hunt the enemy on his own earned the ire of his superiors and the nickname "Krazy Kid." "I expected to die," he said, "but intended to have as much fun and kill as many Nazis as possible in the meantime."

Notwithstanding Righetti's mawkishness, his attempt to lighten the mood of his letter to Doris fell flat. "Sunday, that's tomorrow, has always been a fine day for us. We try to hit Germany about noon and in that way catch thousands and thousands of people coming out of church. They make the finest targets." Of course, the notion of a fighter group gunning down churchgoers was preposterous, but not so outlandish that it worked as humor. Too many innocent people on all sides were being killed for the joke to be funny.

Certainly, there were isolated incidents when Allied pilots did gun down noncombatants. The German authorities took these very seriously and developed the gun camera film from downed fighters whenever possible. German interrogator Hanns Scharff recalled seeing some of these. "In one film, schoolchildren were shot on a street in front of their homes and schoolhouse. In another, a forester and a peasant in a field were hunted like rabbits until both died after this pilot has [sic] made several strafing passes at each of them."[6]

When four women were murdered by a strafing pilot near the town of Greifswald in northern Germany, several Americans who were shot down that day were rounded up for special interrogations. These sessions, conducted by Scharff, lasted for weeks. At one point, as the Gestapo got involved, it seemed that at least one of the fliers would be executed despite his protestations of innocence. Ultimately, the "Greifswald Seven" were exonerated when the Germans developed the gun camera film of another pilot that had been shot down and killed on the same day. The film clearly, "showed four German women in the middle of a small country road being mercilessly and needlessly mowed down by the Mustang's .50 caliber machine guns."[7]

More representative of Righetti's real character was his report to Doris that he, "Just finished a note to Katy telling her what a pretty night it is. There's not a cloud in the sky, no wind, and although it's cold, it's not uncomfortable. On top of that, there's an enormous moon—almost full." He noted that he also, "told Katy of our radio program—source, Heinie [the Germans]. They jam all British programs, which aren't too good anyhow, and then put out some really wonderful stuff. Finest musical program I ever heard, with lots of Jerry propaganda chucked in."

The Americans, like all the Allies, used a variety of slang terms to refer to their German counterparts. Most common were Kraut, Jerry, Hun, Fritz and Heinie. All were carryovers from World War I. Kraut was an obvious reference to sauerkraut, the shredded, pickled and very aromatic cabbage dish that was so ubiquitous throughout much of Germany. Jerry was derived from the word, German, whereas Fritz was simply a shortening of the common German name Friedrich. During the Boxer Rebellion Kaiser Wilhelm suggested that the German army in China should behave like Attila's Huns. Later, during World War I, British propagandists leveraged this reference to portray the Germans as cruel, cold-blooded barbarians.

Righetti used Heinie most often. It was a term that was fairly common during the war but subsequently faded from usage. There was little that was derogatory about it as it was simply an Anglicized form of Heinrich. It is likely he picked up the expression from other pilots in the 55th as it appears quite often in the group's mission summary reports and other official documents.

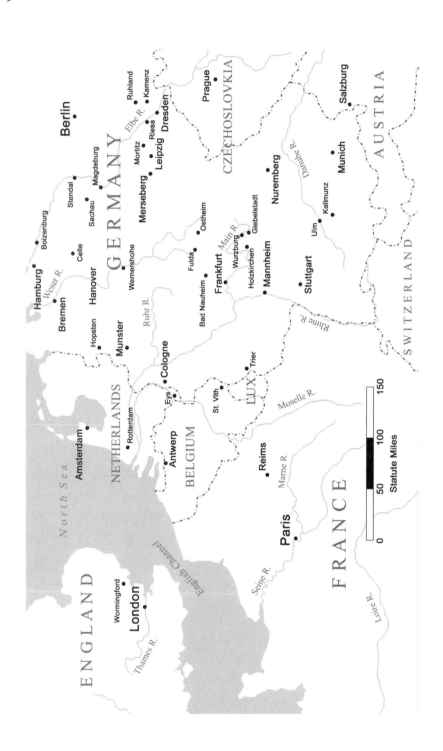

"EVERYONE LOOKS SO WELL"

On December 5, only a week or so after taking command of the 338th, Righetti acknowledged one of the downsides to being in charge rather than among the rank-and-file pilots. "This squadron leading ain't so sharp—I have to sit up topside and call the shots. But then, maybe I shouldn't squawk. There wasn't a single German fighter that got thru to the bombers, so I got commended for the success of the show." Certainly, Righetti was responsible for the performance of his squadron and that performance depended on how he handled and directed it. In some circumstances it was best for him to personally lead the attack, whereas in others the smartest move was to send other elements to engage. Considering his aggressive nature, he was exceptionally disciplined in how he employed his squadron.

"Things have been pretty quiet around here the last two days," Righetti wrote home a few days later on December 9, 1944. "So something ought to pop up in short order. Weather has held us up. This long-range stuff is mean during winter, since it's not always that flying conditions exist both here and on the continent."

Righetti's comment highlighted a characteristic of the air war that vexed Allied planners through the entire conflict. Weather fronts typically moved from the Arctic, through the North Atlantic and across the British Isles before coasting over Europe. Consequently, when a front cleared England and flying operations were possible again, that same front blanketed the continent. And when it finally blew through

Germany, or disintegrated, the Eighth's bases in England were often socked in by a new weather system. Frustrated Allied commanders—air and ground alike—didn't merely chat about the weather. Rather they groused about the "goddamn" weather.

"Have had a tough time locating any Heinie pilots for my own shooting, of late," Righetti continued, "but have really raised hell with their transportation." He noted a new tactic for hitting locomotives: "Got one the other day, head-on, as an experiment. And the whole front end blew down the tracks 100 yards. Looks as though that might be the most damaging approach, and it's better to work because then you can go right down the train."

Righetti apologized for being unable to send Christmas presents. Wartime exigencies precluded the possibility. "But will bring some stuff when, and *if*, I come home."

The following day, December 10, 1944, Righetti led the 55th to south-central Germany. Rather than escorting bombers along specific segments of their route, the 55th was tasked with patrolling in the vicinity of a number of targets, to include Frankfurt and Stuttgart. The group's mission was to intercept German fighters before they could reach the bombers. Such a luxury would have been unthinkable only a year earlier as the Eighth had not had enough fighters of the right sort. Since that time, the wide availability of reliable external fuel tanks and the introduction of the P-51 had changed everything.

The Luftwaffe, for the most part, failed to make an appearance. However, a flight of three Me-262s pestered the group along part of its route as described by the mission summary report:

> Enemy aircraft were content to feint attacks from the rear and head-on, pulling away before coming within range and never firing. Efforts to box them in were unsuccessful. However, one enemy aircraft misjudged by coming in range before pulling away and strikes were scored. They utilized their superior speed to the fullest, but served only as a nuisance and seemed content to harry us. Engagement continued for 20 to 30 minutes.

It was Righetti who scored the strikes on the Me-262. "Tangled with 3 jets and got one damaged. They're a little too fast to destroy but I took all the fight out of him."

The 55th's pilots referred to the Me-262s they encountered as "blows" or "blow jobs"; the latter term carried the same sexual connotations then as today. And beginning in late 1944 they encountered the jets with a frequency that increased until the end of the war. The Me-262 frustrated Allied fighter pilots as its speed allowed it to avoid close-in combat and also gave it the ability to attack the big USAAF bomber streams almost at will. Had the type entered service only a year earlier, the air war certainly would have developed very differently.

That the Me-262 didn't begin combat operations sooner was due to several factors. Among those, the one most commonly offered is that Hitler ordered it to be developed as a fast "Blitz" bomber rather than as a fighter. Certainly this is true, as is the fact that the mandate did cause friction and delays. But it is also certain that Göring and Messerschmitt and others were—initially at least—not big proponents of the jet's potential. Moreover, they misled Hitler about the maturity of the project and the state of the technologies that were required to support its introduction into combat.

In fact, rather than exploring advanced efforts like the Me-262, emphasis was put on producing greater numbers of existing aircraft types in hopes of winning the war sooner. Considering that there was no plan to greatly expand the numbers of pilots available to fly those great numbers of aircraft, it was an ill-considered and naïve decision that caused significant delays in getting the jet into the field. The truth was that regardless of what Hitler did or did not demand, not enough resources had been spent early enough in the design's development. Consequently, the pioneering new aircraft—not surprisingly—encountered a considerable number of technical issues that were impervious to decrees by Hitler or anyone else.

However, even had more resources been put into accelerating the introduction of the promising new type, it is not certain that they would have made an appreciable difference. The various technologies associated with the concept were novel and not well understood. Integrating them into a new aircraft demanded intensive engineering which took time. Moreover, the precision required to manufacture the type's engines was problematic, as was the scarcity of the materials that could withstand the tremendous heat created by the engines.

The end result was that the Me-262—which first flew with a piston engine during 1941, and jet engines during 1942—finally began tentative combat operations with a test unit during the late summer of 1944. The scope of Me-262 sorties remained trifling for several months and increased only in fits and starts through the rest of the year. It was only during the last couple months of the war that the jets started flying in barely meaningful numbers. By then, it was too late.

Nevertheless, from the experience of Frank Birtciel of the 343rd Fighter Squadron, it is apparent how the superior speed of the Me-262 might have neutralized the tremendous war machine the USAAF had become. "The 262 pulled out from underneath the Big Friends [bombers] and headed out ahead of them at about 17,000 feet. This put the 262 and I almost head on. I was coming in about 45 degrees to him head on and started tracking and shooting. I followed him past 90 degrees then pulled in dead astern. Due to his superior speed, he pulled away from me in a matter of seconds."[1]

The performance of the new type was indeed startling. Its two Junkers Jumo 004 turbojets propelled it to speeds of more than 550 mph, while its service ceiling exceeded 35,000 feet. And, although its four 30-millimeter cannon were relatively short-ranged, a couple of strikes were often adequate to knock down a heavy bomber. Later, underwing-mounted R4M unguided rockets were even more deadly. Moreover, rather than burning the same high-octane fuel as its piston-powered counterparts, it used a low-grade benzoil-based fuel that was simpler to produce in smaller refineries. Consequently, it was not hobbled by a lack of fuel to the same degree as the conventional fighter force.

However, the jet was not a good dogfighting machine and an Me-262 pilot who let himself get suckered into a turning fight with P-51s or P-47s, or any of the excellent RAF fighters, soon found himself in trouble. Noted German ace Walter Krupinski recalled, "The only great downside to having the jet was the loss of maneuverability; we could not turn as tight as the other fighters, so speed was our life insurance."[2] Moreover, aside from its limited agility, the Me-262's engines were notoriously unreliable and had to be replaced after only 20 hours of flight time.

The following day, December 11, Righetti again led the 55th on a similar sweep through central Germany. No enemy aircraft were sighted and Righetti split the group and took the 338th down to the deck where he shot up three locomotives. His reputation in the group as a leader who would find action—weather, fuel, ammunition and orders permitting—was growing. Leedom John, who flew most of his missions with Righetti, liked his aggressiveness. "You could bet you were going to be shooting at something somewhere. He was always looking for targets of opportunity—and finding them."

Back at home the same day, Cathryn and little Kyle continued living normal, domestic lives. Kyle had been ill and Cathryn described how a regimen that included laxatives, fasting and various other procedures restored her health. "She has a new lease on life now."

That the labor shortage created by the war was still a problem during late 1944 was evident when Cathryn went shopping. "I was in Sears on Saturday afternoon and before I could get out of the store, three different people asked me if I wanted a job. When I said maybe, they practically had me on the payroll."

When the Eighth's first fighter groups traded in their Spitfires and began flying escort missions with P-47s during the spring of 1943, they typically launched about a dozen aircraft from each of their three squadrons. And, if they were available, a handful of spare aircraft were sent to fill the gaps left by aircraft that had to abort—usually for mechanical issues. So then, once the typical fighter group got airborne, assembled, and underway, it usually motored into Europe with about three dozen aircraft.

However, as the great American industrial complex leaned into the harness, more and more aircraft were delivered to the fighter groups. The receipt of those increased numbers of fighters coincided neatly with the arrival of more and better-trained pilots. Those eager young men were the products of the aircrew training machine within which Righetti had labored so assiduously for the last several years.

Consequently, by the summer of 1944, these greater numbers of pilots and aircraft, together with the men to maintain and support them—and a lower-than-expected attrition rate—gave the fighter groups the ability to launch fifty or more aircraft per mission. In fact, by the end of the war some groups were able to send more than seventy aircraft airborne at a time.

This great surfeit of resources created options. First, of course, VIII Fighter Command could simply task a group to fly as a single large formation to be deployed at the group leader's discretion upon rendezvousing with the bomber stream. Usually, one squadron was sent to patrol along one side of the bombers, while a second was responsible for the other side, and another squadron was kept high. This ensured greater coverage and flexibility as compared to a single, unwieldy and monolithic formation.

Another option was to task a group to fly more than one mission per day which sometimes meant that the available aircraft were split between the missions and not used on more than one. And later during the war, at approximately the same time that Righetti arrived, the fighter groups were often split and tasked to fly as two separate formations, an "A" group and a "B" group. On rare occasions, the units were additionally directed to sortie a third formation, a "C" group. The takeoff times were coincident and generally the tasking was the same. However, splitting the group into two or three formations with their own flight leaders gave a degree of flexibility and ease of handling beyond what was possible with a single formation of fifty or more aircraft.

The 55th and the squadrons that comprised it were all identified by unique radio callsigns. During the period Righetti was with the 55th it was identified as "Windsor." So then, if he was leading the group on a mission, his callsign was Windsor Lead. If there was a "B" group, its callsign was "Graphic." On those very infrequent occasions when there was a "C" group, it was called "Kodak."

Within the group formation, the callsigns of the 38th, 338th and 343rd Fighter Squadrons were "Hellcat," "Acorn," and "Tudor," respectively. If the squadrons were flying as part of a "B" group, their callsigns were "Program," "Richard" and "Saucy." There were no unique squadron callsigns for aircraft flying as part of a "C" group. Finally, the callsign for the airfield at Wormingford was "Fusspot."

The 55th's squadrons were divided into individual flights, designated by color, White—in which the squadron leader flew—and Red, Blue, and Yellow. The corresponding callsigns were complex and cumbersome especially as a pilot's callsign changed between missions depending on which position he flew. For instance, the wingman of the Blue Flight leader in the 338th was Acorn Blue 2. On his next mission he might be the element leader's wingman in Yellow Flight in "B" group in which case his callsign would be Richard Yellow 4. During the heat of battle the pilots sometimes couldn't remember who was using which radio callsign and simply resorted to shouting out names. For instance it was much easier to shout "Bill, break left!" than it was to remember and call out, "Hellcat Yellow Four, break left!" Certainly it was better to drop the naming convention and keep a comrade alive, than it was to see him shot down in flames because a callsign couldn't be remembered.

Individual aircraft also carried unique letter-code markings on their fuselages. All the squadrons in VIII Fighter Command were given two-letter designators which were painted on the side of the fuselage forward of the "Stars and Bars" national insignia. The 38th, 338th and 343rd designators were CG, CL and CY respectively. Additionally, from late 1944, the rudders of the aircraft in each squadron were painted different colors. The 338th's was dark green, and the 343rd's was yellow. The 38th's assigned color was red, and was not used until March 1945.

Aft of the national insignia, on the fuselage, the first letter of the last name of the aircraft's pilot was painted. For instance, Ed Giller's *Millie G* was painted with the 343rd's CY in front of the national insignia, and with a G aft of it. However, as there were usually several pilots whose last names started with the same letter, the letters were modified in various ways, such as with underscores or "bars." Or sometimes the convention wasn't followed at all. For instance, Frank Birtciel's *Miss Velma* was marked with CY for the 343rd Fighter Squadron, and with a D, which had nothing to do with his last name. Similarly, Righetti's *Katydid* was marked CL for the 338th Fighter Squadron, and with an

M for its aircraft unique marking. No matter which way it was turned, there was no M in Elwyn Guido Righetti.

It had long been an axiom that the key to keeping the American fighting man happy was to ensure that he was paid on time, adequately fed and in receipt of regular mail. Whereas Righetti rarely mentioned food or pay, it was obvious that he craved news from home. And he was a demanding correspondent. "Please write me more," he pleaded upon arriving in England, "no letter in several days." This was a request that he made over and over again during his time overseas.

He regularly admonished Cathryn and the rest of the family when he felt they lagged in keeping him caught up: "You can't possibly know how much letters from home mean." And his excitement upon receiving mail was evident in his praise: "Your wonderful V-mails continue to be the spark that keeps me going. Honest, they're wonderful. The pictures arriving today, Sis, are truly tops. Everyone looks so well."

The government definitely understood how important it was for the men to receive reliable and regular mail.[3] Aside from combat, nothing affected morale more. In fact, guidelines were promulgated to families through posters, print ads and movie reels. For instance, chatty news about family and friends was encouraged, as was information about goings-on within the community. Sad or disheartening news was to be avoided or softened. The folks back home were additionally advised to write regularly so that their men felt connected and loved.

Wives were advised that poisonous gossip traveled just fine via the mail and that they were to guard against behavior that might cause their faraway husbands any upset. Also they were to refrain from troubling their men about petty problems about which they could do nothing, separated as they were by time and distance:

> Soldiers are occupied with the fundamentals of existence. Yours, as well as theirs, only most of you are too far away from the terribleness of war and what a Nazi-dominated world could mean, to realize it. Yes, I know. It's very hard to suddenly become a psychologist and an author overnight merely because your man went away. But it's worth your while to try. For just as the right kind of

letters will tighten your romances—or your bonds of affection with son, brother, or husband—so will the wrong kind loosen them"[4]

Cathryn might have been especially good at sheltering Righetti from the typical annoyances or problems that dogged the wife of every man who was overseas. In fact, he had to solicit this information from her: "Tell me about your finances and worries. How are you making out? Can you use more money?" But whatever she shared or didn't, she still owned his heart: "Miss you and love you more than ever—squeeze Kyle for me." He signed off as "Rig."

Much of the mail from mid-1943 until the end of the war was "Victory Mail," or "V-mail." It was used by both the men overseas, and by family and friends back home. Certainly Righetti and his family used it a great deal. It was a concept borrowed from the collaboration between Eastman Kodak and the British that saved cargo weight and space better used for war material.

The mechanics of V-mail letter writing were simple. Specially sized and formatted sheets were picked up at the post office and messages were written on one side, with the delivery address clearly penned at the top. Once the sheet was folded and sealed, the delivery address was also added to the outside before it was mailed.

After arriving at various processing centers, the letter was opened and microfilmed onto a roll of specialty film before being discarded. The state-of-the-art equipment used to photograph and process the letters was manufactured by the Eastman Kodak company. Each roll of microfilm could be imaged with more than 1,500 letters. Accordingly, the rolls of microfilmed letters that filled one postal bag at a weight of 45 pounds would have required 37 postal bags weighing well more than a ton if they had been traditionally mailed.

After arriving at a processing center in the locality of their final destinations, the microfilmed letters were printed onto small sheets and delivered by the postal service. The process proved to be fast and efficient and certainly saved valuable cargo space even if it did require the introduction of a new layer of postal infrastructure and the trained people necessary to operate it.

In practice, V-mail was popular because of its ease of use. Moreover, because there was only limited space on the specially formatted sheets, it was possible to generate many letters at a sitting without the writer feeling guilty at not filling several pages of stationery. And it moved faster than regular mail, as indicated by Righetti in a V-mail he wrote on January 12: "Got your swell V-mails yesterday which is pretty swell service. They were written Xmas eve and day—much faster than air mail." On the other hand, his letter the next day, January 13, underscored how inefficient the postal service could be with traditional mail: "Got five letters from you all and Katy yesterday dated 25 September to 29 October."

Righetti's letters and those of his family are interesting because there are so few spelling or grammatical errors. Although Righetti often truncated sentences or used slang—for example, "tonite" rather than "tonight"—his spelling was nearly always perfect, as was that of his family. It was an indication of the importance the family put on education.

On the other hand, Righetti and his family were direct and to the point. Letters were tools written to communicate, or to entertain, or—certainly on his part—simply to let Cathryn and the folks know he was still alive and thinking of them. Interesting events were shared such as his experience while on a pass to London on December 12, 1944: "V-2 [ballistic missile] last nite flipped us out of our chairs—landed about 400 yards off. I think I'd rather be shot at by bullets." And in a separate letter to the folks: "We've got lots of V-1s [primitive cruise missiles] here yet, but you can hear them coming and hit the shelter if they're close. Quite a war."

And wants were articulated. In particular, Righetti asked regularly for jerky—it was a Righetti specialty that he missed sorely. And he was always interested in news from home: "Sure would like snapshots of home activities if possible. Also jerky."

But rarely was there any attempt to practice florid prose or to explore philosophical complexities. This didn't mean that Righetti didn't deal with emotional issues or conflicts; in his situation he couldn't help but experience some degree of angst or inner turmoil. Perhaps the closest he came to sharing his introspection was in a note he sent just before

Christmas, after nearly two months of combat operations. "Glad you think I'm still tenderhearted, Mom. Sometimes I wonder. I wonder too, occasionally, if I'm changing a little. That frets me."

The V-1s that Righetti mentioned were not uncommon at Wormingford, as recalled by Herman Schonenberg, a young pilot with the 338th. "We were located on a bit of a hill and were on the run to London. The V-1s came in very low over our base. In fact, once we got used to them we tried several times to shoot them down with our .45s. This was really stupid, but there wasn't much else to do."

It was during this time that the Germans made final preparations for a last desperate attack in the West that came to be known as the Ardennes Offensive, or more popularly, the Battle of the Bulge. In strict secrecy—and using the cover of darkness and poor weather—the Germans moved more than two hundred thousand men, hundreds of tanks and more than a thousand artillery pieces into positions across from thinly held American lines in Belgium. Hitler's objective was the Belgian port of Antwerp through which the Allies moved a major portion of their logistics train.

Regardless of Hitler's objective, the Wehrmacht and the Waffen SS simply didn't have the necessary manpower, fuel and equipment. Nor was the Luftwaffe capable of protecting them from Allied airpower once the weather cleared. That being the case, the German plan to encircle and destroy various Allied armies following the unlikely capture of Antwerp was preposterous.

However, the armored thrust that began during the early morning hours of December 16, 1944, caught the defending Americans completely by surprise. Timed to coincide with miserable weather that kept the American airmen grounded, the attack reached deep into Belgium and caused panic and confusion as commanders tried to make sense of reports that described a massive attack where none was expected or even believed possible.

When Righetti wrote home the following day, December 17, it was apparent that he wasn't yet aware that the Germans had launched a major offensive. "Dearest family—Nothing much to report tonite. Led the group again yesterday and English weather forced me into France [Reims] with the whole outfit." Although the weather low over the Ardennes was foul, it wasn't as bad over southern Germany and the 55th was able to escort B-17s of the 3d Air Division to Stuttgart.

After leaving the bombers, Righetti had taken his 338th Fighter Squadron down to the deck in the vicinity of Ulm. "Got three more locos yesterday to bring total to nineteen." He went on to list a grab bag of other target types to include freight cars, trucks and factory buildings. "Stinking weather, but very successful mission."

Righetti also tried to describe the beauty of the snow-covered countryside that, perversely, was made more spectacular by the machines of war. "Some of the most beautiful scenery I've ever seen—in foothills of the Alps, sixty miles from the Swiss border. Wonderful green pine forests, all snow-covered. Locos were similar to our Rocky Malibus. Three-to-four hundred miles per hour over country like that is something I'll never forget. Then, machine guns flashing and great orange flame patches on the ground. Green pine background—beautiful."

"WE TRY NOT TO HIT THE CREW"

Locomotive killing was akin to a sport for the American pilots. Righetti's enthusiasm for it was obvious in his letters in which he described them as, "the prettiest things when they burst. They most always see you coming, so if possible they put the steam to it. You hit them broadside, starting firing at 300–400 yards, and close in to probably 25 to 30. You're on the deck all the way and pull up to go over them. If you're right they go all to pieces—chunks of plate all over. Many, however," he continued, "just break inside and all the steam goes out the stack. We try not to hit the crew, but occasionally get too eager."

There were times when it didn't matter whether or not the pilots aimed at the crew. Crewing the trains was dangerous work and there were apocryphal stories of engineers who were chained to their loco-motives in order to keep them from fleeing. However, it seems that most were dedicated to their work. A case in point was August Grabmann, a 68-year-old engineer aboard a munitions train stopped in the village of Sülzenbrüken, near Arnstadt in central Germany. When American fighters were spotted, the crew hurried to move the train into the countryside lest the village be blown to smithereens in the event the munitions were hit and exploded.

Their instincts were correct, but while the village was spared, the train was attacked and did indeed explode, blowing its crew to bits. Grabmann's obituary recalled him as a "lifetime companion," a "beloved father" and "the best grandfather," who "was taken away from us when he was killed in the line of carrying out his duty during a strafing attack. We are all gripped in the deepest of sorrow."[1]

The locomotives were large, vulnerable targets that erupted with huge plumes of steam when their boilers were hit. And they had no ability to maneuver or hide—they couldn't jump their tracks and travel afield. The disruption caused by the attacks made a real difference to the war effort. Vital supplies and material were delayed or destroyed, and similar hurt was done to the military units that were so desperately shuttled back and forth across the Reich to staunch the crushing Allied offensives.

A 55th Fighter Group mission summary report recorded one of these attacks. "Locomotive pranged [destroyed], at which time uniformed Heinies poured forth from all 20 coaches, heading up a hill to reach the timberline. One full squadron, line abreast, strafed these huddled Heinies, pinning entire gaggle to the ground."[2]

It was terrifying to be on the receiving end of these attacks. Luftwaffe fighter pilot Johannes Steinhoff recalled that his train came to an abrupt halt en route to Berlin, late in the war. "I heard the whine of fighter engines ... Mustangs!" He leapt from his compartment, intent on fleeing the sitting duck that was the train. At the same time a military policeman rushed down the corridor shouting that no one was to leave the train.

Steinhoff's shouts contradicted the policeman's: "Get out, get out—they'll shoot us to pieces!" Steinhoff wriggled through a window and saw many others likewise scrambling down from the passenger cars. "Looking back, I could see the steel-helmeted transport officer waving his pistol and shouting over and over again, "No one's to leave the train!"

The fleeing passengers threw themselves to the ground as the P-51s dove and shot up the locomotive. In subsequent passes, entirely unmolested, they machine-gunned the passenger cars and boxcars. "After ten minutes it was all over," said Steinhoff. "When I got back to the train I saw the transport officer dashing helplessly about looking for a doctor. He had been too late in deciding to evacuate the train, and now we had wounded and dead. We sat for hours and hours in the chilly train, until late in the evening they brought up another engine and we continued our journey toward the capital."[3]

Notwithstanding the fact that the German trains often had no recourse but to endure the air attacks, they weren't always helpless. Particularly important trains were sometimes protected by purpose-built boxcars carrying armored antiaircraft gun turrets. When the train came under attack, the boxcar's sides were dropped and the guns went into action. They were effective and attacking aircraft often discontinued their firing runs and went in search of easier prey.

As spectacular as a blown boiler was, the locomotives were rarely ever destroyed by machine-gun fire. Although the high-velocity rounds might penetrate the boiler and make it impossible to maintain a head of steam sufficient for locomotion, repairs were often readily made. Indeed, most of the components that could be damaged by machine-gun fire could be replaced or fixed. And, of course, there was much that made up a locomotive that couldn't be destroyed by .50 caliber machine-gun rounds.

Consequently, many of the locomotives that Righetti and the 55th and the rest of the USAAF knocked out of action were eventually returned to service. All the same, the disruption caused by the attacks was real. Locomotives had to be repaired on the spot, or moved to a repair depot while an operational replacement was found and shuttled into place. Likewise, railcars that had been damaged sometimes had to be repaired or moved. In the meantime, the section of railway upon which the stricken train sat became a chokepoint beyond which nothing could pass.

Aside from the locomotives, Herman Schonenberg recalled a tactic the 55th used to set the boxcars afire. "We flew line abreast, low and perpendicular to the train. As we got close we released our drop tanks so that they smashed against the train and drenched it with gas. Then, the newest guy in the formation had the honor of coming back around and setting it on fire with his guns."

Through most of 1944, it was typical for the VIII Fighter Command's newly arrived replacement pilots to be sent to training groups that operated the same aircraft types they would fly in combat. Most pilots destined for the P-51 matriculated through a course of several weeks' duration with the 496th Fighter Training Group at Goxhill. However, toward the end of the year, organizational changes, resource reallocations and improvements in Stateside training resulted in the shutdown of the training groups; the replacement pilots were sent directly to the operational fighter groups.

These men were still not ready to be sent to combat and the responsibility for preparing them for action fell to the operational groups to which they were sent. When Righetti had arrived during mid-October he was simply paired up with several different experienced pilots who took him on a handful of training flights—all very informal. Such other information as he needed, he picked up in the pilots' lounge. This worked well enough, considering his experience.

But the group's leadership recognized the need for a more formal training program and commissioned "Clobber College" the following month. It operated around a structured syllabus that introduced new arrivals to aspects of operations that were peculiar to the type of air war then being fought over Europe. There was particular emphasis on high-altitude operations, foul-weather flying, formation work and fuel management. It was equipped with war-weary aircraft that were nevertheless suitable for the task, and it was staffed with experienced pilots who pulled double duty, or who had finished their combat tours or otherwise needed a break from combat. In the end, it proved to be a success as it provided just the sort of "finishing" the new pilots needed to, at a minimum, not be a burden during their first few missions.

While American ground forces battled their German counterparts in the Ardennes, bad weather grounded most of the Eighth Air Force from December 19 through December 22. Righetti was frustrated by the inaction: "Really haven't a durn thing to write about. But four straight days of bad weather with no flying—and the stinking Heinies kicking our boys around just a couple of hundred miles away—kinda puts a guy on edge."

Still, he enjoyed relaxing with his men, with whom he still lived. "In case I didn't tell you all," he wrote, "I passed up the chance of living alone in order to live with my boys in a 12-man barracks. The boys have a heated discussion on women going right now, so I guess I'd better sign off and join in—they're mostly bachelors so need my sage views and advice." He was probably the only squadron commander in the Eighth Air Force who shared living quarters with his youngsters. Of this unorthodox arrangement he wrote: "It's really the life, and certainly a liberal education."

The barracks were concrete structures of British design and were always cold and damp. Each was fitted with a single stove that was unequal to the task of chasing out the chill. Still, as the only source of heat, it was usually surrounded by a circle of men. "Sometimes," said Herman Schonenberg, "some wise guy would get on the roof and drop a cartridge down the chimney." Schonenberg noted that the resultant explosion caused quite a stir. "Nobody got hurt, but it sure scared the hell out of you if you were sitting next to the stove, as you always tried to be."

Unlike Righetti, most of his men were bachelors. And like most young unmarried men, they were interested in female companionship, although the nature of their duties obviously limited such opportunities. Nevertheless, as recorded by one of the group's pilots, opportunities did exist although they were not always of a Norman Rockwellian sort. "In England during the war," he wrote, "there were millions of U.S. soldiers and about six available women. Of course, there was a good supply of whores on the blacked-out streets of London. You could hear the action in every darkened doorway in the vicinity of Piccadilly Circus. We were warned that the girls probably all had syphilis or gonorrhea and that we should not have sexual relations with them. Then we were provided with prophylaxis kits for use when we did."

"My only female encounter," the pilot continued, "began at a dance at the officers' club. I met this girl who had been dating one of the pilots who had just been shot down. She had a pronounced Cockney accent and, considering my Texas accent, we hardly spoke a common language. However, I could understand 'yes' and 'no.' I escorted her home in a chauffeured GI truck. The driver made the rounds, letting out the couples, then made the rounds again, picking up the guys. My date and I had sexual relations standing up in the middle of the dark street in front of her house."

The result of the encounter was predictable. "Pilots returning from the next dance, which I did not attend, told me this girl was pregnant and was looking for me. I missed several dances after that. The English girls had the idea that they could not get pregnant standing up."

Righetti was not a heavy drinker or womanizer. Carroll Henry, one of the junior pilots, recalled how he interacted with his pilots. "I don't know if he won a lot of money or not, but he liked to play poker with us because he liked to be with the boys. He was a fairly good poker player—he wasn't the best we had, but he was pretty good." Russell Haworth seconded Henry's assessment. "Righetti was a very good poker player. His strategy was either to raise or drop out." It was an approach that evidently worked well enough for Righetti. "I've been showing the boys here some card tricks," he wrote, "to the tune of $400 the last three days."

"It was just draw and stud," said Henry. "We never played wild games. And we bet money—English money. But Righetti made us stop because we'd have English pounds lying on the table when girls came to visit in the dining room. He said that there was too much money going to the English girls. He just didn't want us to flash all that money in front of them."

On December 22, with the 55th still grounded by poor weather, Righetti's frustration peaked. "We're all sure that if only the Eighth Air Force could get into the battle, we'd make short work of things." He had a point, although his parochial allegiance to the Eighth discounted the outstanding capabilities of the Ninth Air Force which was specifically tasked to provide tactical air support to the Army units then engaged in Belgium. In truth, Germany's leaders understood the vulnerability of their ground forces very well and grew nervous in the knowledge that sooner or later the weather would clear enough for the Americans to bring the full weight of their airpower to bear.

Notwithstanding his own frustrations, it was Righetti's job to ensure that the morale of his men did not sag. It wasn't easy. "One of my toughest jobs as squadron commanding officer has really been working me overtime of late. Namely, what to do with three hundred officers and men on stand-down days." Righetti's special services officer orchestrated a "quiz contest" between the officers and the enlisted men. "So we ran it in the post theater this afternoon," Righetti recalled. "Five pilots versus their five crew chiefs. The pilots won 595 to 505 points. Things went over swell and [the idea] will be used by other units on bad weather days."

The trivia contest was a mild and apparently worthwhile diversion, but it was only temporary and Righetti and his men chafed to get back into action. It was cold and snowy in England, but they knew that their ground brethren on the continent were enduring far worse. "Haven't killed anyone for four days now, so am getting a trifle bloodthirsty. Hope more than anything else that tomorrow dawns clear and is a clobber day."

His hope was realized as the 55th put up 61 aircraft on December 23, 1944, to escort B-24s from the 2d Air Division to tactical targets in the vicinity of the contested town of St. Vith in Belgium. Although other USAAF units made contact with the Luftwaffe and were credited with downing 133 aircraft, the 55th ended the day empty-handed. It chased after a mixed bag of enemy aircraft types with no luck; an Ar-234 jet was spotted but fled almost immediately, as did an Me-262 and a flight of four Me-109s. Once the group finished its escort duties, the mission summary report noted that it received vectors from supporting radar units and "bounced everything but enemy aircraft—none sighted." Righetti remained exasperated.

Righetti often relied on Nuthouse when leading the 55th, and it was mentioned frequently in the group's mission summary reports. Nuthouse was the radio callsign of the 401st Signal Company that operated radar equipment, also known as Microwave Early Warning, or MEW.[4] The radar—together with radio transmitters and receivers, direction-finding units, telephone switchboards, special listening stations, display scopes, plotting boards, etc.—comprised a large air control system that was used both to assist the Eighth's escorting fighter groups to rendezvous with their assigned bombers, and to monitor the progress of a given raid.

Importantly, it was also used to vector the fighter groups onto enemy fighter formations.

Developed in the span of just a couple of years, it was rushed into service from the United States and started operations at Greyfriars, England, shortly after D-Day on June 13, 1944, with the callsign of Dwarfbean. Although it could detect high-altitude targets at ranges that exceeded two hundred miles, that range wasn't enough as the Eighth penetrated ever deeper into Germany. Consequently, during November 1944, the heavy, complex and sensitive radar equipment—and its support components—was moved across the North Sea and atop a hill near the small town of Eys, in the Netherlands.

From its new location, Nuthouse began operations on November 23, 1944. The unit was surprisingly effective considering that the technology had been developed only a few years earlier, and the additional fact that virtually none of the men had operational experience that predated their arrival in England earlier that year. Not only was the equipment very basic—even crude—but the concept of radar control had only been evolving for a very short time. Operations inside the control center were operatic in their complexity and the demand for timely and accurate transmission of information to the air units being supported was very high.

And it quickly became indispensable as noted by the head of the United States Strategic Air Forces in Europe, Carl Spaatz: "Our war is becoming a radar war. We depend heavily on the operational capabilities of a small number of radar sets of extraordinary performance."[5] Indeed, Righetti was often the beneficiary of the control provided by Nuthouse, especially in joining the bombers at the correct time and place. And, with the help of radar control, the 55th engaged enemy aircraft that would have otherwise gone unnoticed. However, because of the radar horizon, or curvature of the earth, Nuthouse was of no use when Righetti operated where he liked flying best—low to the ground. The radar was simply blind to anything that happened at low altitude.

Righetti and the rest of the 55th finally found action on December 24, as the weather over Europe continued to clear. The group's mission summary report stated: "There were still plenty of Heinies for the last minute shoppers." The German fighters were encountered as they attacked 3d Air Division B-17s near St. Vith. The 55th was vectored to them by Nuthouse who called out "Rats! Heinies! Rats!" The mission summary report noted that German fighters, "were observed in the distance attacking violently from the down-sun side."

By the time the 55th engaged the enemy fighters, there were only about fifteen of them remaining in small, scattered groups. A group of four was attacked and two were destroyed, but the 55th's fighters "were in turn bounced" by four Me-109s, "the latter attacking aggressively and determinedly down to the deck. At the same place, one FW-190 jockeying for a sneak attack from 5 o'clock level on the bombers was in turn snuck up on and clobbered. A runaway 190 was sighted at 13,000 feet and pranged [destroyed] in the same area."

Fighters from other units arrived to the fight. "Three more lone Krauts were sighted at 10,000 feet, but in the ensuing bounce, 8 Mustangs of another group bounced us ..." The other P-51s were from the 357th Fighter Group and dived on aircraft from the 55th's 343rd Squadron. As the 357th's aircraft came down from high on their left side, the four pilots of the 343rd's Yellow Flight turned and climbed into them, probably unsure as to whether or not they were Germans. The pilots from the other group subsequently realized their mistake and turned away to the left, "with the exception of a straggler, who was pushing his nose up and down, apparently having trouble in deciding which way to go."

The straggler was the 357th's Wendell Helwig, who smashed directly into Kenneth Mix. One of Mix's comrades observed that the engine was "pushed back into the fuselage, and the right wing torn off. No chutes were seen."[6] In whirling, confusing fights of this sort, midair collisions were a constant danger and occurred throughout the war. So did mistaken attacks on friendly aircraft. In fact, aside from the 357th's abortive bounce, a group of Spitfires had also attacked the 55th earlier during the mission which caused a number of pilots to drop their external fuel tanks.

As it developed, there weren't enough enemy aircraft to go around and Righetti descended with five other aircraft of his 338th Fighter Squadron to attack targets of opportunity in the vicinity of Frankfurt and Mannheim. There, they bagged five locomotives and shot up about thirty boxcars, or "goods wagons."

"Following these attacks," Righetti said, "one of the six planes was completely out of ammunition and the remaining planes had approximately half their ammunition left. We were flying north at deck level in the haze because visibility was sufficient to pick out targets and at the same time give us additional security from ground AA [anti-aircraft] positions."[7]

Righetti led the flight of P-51s in a line-abreast formation with his aircraft slightly in the lead. He found what he was looking for about fifteen miles southeast of Munster. "We saw 20, FW-190s flying four-ship flights in close trail formation approximately at 3 o'clock at our altitude. All of the enemy aircraft carried belly tanks. I believe we saw the enemy aircraft before they identified us."

Someone called out, "Oh boy, a field day," but the two formations held their courses until the Germans passed less than half a mile in front of Righetti and his little group. He made a turn to get behind the FW-190s and it was then that the German pilots reacted, as Righetti noted in his encounter report. "I closed on the nearest 190 which was in a tight left turn." He fired a short burst and observed strikes on the enemy aircraft's left wingtip. "I turned with the enemy aircraft, and as I did so, I saw two FW-190s directly ahead belly in, one heading due west and the other northwest. Both raised large dust clouds as they hit, but did not explode. Their airspeed was in excess of 150 mph." It was telling that the two German pilots, although they were part of a formation that was more than three times the size of the attacking American group, chose to throw themselves onto the ground at high speed rather than to fight, or even to flee.

Righetti continued after the FW-190: "The enemy aircraft I was pursuing continued to tighten his turn to the left, and when he reached a bank of 70–80 degrees he snapped under and went straight into the ground from 600 feet." This propensity of the FW-190 to go out of control under heavy maneuvering had been noted by Allied pilots who tested captured examples. Recovering the aircraft while at high altitude was generally not a problem. However, so low to the ground, Righetti's opponent never had a chance.

"I continued my turn," Righetti said, "and observed my wingman, Lieutenant [Kenneth] Griffith, in trouble with a 190 on his tail. I turned to engage this enemy aircraft, and as I did so took short bursts at two other enemy aircraft which crossed my path, and secured scattered strikes on both, which I claim as damaged."

Righetti continued after Griffith's pursuer. "Lieutenant Griffith was in a tight left turn, and as I approached the 190 on his tail, I secured a good group of hits on the enemy aircraft." The German pilot spotted Righetti and broke off his attack on Griffith with a climbing turn to the right. Righetti followed him and began firing from three hundred yards as he rapidly closed the distance. "I secured a scattered set of strikes all along the enemy aircraft, and when he reached 1,600 feet he rolled over on his back and went straight into the ground, crashing and exploding."

Although Righetti had shot the attacker down, Griffith was still in trouble. "Just after the last enemy aircraft crashed," said Righetti, "Lieutenant Griffith called that he was hit in the arm and that his engine was out. Due to the haze I could not locate him so I advised him to bail out. He stated that he was too low but was very calm as he wished me a Merry Christmas. I feel sure that Lieutenant Griffith was able to belly in as the terrain was suitable." Nevertheless, German records indicate that Griffith and his aircraft were found completely destroyed and burned.[8]

Another pilot in the flight, Paul Reeves, was also very nearly killed during the fight. "I began firing at an FW-190 but before I could do much damage, my ship was hit."[9] A 20-millimeter shell exploded in Reeves's cockpit near his left foot and a large hole was blown out of his right wing. "I tightened my turn and managed to keep the German from getting any more hits. We made a couple of complete turns with neither of us able to put the other away. Someone called on the radio and said 'Let's get out of here.'"

But Reeves could not. "I called that a German was on my tail. Frank Bradford acknowledged that he could see the action and he made a pass at the 190, which broke off and ran. Bradford was about out of ammo and my plane was so crippled that neither of us could pursue the guy."

Reeves became separated from Bradford. "I leveled out and headed in the general direction we had been flying previously but I had no compass—it had been shot out. A coating of oil covered the windshield and the canopy on the top and right side." Reeves started a climb and tried to determine whether or not he would have to abandon his aircraft. "The plane was performing well and it seemed that I had a chance to limp back to Allied territory, so I called Righetti and asked him to make a 360-degree turn so that I could see and join him."

Instead of turning, Righetti asked Reeves where he was. "I replied about ten miles north of where we had the fight. He said 'Roger, I don't see you.' That he didn't consider making a circle to pick up one of his men was disappointing." It is peculiar that Righetti didn't reverse course and try to collect Reeves. His failure to do so might indicate that he didn't understand Reeves's situation and believed that he was simply separated rather than shot up and alone.

With his canopy covered by oil and his aircraft punctured with more than forty holes, Reeves climbed and discovered that his engine performed reasonably well. "Bradford called me and told me to point my nose at the sun and set my gyro compass at 240 degrees. He had checked this with his own compass and it was a great help to me." As Reeves nursed his ship westward he heard Russell Haworth—the "Krazy Kid"—declare that he was chasing an Me-109. "I saw a 109 being chased off to my right, followed by the 51 about two thousand yards behind."

Reeves considered landing at one of the many Allied airfields on the continent, but his engine seemed to be running reasonably well. He continued toward England and crossed paths with a four-ship of 4th Fighter Group P-51s, but decided to proceed to Wormingford on his own. "I rolled to a stop at the end of the runway and hit the left brake to turn onto the taxi strip but I had no left brake. It too, had been shot out." Using only his right brake, Reeves gingerly made his way toward his revetment. Another 55th pilot recalled, "I had just parked and was not yet out of my airplane when I saw a P-51 taxi by that was all covered with oil and as it passed, I could see the valve rocker arms moving up and down through a jagged hole in the engine cowling from a cannon hit on the top right portion of the cowling."[10]

When Reeves reached his parking revetment, his engine finally seized.

True to form, and as noted by Paul Reeves, Russell Haworth had gone hunting the Luftwaffe on his own. He found himself over an airfield near Vogelsberg, in central Germany. "I started circling the field," he said, "saw a plane landing, and realized the planes were Me-109s. Then I saw a second plane on his downwind leg in the landing pattern with wheels down and about 50 feet off the deck. I pulled in behind the enemy aircraft as he turned on the base leg, firing a short burst in the turn."[11]

Haworth closed the range until he was nearly atop the enemy fighter and fired his guns once more. His rounds tore into the Me-109. "I pulled up, rolled over, and watched the pilot attempt to belly land the enemy aircraft. However, his wheels were still partly down and his airspeed was too high. The enemy aircraft rolled over and broke apart, pieces being scattered over a considerable area."

"TONITE THIS LAD IS A TIRED GUY"

The 55th was airborne again the following day to escort the same 3d Air Division B-17s to the same tactical targets in the vicinity of St. Vith. Enemy fighters were encountered as they climbed to meet the bombers. Righetti and his 338th Fighter Squadron were held in reserve while the 343rd attacked and downed five Me-109s.

Later that night Righetti wrote a Christmas letter home: "Just a V-mail quickie, for tonite this lad is a tired guy. Got 16 hours in combat during the last three days, including today." He noted his downing of the two FW-190s the previous day against his total accomplishments up to that date. His attitude was typical of a combatant who had experienced nothing but victory and who knew little of the despair that accompanied defeat. "Words can't express what a really wonderful game this is."

Such words were simple, high-spirited bombast. Intellectually and morally, he knew that the killing was not a "wonderful game." Certainly it was not a game to his wingman, Ken Griffith—who had arrived at the 55th at the same time as he had—or to Griffith's family, or to anyone that suffered during the war.

In fact, during the course of Righetti's combat career, dozens of pilots from the 55th were lost while flying missions in which he had a leadership role of some sort. Such losses were an inevitable part of the war and certainly weighed on his conscience to a degree. Nevertheless, he never shared details in his letters home as to how the men were killed, nor did he write of any feelings of grief. Certainly this was due in part to censorship sensitivities, but he was also aware of the worry that such shared feelings would invariably cause Cathryn and his family in San Luis Obispo. And perhaps he might have been coping—shielding his own psyche by not dwelling on the lost men.

As his family worried about him, he also worried about them. He worried about his parents' health. He worried that so much of the responsibility for the ranch was on brother Ernie's shoulders. He worried about the happiness and well-being of his sisters—especially Lorraine who was in the Women's Army Corps. And he worried about Maurice—not just about his safety, but about how and what he was doing.

And of course he worried about Katy and Kyle. He worried that Katy might be overwhelmed and lonesome. He worried because he knew she worried. He worried about Katy's finances, and he especially worried—during a time of childhood diseases that included polio—about Kyle. "Kyle's illness gave me a quite a scare," he noted after receiving a telegram alerting him that his daughter was ill and that Cathryn needed money. As it developed, he received a second telegram a few days later reassuring him that Kyle was "recovering beautifully," and that the "crisis" was over. "I had a rough 96 hours," he wrote. "Wish they were in California where the weather is better."

In fact, Katy and Kyle moved back and forth between San Antonio and San Luis Obispo. Righetti preferred them in California—he knew that his family would love and care for them. Certainly, he knew that Katy's family also loved them, but he was understandably biased toward his own clan.

Following the Christmas Eve dogfight, Righetti made claims only for the two FW-190s he actually engaged. Of the two FW-190s that were destroyed when their pilots preemptively crash-landed, he wrote in his encounter report: "2 FW-190s destroyed by the flight, to be awarded as the Group Commander desires." Because he was the senior man in the formation, and because he led the attack, he could have legitimately claimed both as his own. He did not, and never made mention of them again in his letters home. However, the 55th's commander, George Crowell, was evidently motivated to give Righetti credit for one of the enemy aircraft as the records show that three aerial victories—rather than two—were attributed to Righetti on that date.

The original plan for the German ground assault into the Ardennes included a massive, surprise air attack against Allied airbases on the continent. Luftwaffe planners hoped to catch American and Allied aircraft on the ground and, if not wipe them out, deal them a crippling blow. However, the foul weather that shrouded the launch of the German thrust on December 16, 1944, also kept the air forces of both sides on the ground. When the weather finally cleared and the Allied air forces started shredding the German ground units, the Luftwaffe was too weak to stop them. The ground advance faltered and consequently the imperative to neutralize the Allied air advantage over the battlefield grew critical.

Operation *Bodenplatte* was the product of that imperative. At first light, on January 1, 1945, the Luftwaffe launched just more than a thousand aircraft—virtually all of them fighters—on a low-altitude attack against more than a dozen Allied air bases in France, Belgium and the Netherlands. To its credit, the Luftwaffe's leadership maintained strict secrecy during the period leading up to the actual operation and consequently achieved complete surprise. On the other hand, that secrecy was so complete that trigger-happy German antiaircraft gunners misidentified and shot down many of the Luftwaffe aircraft as they flew to their targets. Moreover, many of the pilots were so ill-prepared and poorly briefed that they had little idea of what their mission was.

In the event, although many of the attacking units became lost, or were engaged by both hostile and friendly forces prior to reaching their targets, the operation achieved a degree of success. Approximately three hundred Allied aircraft were destroyed on the ground and another two hundred were damaged. Had the German flyers been better trained, the results would have been even more impressive. Regardless, the size and scope of the effort caused Allied planners to reconsider their earlier assessments of the Luftwaffe's strength and capabilities.

Still, the short-term results were far overshadowed by the costs. More than two hundred German pilots were captured or killed—the largest single-day loss of the war. These airmen, especially those who were experienced, could not be replaced. It was a blow from which the Luftwaffe simply could not recover. On the other hand, most of the Allied aircraft that were destroyed were parked. As most of their pilots were still sleeping or at breakfast during the attacks, few were killed. The aircraft were easily replaced and the effects of *Bodenplatte* beyond the day of the attack were essentially nil.

Bodenplatte had virtually no effect on the England-based Eighth Air Force or the 55th Fighter Group other than to make clear that the enemy was resourceful and capable of mounting large, complex air operations. For his part, Righetti never even mentioned it in his letters home. Indeed, although there was little doubt that the Luftwaffe was on the ropes, to what extent was still uncertain. Accordingly, Allied air operations continued unabated, and the German air force was engaged at every opportunity both in the air and on the ground.

It was the weather—the worst in decades—that was the biggest factor in determining when and where those engagements occurred. Combat operations aside, the misery that the cold and wet and wind created was inescapable at Wormingford where the 55th's men lived and worked. One of the 38th Fighter Squadron's monthly narratives noted that high winds blew the door from one building and lifted the roof from another that housed some of the unit's officers. "The door was soon reinstalled but the roof has to date defied the efforts of our English friends to fix it. And although they've stopped the rain from coming in, a fine grade of black tar continues to drip on any unfortunate officer that tries to use this part of the barracks. Suggestions that the officers move into tents has so far met with nothing but abusive language and flying shoes, stones, etc."[1]

Aggressiveness oftentimes pushed common sense aside during the fight against the Luftwaffe. This was the case with one of the 55th's airmen on January 3, 1945, during the mission to Fulda. After seeing the bombers across their target, the 55th went looking for trouble. Righetti led the 55th's

B group through Kassel and then back across Calais and home without finding any trade. However, Crowell's A group spotted three Ar-96 training aircraft headed east at low level near Stuttgart. "We peeled off to the right, went down and clobbered all of them," noted the 38th's mission summary report. "Two were seen to blow up in the air, and the third augured in." A fourth Ar-96 was subsequently spotted and also knocked down.

Righetti's letter home that evening wished everyone "a Happy New Year," and expressed hope that "this one will finish things over here." He also—after just more than two months in combat—had already started counting down the number of combat hours until his tour was over and he could go home. "Total time now is 122 hours, 148 to go." He estimated that he would complete the requisite 270-hour combat tour in time to be home by April. Notwithstanding his desire to get safely back home, he still wanted to bag more enemy aircraft. "If I don't get them in that time, and if the war still needs me, I reckon I'll sign on for an extension—50 hours is all I can get."

Combat hours were those hours flown while on an actual mission. At that point in the war missions generally exceeded four hours, and occasionally stretched to six hours or beyond. Mission paperwork was occasionally fudged as some men "fat penciled" their combat time in order to leave for home sooner. Others logged less than they actually flew so that they could fly more missions.

Righetti mentioned the downing of the German training aircraft that day only in passing. "Weather's been quite tough [the] past few days so Heinie fighter opposition has been almost nil. We got three today. However, I didn't score." He also noted the length of the mission which, at 5 hours and 40 minutes, "was a long time to sit strapped and squirming in one spot."

One event that Righetti did not mention was the downing that day of one of the group's pilots. That man was Captain John Coonan. Righetti was not aware of the details surrounding Coonan's loss, but another of the group's pilots, Dudley Amoss, was. And that night as Righetti penned his letter, Amoss was no doubt enduring a guilty hell.

The group's mission summary report described only part of what had happened: "Captain John F. Coonan [was] hit by flak and was seen to belly land in vicinity of Kellmunz. He called in and said he was hit when he passed over a small town. His ship was in good condition after landing except that [the] canopy was off. He was not seen to get out of his plane." The 38th Fighter Squadron's monthly narrative noted that the loss of Coonan was, "the first low blow of 1945."

Coonan, an old hand who had not only shot down one of the Ar-96s, but had also been credited with a victory against the Japanese earlier in the war and with an Me-109 the previous summer, survived the crash landing and was made a POW. Robert Jones, one of the pilots in Coonan's White Flight recorded, "Captain Coonan led the attack, and shot down one enemy plane. Several seconds later he said he had been hit." Jones spotted Coonan's aircraft in the snow and made a couple of camera passes. He observed that Coonan's aircraft "seemed to be in good condition."[2]

A German report, J2735, confirmed that the aircraft was only slightly damaged at "12–15%." It further stated—in a direct contradiction to the 38th's mission summary report—that Coonan had been shot down by "machine-gun fire from another Mustang." This information was shared with Coonan who promised to "kill the son-of-a-bitch" who shot him down if he was ever able to determine who it was.

As it developed, he later had that opportunity. Dudley Amoss was shot down by antiaircraft fire on March 21 while strafing the airfield at Hopsten. He was made a prisoner and was eventually put into the same POW camp as Coonan. "He [Coonan] told me that his wingman had shot him down," said Amoss. "I had to level with him and tell him that it was me that shot him down!" Amoss, who had not previously admitted his mistake, told Coonan that he had incorrectly identified his aircraft as an Me-109. "It was a long, long shot. I gave him a lot of lead and fired."

"Much to my horror," said Amoss, "as I passed over him, I recognized the plane as a P-51." Coonan grimaced when Amoss told him the truth. But he neither killed him nor even became angry.[3]

Mail call was good to Righetti on January 5, following the group's mission to Trier, during which he shot up three more locomotives near

Fulda. "Xmas presents arrived last evening and I loved them all. They were picked with such good judgment. Thanks too for the swell letters."

An official document explained how VIII Fighter Command's pilots—virtually on their own initiative—came to be so heavily engaged in strafing operations:

> Plainly our fighters, being there for the purpose of fighting Germans, were determined to join the battle, be it on our terms or on theirs. If the high-altitude strategic escort didn't produce enough combat and enough victories to satisfy the healthy appetite of the Eighth, then there'd be some fighting lower down.[4]

Strafing attacks by Eighth Air Force fighter pilots before 1944 were mostly ad hoc hit-and-run affairs by one or two or a handful of pilots that achieved little of note. In fact, early in the Eighth's operations it was discouraged as too dangerous—the emphasis was on protecting the bombers. However, on February 22, 1944, elements of the 353rd Fighter Group made a planned attack on their own initiative after completing their escort duties. Eight aircraft hit the airfield at Ostheim and achieved some success. Believing that real hurt could be achieved against the Germans by more thoroughly developing "the art of ground strafing" and subsequently disseminating appropriate tactics throughout VIII Fighter Command, the 353rd's leadership approached its head, Major General William Kepner.

Kepner embraced the notion and directed the formation of a temporary unit made up of sixteen volunteers from several different fighter units during March 1944. The group of enthusiastic strafers honored Kepner by dubbing themselves "Bill's Buzz Boys." They threw themselves into their work and flew six strafing missions from March 26 to April 12 while developing and testing different tactics. That developing and testing resulted in a tally of thirteen German aircraft destroyed on the ground—together with an assortment of other targets—at a cost of two pilots and three aircraft. Their emphasis, however, was on airfields as the neutralization of the Luftwaffe prior to the invasion was an imperative.

Importantly, the work served as the basis for a document, *Down to Earth*, from which the Eighth's fighter pilots—as intended—took lessons and, as they gained experience of their own, refined the work of the Buzz Boys. Righetti certainly identified with much of what was written. The following excerpt applied as much to him as to his men:

> The qualifications for a successful strafing pilot are plenty of daring, the ability to size up a situation and to arrive at a plan of attack quickly and on the spot, and, of course, he must be a cool shot. He must know when not to attack as well as when to attack. Many pilots enjoy ground strafing much more than escort work due to the certainty of action when they start out.[5]

Another official document, *Light, Intense and Accurate: U.S. Eighth A.F. Strategic Fighters versus German Flak in the E.T.O.*, described Righetti almost perfectly when it noted: "Because if there is anything a fighter pilot likes to do more than anything else, it is to get down on the deck, going like hell with all guns blazing, shooting up everything in sight."[6] Darrell Cramer, who credited Righetti with "great combat flying skills," recalled his fighting spirit: "He was always aggressive and a good offense is better than a good defense in air combat. He inspired a sense of aggressiveness in the pilots he led and they were always spoiling for a fight."

The 55th, with Righetti at its head, escorted a group of 3d Air Division B-17s to Germersheim, south of Mannheim on January 6, 1945, as the German thrust into the Ardennes stalled. The escort was uneventful and after seeing the bombers clear of the target, Righetti broke the group into smaller elements and sent them to hunt on their own. He took the 338th in tow, descended to fifteen hundred feet and headed east—deeper into Germany.

It wasn't long until Righetti noted fresh, muddy, vehicle tracks around the airfield perimeter at Giebelstadt. Closer inspection showed more than a dozen twin-engine aircraft and nearly that many single-engine types, "well-dispersed and camouflaged." He wasted no time and sent half the squadron down "to make the initial and surprise attack while he acted as top cover and observed the attack as it progressed."

There was no established protocol as to whether a squadron or group leader should make the first firing pass when he might catch the defending gunners by surprise and complete one or more runs unmolested. However, there was also the possibility that the airfield defenses would be ready and alert, in which case the unlucky pilot would receive the full attention of the enemy defenses and might very well be shot to pieces. Another very real risk was that he might do little more than alert the enemy gunners so that they would be ready for the rest of the pilots when they eventually made their attacks.

In truth, there were at least as many different sets of tactics for attacking airfields as there were fighter groups, and nothing was mandated by VIII Fighter Command. Contemporaneous documents outlined the benefits in carefully studying photographs of a given airfield, locating its aircraft and defenses, and creating definitive—and often complex—strafing plans. For instance, some plans called for shooting up the enemy antiaircraft guns before beating up the rest of the airfield. Others called for distracting the gunners with a high flight while the rest of the group made a low, fast, surprise attack. Many schemes described attack headings, altitudes, patterns, and sequences in great detail.

Few argued against the notion that it was better to have a plan than not, but the Luftwaffe's situation late in the war was extremely fluid and a base crowded with aircraft one day might be deserted the next. Likewise, airfields that were seemingly only lightly defended might be greatly reinforced overnight. Or, weather or operational considerations might compel a group to attack a different airfield, thus making a carefully wrought plan useless.

In truth, most airfield attacks were spontaneous affairs made as the fighters headed home after fulfilling their bomber escort duties. It was often the case that the pilots stumbled upon airfields about which they knew nothing and immediately attacked, trusting in surprise and luck. Or sometimes a simple scheme was quickly put together and executed, literally, on the fly.

There were basic principles followed by many of the pilots. For instance, some advocated attacking, "from down sun so that if the attacker chooses to pull up he can climb directly into the sun, thereby making a very difficult target for the ground gunners." Another factor was the wind: "When the attack on an airdrome is started, the direction of the wind should be taken into consideration so that smoke from burning aircraft may be used to advantage in providing a cover for attacking planes." The downside, of course, was that the drifting smoke sometimes obscured the enemy aircraft that the fighters were trying to destroy.

One group declared that, "all passes should be made at high speed and minimum possible altitude."[7] Another group commander agreed that attacking aircraft must, "maintain high air speeds. There is a tendency after a few passes to let the airspeed in the pattern drop off to slightly over 200 m.p.h. This is dangerous because a plane is much more vulnerable to ground fire at reduced air speed." Probably the best but most ignored bit of advice was, "If the field has too much flak, use your head: Go home."[8]

Aside from officially promulgated documents and memorandums, experience was shared pilot-to-pilot. Russell Haworth recalled a discussion with Righetti. "I pointed out from my observations of combat films how others would start firing out of range, see their hits fall short, and then try to correct by pulling up, only to have their rounds rake through to the other side of the target."

Not surprisingly, although he was canny about how he used his men, and about the risks to which he subjected himself, Righetti sometimes attacked airfields in ways that violated these tactics and principles. In fact, they were regularly broken by pilots from all the fighter groups as circumstances sometimes precluded making a perfect attack. Moreover, the prospect of easy targets was, time and again, simply too great to resist.

The pilots had to be especially aware of what was going on around them, aside from enemy fire. When attacking in line-abreast formations, they had to concentrate on, or accept, whatever targets were generally in front of them. A turn to fire on an attractive target might put a pilot in another's line of fire. "Everyone had to know where everybody else was," said Herman Schonenberg, "and be very alert so you either did not shoot down a buddy, or get shot up by one. It was exciting."

The outcomes of these airfield attacks—both planned and spontaneous—were never predictable. There were instances when groups were savaged despite having made meticulous preparations. There were other times when formations threw themselves pell-mell across an airfield without any plan whatsoever and created tremendous destruction while suffering few or no losses. For his part, Righetti seemed absolutely unable to let pass any opportunity to shoot up German aircraft, or indeed, any worthwhile target.

His attitude seemed similar to that of Donald Blakeslee who was one of the USAAF's most successful fighter pilots in Europe, having started flying combat first with the Royal Canadian Air Force out of England in 1941. Blakeslee offered much wisdom about the art of strafing but put little stock in by-the-number tactics. "... I want to say a word about tactics. My feeling is that there is entirely too much emphasis placed on methods of strafing and on so-called tactics. Strafing is a simple process. You pick a target and shoot it up. As long as you are comfortable and get away with it, that's all there is to it. Every pilot probably has a different idea on how to do it. A general rule just can't be laid down, for one method is probably no better than another."[9]

Notwithstanding the volatile nature of airfield strafing, there was no doubt that the attacks were effective. In effect, the Americans were taking the fight to the Luftwaffe. Whereas, during 1944, of the 7,977 German aircraft the USAAF's fighter pilots claimed destroyed, 70 percent, or 5,602 of them, were aerial victories, while only 2,375 were strafing claims. But of the 5,783 German aircraft claimed destroyed by the Americans in 1945, 76 percent, or 4,421, were ground victories and only 24 percent, or 1,362, were aerial claims. In other words, more Luftwaffe aircraft were destroyed on the ground than in the air.[10]

High-ranking Luftwaffe officers underscored this fact—and its effects—to Allied interrogators following the war:

> Your ever-present fighters with their constant strafing attacks on our airfields kept the GAF [German Air Force] grounded in the later stages of the war. Strafing affected the morale of the Luftwaffe personnel more than bombing. While communications were not interrupted and casualties were light, strafing had a disrupting effect on efficiency. It seemed to impress on those involved, the matter of your superiority more effectively than any other means.[11]

In fact, when it is considered that a single fighter brought to bear as many heavy machine guns as a U.S. Army infantry battalion, there is no wonder that the Luftwaffe men grew disheartened.

Above: The Righetti children learned a great deal as they grew to adulthood on the ranch. Pictured are Ernie, Doris, Maurice, Lorraine, Elizabeth and Elwyn. *Righetti family*

Below: Righetti learned to operate various types of machinery while growing up on the family's Edna Valley ranch, near San Luis Obispo, California. *Righetti family*

Above: The Righetti family circa 1936. From left: Doris, Elwyn, Pop, Elizabeth, Mom, Ernie, Maurice and Lorraine. *Righetti family*

Above: Righetti, far right, enjoyed studying at the California Polytechnic College at San Luis Obispo. Here he is participating in the stock horse judging during the Poly Royal event. *Righetti family*

Above: Aviation Cadet Elwyn G. Righetti, 1940. *USAAC*

Right: The North American AT-6 Texan was perhaps the most widely used trainer in history, and was an aircraft with which Righetti was very familiar. *USAAC*

As a young instructor, Righetti, second from left. and his peers led the way in creating the biggest, most effective air force in history. *USAAC*

Newlyweds, Cathryn and Elwyn Righetti. *Righetti family*

Righetti's wife Cathryn, or "Katy," with their daughter, Kyle, circa 1944. *Righetti family*

Righetti, his wife Cathryn, and their daughter, Kyle, in 1942. *Righetti family.*

Righetti likely participated in this flyover of the "Taj Mahal" at Randolph during 1942. *USAAF*

Above: Righetti's rank and position in the training command led to many perks. Here, he is pictured with Irene Dunn and Spencer Tracy on the set of "A Guy Named Joe." *Righetti family*

Righetti made rank very quickly. Here, he is a major during 1943; it would have taken more than ten years to have made the same rank prior to the war. *USAAF.*

Above: Righetti received gunnery training in the Curtiss P-40 Warhawk before heading overseas in 1944. *Righetti family*

Below: Darrell Cramer helped mentor Righetti during his introduction to combat. The two downed an Me-109 on Righetti's first full mission, November 2, 1944. *USAAF*

Elwyn at home with Pop and Ernie. *Righetti family*

Righetti took over the 55th from George Crowell who had flown with the unit since the time it operated P-38s. *USAAF*

Righetti presents an award to one of his young lieutenants, Herman Schonenberg. *USAAF*

Righetti was well-pleased at flying P-51s with the 55th Fighter Group.

The FW-190 was a contemporary of the P-51, adept at ground attack and air-to-air combat, and was arguably a better fighter than its stable mate, the Me-109. *Imperial War Museum*

The Me-109 was a capable opponent through the entire war, despite its age. This was a late-model variant with a Galland hood-style canopy. *Grosse, Bundesarchiv Bild 101l-674-7774-25*

Above: Russell Haworth, known as the Krazy Kid, had no expectations of surviving the war. *USAAF*

Below: Righetti, with the first *Katydid*. The overtly sexy cariacture painted in green and black on the left side of the P-51's nose is readily visible. *Righetti family*

Above: A pair of Mistel combinations being chased by the 55th. *USAAF*

Right: One of the Ju-88 Mistel aircraft without its fighter, just before being downed by Righetti and the 55th. *USAAF*

Below: An intact FW-190/Ju-88 Mistel combination. *USAAF*

Above: Richard Gibbs was Righetti's wingman on February 3, 1945 and was credited with downing a Mistel and its controlling fighter. *USAAF*

Below: Herman Schonenberg strafes a train. One of the dangers in strafing was the close proximity of squadron mates as evidenced by the P-51 in front of him. *USAAF*

Above: The 20 millimeter cannon, in various forms, was the weapon most encountered by Allied pilots when strafing German airfields. *Bundesarchiv Bild 183-J08338*

Below: Frank Birtciel recalled that Righetti imbued the 55th with a newly invigorated spirit of camaraderie and aggressiveness. *Frank Birtciel*

The winter of 1944–1945 was not only difficult for the pilots, but also their aircraft maintenance crews. *USAAF*

Above: The Me-262 was fast and difficult to shoot down except while it was taking off or landing. *USAAF*

Below: Righetti, Clayton Peterson, George Crowell, Darrell Cramer and Edward Giller enjoy themselves at a social gathering. *Righetti family*

Left and below: John Cunnick downed this Me-262 on March 22, 1945. The 55th held the record for most Me-262s downed in a single day—seven, on February 25, 1945. *USAAF*

Above: Frank Birtciel's *Miss Velma* wore the green-on-aluminum livery sported by some of the 55th's 343rd Fighter Squadron aircraft. *Frank Birtciel*

Right: Robert Cox downed two Do-217s and shot up an additional five Do-217s on the ground on March 3, 1945. There were no witnesses and his gun camera film failed; his claims were subsequently denied. *USAAF*

In order to keep him from harm, Righetti sent Paul Reeves back to base early on April 17, 1945, which was scheduled to be the last mission of Reeve's tour. Five 55th men, including Righetti, were lost that day. *USAAF*

Millard "Doak" Easton was Righetti's crew chief. He recalled that Righetti was easy to satisfy. *USAAF*

Above: Righetti's sisters, Lorraine and Doris. Righetti was especially proud of Lorraine's enlistment into the Women's Army Corps, or WAC. *Righetti family*

This Hitler Youth pilot and glider are representative of the young men and aircraft strafed on the ground by the 55th on March 3, 1945.

As the commanding officer of the 55th, Righetti was responsible for virtually all the units on Wormingford— nearly two thousand men. He was 29. *USAAF*

Although he preferred to fly, Righetti appreciated that his leadership position allowed him to influence plans for the air war. *USAAF*

It was believed by some that Righetti and John Landers, seen here in the cockpit of his P-51, engaged in an unofficial contest to determine who could score the most strafing victories against enemy aircraft. *USAAF*

Below: A rare photo of Righetti's *Katydid* in the air. This was the second *Katydid*, a P-51D, Serial Number 44-72227. *Righetti family*

Above left: Righetti took his administrative duties seriously, despite the fact that they detracted from his ability to fly as many missions as he would have liked. *USAAF*
Above right: Righetti and John Cunnick pretend to review a map in this USAAF publicity shot. *USAAF*

Right: The Luftwaffe's airfields were wrecked by a combination of Allied bombing and strafing attacks. *USAAF*

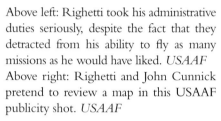

Above left: Chester Coggeshall flew P-38s and P-51s with the 55th and was murdered by the Germans on the day he was shot down, April 16, 1945. It was the last mission of his second combat tour and the day before Righetti was shot down. *USAAF*

Top right: Righetti watched younger brother Maurice's career closely. Maurice eventually flew B-29s in the Pacific. *USAAF*

Righetti's daughter Kyle is presented with his decorations at a military ceremony held at Fort Ord, California on November 6, 1946. *Righetti family*

Righetti, perhaps wanting to underscore to his men that he would and could do anything he asked of them, sometimes was the first one to attack, and sometimes was the last. However, on January 6, the surprise at Giebelstadt was not complete and Claire Buskirk, at the head of the four-ship Righetti sent to open the attack, was hit on his first pass. He climbed away to the west with his wingman.

Meanwhile, Righetti orbited overhead and watched the remaining pilots destroy seven enemy aircraft during the course of three separate firing passes. Smoke from the burning aircraft drifted across the airfield, greatly reducing visibility and increasing the risk of midair collisions. At the same time, the streams of cannon fire that laced the sky over the airfield intensified. It was then that Righetti dove on Giebelstadt with the rest of the squadron.

The formation of silver Mustangs leveled off just above the ground and scythed through the smoke and haze and enemy fire. Righetti rested the illuminated pipper of his gunsight on a twin-engine Ju-88, and held forward pressure on the control stick to keep it there. Once in range, he squeezed the trigger and felt the barking rumble of *Katydid*'s guns vibrate into his seat.

He released the trigger a couple of seconds later. To both sides he saw muzzle flashes as the rest of his formation fired on other targets. Ahead of him, his gunfire spattered into the Ju-88 and the ground around it. The armor-piercing incendiary rounds sparkled and flared and set the enemy ship ablaze as he roared past.

Righetti pulled *Katydid* into a hard, climbing turn and looked over his shoulder and down at the seething, smoking mess that was the airfield. The antiaircraft fire that had earlier lashed out at the speeding aircraft in individual streams now came together to form a seemingly impenetrable curtain. Nevertheless, the last of his formation punched unscathed through the deadly veil and climbed after him.

Save Buskirk and his wingman, the squadron was safely back at altitude and out of range of the enemy guns. Righetti considered the flaming wrecks on the airfield below. Notwithstanding the destruction that he and his squadron had wrought, he saw through the smoking pall that several enemy aircraft remained undamaged. He called over the radio that he was readying for another pass, and that any others who wished to chance the enemy fire again, could join him.

Righetti dove for the deck a moment later. One other pilot followed in trail. The smoke that drifted across the airfield made it difficult to find the aircraft he had spotted earlier and he sped through it without hitting anything worthwhile.

There was a flash and a deafening crack as a foot-wide section of Righetti's windscreen disintegrated under the impact of an antiaircraft round. A breath-snatching gale of air rushed through the hole. Momentarily stunned, Righetti blinked through his goggles against the shards of Plexiglas and dust and other debris that swirled around the cockpit. At the same time he hauled *Katydid* skyward and grabbed reflexively at the map that blew into his face.

The citation that accompanied Righetti's recommendation for the award of the Distinguished Flying Cross described his subsequent actions:

> Undaunted by this damage, Lieutenant Colonel Righetti, in complete disregard for his personal safety, carried on his onslaught and made another pass, this time alone. On pulling up he observed two Junkers Ju-88s parked in the same small area and as yet undamaged. Peeling around, he came down in a return pass, his fourth and last, and destroyed both of these German aircraft, one exploding almost immediately, and the other bursting into flame, having received a considerable concentration of strikes.

On the way home, the 338th shot up six locomotives and a truck. Righetti made it back to Wormingford, although Buskirk did not. His damaged engine eventually failed and he was forced to bail out and was quickly captured and made a POW.

Righetti never mentioned this specific mission in his letters home, other than to note that he had been recommended for the Distinguished Flying Cross.

Virtually every important population center, industrial plant and military installation in Germany was protected by various types of antiaircraft weapons, collectively known as *Fliegerabwehrkanone*, or "flak."

The most famous and ubiquitous of these guns was the 8.8-centimeter, or 88-millimeter, cannon that fired 20-pound shells at a rate of nearly 20 rounds per minute. Most commonly called "eighty-eights," they were universally hated by American airmen, especially the bomber crews who had no choice but to punch through dense curtains of exploding shells, any one of which had the potential to blow them out of the sky. The bomber men could shoot at the Luftwaffe's fighters, but against the highly coordinated, computer-aided and sometimes radar-guided heavy flak guns, there was little they could do other than pray, hunker down and endure.

Although the USAAF's fighters were sometimes targeted by these heavy German cannons, it was the lighter flak guns that caused them so much grief as they trolled the countryside at low altitude looking for targets, or when they attacked military convoys, troop concentrations and, particularly, airfields. The most common of these weapons were the 20-millimeter Flak 30 and Flak 38 guns which fired explosive shells at rates of up to 180 rounds per minute. Employed in single, dual and quad mounts—both mobile and static—they were relatively simple to maintain and operate. In adequate numbers, and complemented by the 37-millimeter Flak 43, they could be, and often were, deadly against the types of strafing attacks practiced by the American fighter groups.

Still, they often were not effective enough as evidenced by the fact that the 55th and other fighter groups regularly made successful attacks against defended targets. The Germans were hard pressed to concentrate antiaircraft guns in numbers large enough to deter forty or fifty or more aggressive Allied fighters. This was especially true when the fighters made the antiaircraft guns and crews their first targets. Of course, it was exceedingly risky for a fighter pilot to duel with an antiaircraft gun, but the odds of success increased when he was joined by multiple squadron mates.

Moreover, solving the physics required to shoot down an aircraft flying at treetop level at three hundred miles per hour or more, although less complex than air-to-air gunnery, was still not simple. Approaching aircraft could be engaged by the 20-millimeter guns from as far away as half a mile. However, keeping a weapon properly trained against a fast-flying aircraft became increasingly difficult as the firing angle increased and the aircraft flashed past and sped away. In reality, the time available to engage a single aircraft was only about a dozen seconds.

Although advanced sighting equipment was available for these lighter guns, it was expensive, temperamental and difficult to use and maintain. In most instances antiaircraft units in the field resorted to using simple visual sights. And often, rather than trying to track individual aircraft, all guns were aimed so that their fire intersected to form a deadly shroud through which attacking aircraft were forced to fly. Such barriers made a fearful sight as tracers crisscrossed the sky and cannon rounds detonated upon reaching maximum range. Few were the pilots who did not instinctively duck low in their cockpits as they passed through these linked streams of gunfire.

All these weapons—heavy and light—cost Germany dearly. There was no arguing that the resources to manufacture not only the guns, but also the ammunition and other necessary material was expensive and could have been useful elsewhere. But more important was the human capital necessary to operate it. More than half a million men were committed to manning the guns—men who were desperately needed at the fighting fronts. Indeed, as the war dragged into its later years, many of the purpose-trained soldiers making up the antiaircraft organizations were transferred into infantry and armored units only to be replaced by older men, adolescent boys, women and even POWs.

Gerhard Oberleitner, a 15-year-old boy, served with an antiaircraft unit in Austria. "My mother was a particularly frequent visitor and brought me, her youngest, provisions and fresh underwear as often as possible, and looked after my well-being. She was obviously the most diligent of the mothers and I used to get teased by my comrades because of it, but I didn't give a damn."[12]

Armin Langheinrich was a schoolboy drafted to help operate the light antiaircraft weapons that protected the huge flak tower at Humboldthain in northern Berlin. "We had to live in those towers with the regular air force personnel, the antiaircraft people ... and in the morning the teacher came. When it was summer, we would sit out on the grass outside for class. And sometimes we hoped for the air raid, so we could get out of class.... You know how young people are, we were stupid."[13]

Notwithstanding the fact that Germany's antiaircraft units were in large part manned by a nontraditional mix of personnel, they were still effective. The 55th's men never belittled the capabilities of the guns that targeted them. Indeed, when they were mentioned it was because the fire they put up was so fearsome: "Flak barrages of a type more intense than heretofore encountered belched from all sides of this Enemy Landing Ground and to a point 10 miles south."[14] Ultimately, it was antiaircraft fire rather that German fighters that shot down the majority of the Eighth Air Force's fighters.[15]

"IT ALL HAPPENED PRETTY FAST"

Righetti's eagerness for air combat was such that he actually flew with another fighter group on one occasion. On January 7, 1945, he flew to Duxford to visit his old friend and boss Fred Gray, the commander of the 78th Fighter Group. The following day he flew an escort mission to Stuttgart on Gray's wing. Regardless of his hope for action, the mission was a dud and he returned to Wormingford that afternoon.

By mid-January 1945 the Germans were being turned back out of the Ardennes. Notwithstanding the successful penetrations that were made during the first few days of the assault just a few weeks earlier, stiff Allied resistance on the ground and in the air—together with limited supplies and poor roads—confounded the German effort. Despite a renewed push on January 3, the Wehrmacht was simply outmanned, outgunned and desperately short of fuel, ammunition and other supplies. Moreover, the Luftwaffe, especially after the Pyrrhic victory that was *Bodenplatte*, was virtually impotent over the battlefield.

However, the Eighth Air Force's focus during this time was still directed against transportation targets. The objective was to keep reinforcements and supplies from reaching the embattled German forces in the Ardennes, while also bottling up the movement of needed war material throughout the Reich. On January 13, more than 1,500 bombers were sent against rail bridges and marshaling yards along the Rhine and in western Germany. The 55th was not tasked with escorting any specific bombing organization but instead was directed to sweep the area between Bad Nauheim and Mannheim.

The Luftwaffe declined to meet the group as it patrolled under the control of Nuthouse. When the bombers finished their work and Nuthouse released the 55th, the three squadrons separated to hunt on their own. Righetti led nine aircraft from his 338th Fighter Squadron to the airfield at Giebelstadt where the group had enjoyed such success the previous week on January 6. On this day there were approximately 20 enemy aircraft parked around the airfield.

As he had on January 6, he directed one of his four-ships to initiate the attack while he stayed back and choreographed the action. "We let down and I instructed Red Flight to attack the field while I covered with White Flight." The four pilots making up Red Flight made a strafing pass before pursuing a twin-engine aircraft that was just taking off. "As the airdrome was clear," Righetti said, "I sent Lieutenant Miller [Roy] and Lieutenant Henry [Carroll] down for an attack." The two lieutenants made a couple of passes, flaming an Me-262 in the process.

In the meantime Red Flight returned to the airfield, having downed the enemy aircraft, another Me-262.[1] Righetti watched as the four aircraft, together with Miller and Henry, shot up the airfield. Finally, with the enemy gunners fully alert, he took White Flight down. "Captain McGill [William] and myself were the last to strafe the field, and we made two passes, the first from northwest to southeast and the second from southeast to northwest. On the first pass I placed a 4-second burst in the engines and fuselage of a Ju-88 and saw it blaze up as I pulled away."

The squadron's pilots finished their work at Giebelstadt just as antiaircraft fire struck Phillips Eastman's aircraft in the engine. It also punched through his cockpit, lacerating his left arm and disabling his throttle. Nevertheless he chased after an Me-262 for which he claimed credit after setting the jet's right engine afire.

Eastman's account conflicted with that of Kenneth Schneider: "We strafed the airdrome and as I was making my second pass I heard Lieutenant Eastman say he had been hit and might have to bail out,"

Schneider said. "When I finished my pass I saw an Me-262 and started to chase him. I looked around and spotted Lieutenant Eastman was chasing the same jet. We chased him east for about three minutes. We could not catch the jet so Eastman called and said he was heading out on 270 degrees and repeated that he might have to bail out."[2]

Schneider pointed out to Eastman that he was actually headed north rather than west. Eastman subsequently turned to the left to take up a westward course. However, his engine was overheating and it was apparent that it would not get him back to Wormingford. Schneider reported that Eastman made a radio call before parachuting from his aircraft: "He said that he had destroyed three enemy aircraft and to tell his wife he was OK and that he was bailing out." Righetti's account echoes Schneider's. "It is believed that Lieutenant Eastman clobbered two or three enemy aircraft also, as he later had to bail out as the result of a flak hit, and his last words over the R/T were, 'tell my wife I'm OK and I got three of them.'"[3] Eastman was quickly captured and treated for his wounds. "The next day they took me to see the large crater my P-51 made. They then took me to an airdrome—Giebelstadt from the looks of it, I didn't ask—on my way to Dulag Luft.[4] He received no official credit for the aircraft he claimed as destroyed that day.

Meanwhile, Righetti headed northwest and encountered an Me-109. In a letter home he described the German pilot as "damn near as cagey as I am." Indeed, he was nearly caught unaware by the Me-109 pilot. "It all happened pretty fast. I was intent—fat, dumb and happy—on busting a loco. All alone, which was my first mistake. Darn train was in a canyon and I couldn't get at him on my first pass. Pulled a big, hairy Chandelle to come in again at him and spotted the Heinie just sliding in for the thrust." A chandelle was a sharp climb followed by a quick reversal in direction and a steep dive.

Righetti reacted instantly. "Split-essed out [rolled upside down and pulled toward the ground]. He didn't expect the maneuver at all so he was almost caught flat-footed. He tried to turn with me, but once around and my 2,200 [flight] hours, and *Katydid*, was a little too much for him. He chickened out and broke for home, so I slid on his tail and clobbered him. Easiest one I've had yet."

The crash was gruesomely spectacular. "He went in pretty hard on fire. Impact broke the chute open and it spilled—on fire too—across the snow."

In describing this encounter Righetti noted the superiority of his experience and training, and additionally showed pride in *Katydid*. But he did not denigrate the aircraft his opponent flew. And that is because the Me-109 was a good fighter. To be sure, although the majority of the USAAF pilots who flew the P-51 were smitten with it, few of those same pilots dismissed the two main German fighters—the Me-109 and the FW-190—as inferior.

The Me-109 was the most dated of the three aircraft, having won the Luftwaffe's competition for a new fighter during 1936, almost a decade before Righetti encountered it for the first time. When it debuted as a mostly metal monoplane with an enclosed cockpit, retractable landing gear, and inline engine, it was far and away the best fighter in the world. Moreover, it was menacingly modern in appearance whereas many fighters in service at the time were biplanes that more closely resembled their World War I forebears.

The Me-109 performed well during the Spanish Civil War beginning in 1937, and later dominated its opposition during the invasions of Poland and the Low Countries. It likewise swept aside the fighters operated by France's Armée de l'Air. It met its equal only when it encountered the RAF's Supermarine Spitfire over Dunkirk in 1940.

It was a sleek, powerful and very small aircraft that, despite having met its match in the Spitfire, continued to perform well through the war as it was continuously evolved with more powerful engines, heavier armament and updated equipment. However, its small size did not readily accommodate many of the modifications and it was consequently scabbed with bulges, bumps and fairings that only partially mitigated the weight and drag of equipment that was too large to be incorporated entirely inside its airframe. Later in the war, due to shortages of aluminum, the Me-109's tail section was made of wood. Indeed, as time passed and the Allies fielded ever more capable types, it grew more difficult to maintain the Me-109's viability as a frontline fighter.

The cockpit, covered by a heavily framed canopy, was very cramped—almost claustrophobic. The Me-109's pilots did not have the same clear

fields of view enjoyed by the pilots of its more modern counterparts—
especially the P-51D with its bubble canopy. The windshield was small
and the canopy was mullioned with thick, vision-blocking members.
The nose, with its two protruding fairings, was long and further obstruc-
ted the field of view. An American pilot flying a captured example
noted: "This airplane is as blind as any fighter I have seen. Vision in
all directions is restricted and no rear-view mirror is provided. In the
air the visibility over the nose does not appear sufficient for deflection
shooting."[5]

Moreover, the Me-109's narrow-tracked landing gear made it difficult
to handle on takeoff and landing. It was the cause of many accidents,
especially with the ill-trained pilots that were so typical of the Luftwaffe
late in the war. On the other hand, the Me-109's handling characteristics
once it was airborne were honest. At low airspeeds, despite leading
edge slats on the outboard wings that sometimes extended themselves
asymmetrically, it was very responsive and true. Its climb performance
was very good, it dove quickly and it rolled and turned as well as most
of its opponents. Indeed, at airspeeds below 250 miles per hour its
performance was exceptional. This was an important attribute as, after a
few hard turns—typical of dogfighting—the airspeed of all aircraft bled
down to the lower ranges where the Me-109 excelled.

However, Allied pilots flying captured examples noted that the
Me-109's controls were very heavy at high speeds. Accounts of Me-109s
flying into the ground were numerous and no doubt due to the fact that
the pilots simply could not wrestle their aircraft out of high-speed dives.
At airspeeds greater than three hundred miles per hour the rudder and
aileron controls were so heavy as to feel locked in concrete. The same
American pilot who complained about the poor visibility noted that, "It
is very hard to maneuver at high speeds," and, "The forces increase at
high speed becoming very heavy around 500 kph [310 miles per hour]
indicated. The elevator force is extremely high at the higher speeds
and is one of the most objectionable features of the airplane."[6] Indeed,
at four hundred miles per hour it required four glacial seconds to roll
the Me-109 through only 45 degrees.[7] In comparison, the P-51 could
complete nearly a full, 360-degree roll during that same time.[8]

The type's maneuverability and general performance declined still further when encumbered with heavy guns designed to better bring down the big American bombers. These guns were accommodated in draggy underwing pods. "I refused to fly it with the additional 20-millimeter cannon slung in pods under the wing," recalled one Luftwaffe ace. "Worst of all, when we met escorting fighters of any kind, and P-51 Mustangs in particular, we were at a mortal disadvantage."[9]

Still, the Me-109 remained the favorite mount of many of the Luftwaffe's great aces, perhaps as much due to their familiarity with the type—and a sense of loyalty—as much as anything else. This familiarity certainly must have been very powerful as, on paper, the Me-109's stable mate, the FW-190, was a superior fighter.

Ultimately, despite its age, Messerschmitt's engineers squeezed the design for every bit of performance possible, and the Me-109 remained competitive through the end of the war. Although the Me-109G, the most produced variant, was less capable than the P-51 in most respects, its deficiencies were not readily apparent in the swirling hit-and-run frenzy of air combat.

The late-war Me-109K—successor to the many subvariants of the Me-109G—was given a more powerful engine as well as many improvements and refinements to include a better canopy, the Galland hood. It was described as a "very dubious modification" by Walter Wolfrum, the famous Luftwaffe ace. "The visibility was much better with the new design, but the emergency release of the one-piece canopy had a high rate of failure."[10] Wolfrum estimated that the new canopy failed to release at least half the time it was called upon, and that he was forced to crash land rather than bail out on two different occasions because the balky canopy had trapped him in the cockpit.

The Me-109K had a higher service ceiling than the Mustang and was faster in some regimes while being similarly maneuverable at lower airspeeds. It also carried heavier armament. Ultimately, notwithstanding the fact that its roots reached back to the early part of the previous decade, and despite its many shortcomings, the Me-109K—when flown by an experienced pilot—was still a capable fighter during the war's last months.

Unlike the Me-109, the FW-190 was a near-contemporary of the P-51. It entered service in August 1941, only a few months before the RAF's Mustangs, which went operational during January 1942. Also, unlike the Me-109, the FW-190 was powered by a radial engine and, with widely spaced landing gear, was much easier to handle on the ground. Unusually, it featured automatic controls for the propeller pitch, engine mixture and boost, and the pilot only had to operate the throttle lever. Flight controls were light, visibility through a vacuum-formed canopy was good and it had an excellent roll rate. Except for a tendency to snap into a stall when snatched too abruptly into a hard turn, it was a predictable and easy aircraft to fly.

Larger than the Me-109, the FW-190 was more readily modified, especially with heavier armament and greater bomb loads. Although its performance dropped off at high altitudes, it was still reasonably effective against the American heavy bombers. In fact, Adolf Galland, the commander of the Luftwaffe's fighter forces and a renowned Me-109 ace, recommended that production of the Me-109 be stopped in favor of the FW-190 in order to streamline production, logistics, and training. Late in 1944 the FW-190D, with an inline engine, began to appear in numbers. Known as the "long nose" because the forward fuselage had to be extended to accommodate the new engine, this aircraft was essentially equal to the best American fighters.

Ultimately, however, the performance of the best fighters operated by all the belligerents was similar enough that the difference between victory and defeat rested primarily with the pilots. An experienced and aggressive Me-109 pilot was likely to prevail over a neophyte P-51 pilot in one-on-one combat. Likewise, Righetti was exceedingly experienced, and at the controls of the P-51 would have been very difficult to defeat by anyone in an Me-109 or FW-190. Accordingly, as the number of experienced Luftwaffe pilots was small and declining, it was the better-trained American pilots who generally triumphed in air combat during the last year or so of the war.

There was one other equalizer that rendered moot the advantages that different fighters had over their competitors. That equalizer was the big air battle. When large formations clashed, attackers often had only a few seconds before they came under attack themselves. In these twisting, spiraling, death-at-every-turn melees, it didn't matter if one aircraft was twenty or thirty miles per hour faster, or could roll a few degrees more per second, or had a moderate climb advantage over other aircraft. In these confused fracases, most of the pilots who were shot down never saw their attackers until it was too late—if at all—and the victors were usually those with the experience and level-headedness necessary to maintain their awareness during situations in which it was very difficult to do so.

Herman Schonenberg, a young lieutenant in Righetti's 338th Fighter Squadron, recalled one such enormous melee. "One day we saw an enormous gaggle—it must have been a couple of hundred enemy fighters. Some estimates put it as high as four hundred. It looked like an enormous swarm of bees and we went barreling right into them. There were airplanes everywhere, a lot of people bailing out, parachutes all over the place. I think it was just a bunch of German kids that were bailing out as soon as someone fired at them. This was early on for me too, and I didn't shoot anybody down. I think I was just glad to get out on the other side of that mess."[11]

An illustration of how magnificently the air war had changed in just one year starts with the air combat of January 31, 1944, when the 55th was still flying P-38s. On that mission the group lost seven aircraft to enemy fighters. This single-mission loss was almost double the number of aircraft—four—that the 55th lost to enemy fighters from the time Righetti joined the unit in late October 1944 until the end of the war.[12] Indeed, during that time the 55th lost ten times as many aircraft—forty—to ground fire. Another sixteen were lost to other causes such as mid-air collisions, mechanical failures and fuel starvation.

Aside from their superior numbers and training, the USAAF's fighter pilots also enjoyed other smaller advantages that further padded the margin over their German counterparts. One was the gyroscope gunsight—the Luftwaffe did not have a widely used equivalent; another was the Berger Anti-G suit, more commonly known as the G-suit.

During aggressive, high-speed turns and climbs, or diving pullouts, the force of gravity (g-force) increased dramatically and caused the pilot's blood to be pulled from his head and down into his lower extremities. With his brain starved of oxygen, the pilot's vision faded, as did his sensibilities. If the g-forces were too great, the pilot lost consciousness. Although this loss of consciousness seldom lasted more than ten or fifteen seconds once the g-forces returned to normal, many men smashed into the ground or were shot down during this brief period.

Consequently, the advent of the G-suit during the spring of 1944 was most welcome. It was a set of chaps or trousers that wrapped around the lower abdomen and both legs all the way down to the ankles. Sewn into the ensemble were air bladders connected via the G-suit's hose to a pneumatic system in the aircraft. As the aircraft sensed increased g-forces it pumped air into the suit which expanded and wrapped itself tightly around the pilot's body. This kept more of the pilot's blood in his head and forestalled the onset of unconsciousness by up to two gs.

Although some pilots resisted the addition of another piece of flying gear, most were soon convinced of the G-suit's value. The 339th Fighter Group was the first group in the Eighth Air Force to adopt it during the late spring of 1944, and its pilots acknowledged that they scored more aerial victories than they otherwise would have.[13] The Eighth's other fighter groups quickly followed the 339th's example.

The 55th was among them and Righetti readily adapted to the new suit as soon as he joined the unit. In answer to a question from home, he wrote: "I have never flown a mission without my G-suit. And if I couldn't get another, I honestly wouldn't sell it for $7,000."

"JERRY WENT OUT OF CONTROL"

Righetti went to a rest home on January 14. "Doc is sending me to a flak home, starting Sunday," he wrote. "It's routine. We have to take it so I reckon I'd better be nice and go while the weather is still bad—miss less war that way."

The rest home concept was something the USAAF borrowed from its British counterpart, the RAF. Recognizing that its combat crews needed more respite from combat than a weekend furlough might provide—and because allowing men to go back to the States would have been too costly in time and resources—the USAAF eventually set up sixteen rest facilities in England. Variously referred to by the men as flak shacks, flak houses, or funny farms, they were demilitarized to the maximum extent possible, with an almost obsessive emphasis on rest and relaxation. Indeed, the men were issued civilian clothes upon arriving, and references to rank were discouraged.

Staffed by officers and enlisted personnel from the Air Service Command, as well as Red Cross hostesses, the homes were typically hotels, or large estates especially requisitioned for the purpose and usually located in pastoral settings far from the hubbub of the war. For physical recreation there were outdoor sports such as canoeing, cycling, tennis, and horseback riding—among other activities. Inside, the men could sleep, read, play snooker, billiards, cards or board games, write letters or simply do nothing. There were separate homes for the enlisted men of the bomber crews, however special pains were taken to ensure there was no difference in the quality of their experiences.

Men were typically sent to a home halfway through their combat tours, or earlier if they showed especially pronounced signs of weariness, fatigue, or mental stress. Righetti was sent because it was his turn, rather than because of any problems with his performance. The Eighth Air Force's brass was serious about the program and orders to the homes could not be refused. Ultimately, the homes proved to be quite successful and virtually everyone enjoyed the respite.

Although no records confirm it, Righetti probably went to Moulsford Manor where many of the 55th's men were sent. Located in Oxfordshire on the banks of the Thames, the estate claimed a history dating back to the 12th century. Righetti did not name or describe it, and evidently did not use his time there to write letters. "Long time since writing," he finally wrote on January 20 upon returning to Wormingford, "but nothing doing here to talk about. Been laying off for a week now at the flak shack. Enjoyed it plenty, but became quite bored—missed my guys and *Katy* [his aircraft] and Jerry's dirty tricks too much to sit around an old castle and be waited on."

Indeed, he wanted to get back to the work at which he shined. Aside from shooting up enemy aircraft, the neutralization of the German transport system was high on the list of the Allied planners. And the 55th, especially Righetti's 338th Fighter Squadron, excelled at it. "General Doolittle personally commended my outfit for loco busting three days ago. Since I've led the 338th, we've become the high scorers of the war."

A couple of days later, Righetti had news. "Our [combat] tour was extended 30 hours [from 270] to 300. And I was made assistant group commander. Both will throw off my 'Home in April' schedule. As second-in-command it won't be possible for me to fly so much since I'll only be up when leading the group. The 30 additional hours means six or seven additional missions, or some two-to-three additional weeks. New date of arrival in the States is June 1, or thereabouts. It is a promotion for me, though," he continued, "and sitting in a group executive spot puts me within yelling distance of a group of my own, and a pair of eagles [promotion to colonel] which I do want for my homecoming uniform."

The men who fought World War II were aware of the history they were making. Like most history makers, they were keen to capture their personal places and roles, and they did so through letters and photographs. Righetti included photographs in a letter to the family on January 29. He explained that his "unshaven and beat out" appearance was due to the fact that they were taken after a mission that spanned nearly six hours. In fact, he had a very thick beard and was self-conscious—and sometimes apologetic—of the fact that he often looked as if he hadn't shaved, particularly as it was noticeable to his men. "Righetti had a heavy beard," recalled Carroll Henry, a young lieutenant who often flew as his wingman. "He shaved, but you could see it."

Righetti noted that the group had enjoyed decent luck on that day's mission: "Fared better today—outfit got four [Me-]109s in the air. I led, called the shots, but did no shooting. That's the trouble with this new position of mine. Can't fly unless I lead the group, and in that capacity don't get in on the kill quite so often. Ah well, I only want 35 more anyhow."

In fact, as the leader that day, Righetti could have chased after any enemy fighter within reach of the group. There were no hard and fast rules as to how and where the group leaders were required to fly and the fact that Righetti didn't chase after the enemy fighters was proof against those who might have considered him too aggressive, or a glory hound. Certainly he wanted to rack up a big score, but so did every other fighter pilot in the Eighth Air Force.

Instead, he let the group perform as it was designed to do; the elements best positioned to engage the enemy were allowed to do so. This was tactically sound and spread both the risks and opportunities of air combat equally. And finally there was the fact that as the formation leader that day, the successes of the men also reflected well on him.

And to his credit, he took his job as a leader seriously. The group's photographer and public relations officer, Frank Stich, remembered that

Righetti approached him and noted that they shared the same birthday. "In his usual searching manner and thoroughness, he had been assiduously checking the group's personnel files to learn more about the men in his command." Stich was keen on the way that Righetti conducted himself and recalled that the men, "admired his sparkling bounce—officers as well as enlisted men. He had an unflagging give-and-take sense of humor, contagious and epidemic to all."[1]

When she wasn't staying with them Cathryn stayed in touch with the Righettis and forwarded the information about her husband that he shared with her. Her pride in his accomplishments was evident in her letter of January 26, 1945. "I got a letter from Elwyn dated the 13th of January. He expects the D.F.C. [Distinguished Flying Cross] for his victories on the 6th. The day he wrote it he had just gotten two more. There's just no stopping the boy."

She also wanted him home—and for good. "He still expects to be home in a few months. Oh, what a happy day that will be. I only hope that it's for reassignment to the training center instead of leave." In fact, the USAAF was at that very moment struggling with the notion of what it would look like in the near term. Already, in anticipation of the war's end, it had dramatically curtailed pilot training. It was only a fraction of what it had been just a year earlier and there was little guarantee that there would be a need for her husband in the training center even if that is what he had wanted. On the other hand, the USAAF still had to make war in a world within which Germany was still fighting with vigor, and Japan was not expected to surrender any time soon.

Cathryn and the Righettis obviously claimed Elwyn as their own. But the rest of the nation also wanted to identify not only with him but all of its fighting men. Never in its history had the United States been so singularly committed to a common cause. Because virtually every family had someone in uniform overseas, there was a ready market for news of the war and the media was ready—indeed, encouraged—to meet the demand. Hometowns were eager to publicize the accomplishments of local heroes and were not bashful about adopting outsiders as their own.

As Cathryn, a native Texan, noted in a letter to his parents, Righetti was claimed by Texas citizens as their very own. "I'm enclosing an article that was clipped from the Fort Worth paper. Of course, it's old news and you will probably resent them saying he's a Texan, but how else would we get our Texas heroes if we didn't adopt them?" Another news release accompanied a photo of Righetti with his friend Fred Gray and a snow-covered P-51. The release described how, "two San Antonio colonels," had the opportunity to meet up again in faraway England.

At the start of the fighting in 1939—the same year that Righetti enlisted as an aviation cadet—the Luftwaffe leadership failed to anticipate what the war would become. And that failure to anticipate translated into a failure to plan and provision. The result was that during the closing months of the war, Germany was fighting the Allies with an air force that didn't have enough aircraft of the right types. And aircraft numbers and types notwithstanding, the Luftwaffe didn't have enough pilots. Even then, the majority of the pilots it did field were woefully undertrained when compared to their American and British—and even Soviet—counterparts.

That Germany was desperate is an understatement. A sign of that desperation was that the Third Reich committed wholesale to a broad spectrum of "wonder weapons." In reality, most of these schemes were little more than ill-considered shortcuts and hackneyed concepts that Germany's leadership hoped would substitute for the difficult work it had neglected to complete years earlier. Even the much-feared V-1 flying bomb and the V-2 guided ballistic missile—both of which had pre-war origins—were examples of misguided efforts that consumed tremendous resources but had little effect on the war.

The Me-163 rocket-propelled fighter was another interesting but flawed concept, with results that came far from justifying the people and material that were spent on it. Despite its high speed and heavy armament—two 30-millimeter cannon—it knocked down only about a dozen American bombers. Likewise, the He-162 and Ba-349 were designed as easy-to-fly fighters readily manufactured from non-strategic materials. They were intended to be produced in prodigious numbers and flown by pilots who had received only rudimentary training. Neither became operational and the notion that they might have been effective against the massive American bomber formations and their aggressive fighter escorts was absurd. In the aggregate, these many failed schemes were a waste that reflected the inability of the Luftwaffe's leadership to understand what the Allies were capable of, and to prioritize resources against them.

Righetti encountered another of these ill-considered concepts on February 3, 1945, when the 55th escorted the Eighth's heavy bombers to Berlin. The group's mission summary report noted that the bomber men made quite an impression: "Bomb results exuberantly observed, as fires, explosions and smoke gutted city." Still, it came at a cost as the report counted five bombers and one fighter down in the target area.

After escorting the bombers out of the Berlin area and through Bremen, Righetti, at the head of the 55th, redeployed the group. He left one formation with the bombers and took two squadrons "downstairs" for a low-altitude sweep on the return route. When the 38th Fighter Squadron called out targets that he couldn't see, he cleared it off on its own.

His formation continued to shrink: "In the area of the Muritz See, my Red Flight leader called in a Ju–88 below the undercast which was not visible to me, but as my radio was working only intermittently, I did not receive his call."[2] William Lewis, the leader of Red Flight, dived on the enemy aircraft. "It was a Ju–88 night fighter. The turret gunner fired a short burst as I was closing in," reported Lewis. "However, he scored no strikes on my aircraft. I opened fire at about 75-to-100 yards and closed to about 25 yards. I saw many strikes about the canopy and both engines."[3] As Lewis pulled away he noted that the German aircraft's right engine was afire. It is likely the pilot was dead or wounded as the Ju-88 made only a couple of shallow turns before it smashed into a field and exploded.

Meanwhile, Righetti pressed westward on a course that took the formation about twenty miles southeast of Hamburg. "White Flight, which I was leading, continued on seeking targets of opportunity," he recalled. "Near Boizenburg on the Elbe River, I located a small, clear hole in the otherwise unbroken undercast. In this hole there were two locomotives. I called them in and started down, needing only one ninety-degree turn to starboard to set me up in firing position."

Flying conditions below the clouds were poor as the visibility was only about two miles. At a cruising speed of more than 250 miles per hour, the flight could cover this distance in less than thirty seconds. Moreover, the bases of the clouds were ragged and reached down to only about six hundred feet in places. Consequently, the men had to watch not only for the enemy, but also for obstacles such as power lines, or rising terrain.

Righetti pointed White Flight—echeloned to his right in a half-mile-long string—at the two trains. At the same time he called out assignments over the radio. This served two purposes. First, it helped ensure the formation's firepower was maximized across the targets. Second, it reduced the risk of midair collisions; aircraft firing on the same target tended to converge on the same point in the sky. It was then that Righetti spotted three, odd-looking, aircraft-on-aircraft combinations to his left-front and below, flying in the opposite direction in a loose, inverted-V formation. Each combination appeared to be a bomber with a fighter mounted atop.

The contraptions that caught Righetti's attention were actually hybrid combinations of fighters affixed to Ju-88 bombers. German pilots informally called the arrangement a *Huckepack* (piggyback), or *Vater und Sohn* (father and son). More generally, the arrangement was called a Mistel. Mistel was the German word for mistletoe, a parasitic plant. Regardless of what it was called, it was the flawed realization of a proposal to use worn-out Ju-88s—aimed from attached fighter aircraft—as unmanned aerial bombs.

When the concept was originally presented during 1941 the German Air Ministry dismissed the idea as impractical, if not outright bizarre. However, by 1943 the Luftwaffe was increasingly hard-pressed and regularly grabbed at straws that showed even a glimmer of promise.

Consequently, the Mistel concept was no longer considered quite so outlandish and the go-ahead was given to proceed with development. The first flight occurred during July that same year.

No matter how much engineering went into the concept, the result could never be better than awkward. The fighter, either an FW-190 or an Me-109, depending on the variant—and there were many—was attached via explosive bolts to an arrangement of steel struts that were, in turn, attached to the Ju-88. A rudimentary electrical control system connected the fighter to the bomber and allowed the pilot to fly the combination. The engines of both aircraft were usually running and the fighter typically drew fuel from the bomber to extend the reach of the strange weapon; although it was a one-way trip for the bomber, the pilot in the fighter was expected to return to his base.

During training, or when moving between bases, the Ju-88s often carried support personnel. However, in the operational configuration the bomber was unmanned and the cockpit and crew were replaced by a shaped-charge warhead of approximately four tons. It packed enough power to penetrate virtually any bunker or ship hull in existence. As the contraption approached the target in a shallow dive, the fighter pilot lined up as best he could before—at close range—firing the explosive bolts that connected the two aircraft. Once he was safely separated from the Ju-88, he exited the area as quickly as possible while the bomber's three-axis, gyro-controlled autopilot held it on course until it hit its target.

The Luftwaffe's leadership hoped to use the Mistel in long-range attacks on strategic targets. The British Home Fleet at Scapa Flow was one such target and a number of Mistels were staged in Denmark during much of 1944 before the idea was given up in the face of uncooperative weather and changing operational conditions. A group of massive Soviet power stations was also considered but the Red Army's rapid advances during 1944 overran suitable airbases and made the scheme impossible. Instead, beginning on the night of June 24, 1944, when ships supporting the Allied invasion in Normandy were attacked, the Mistels were frittered away in small inconsequential operations that achieved virtually nothing. The last Mistel attack was made against bridges across the Oder River on April 26, 1945, in the face of the onrushing Soviets.

Righetti knew none of this. He immediately abandoned his attack on the locomotives and turned to engage the enemy curiosities: "I mistakenly called them in as Buzz-Bomb [V-1] equipped He-111s and broke rapidly left and up in a 200-degree chandelle, positioning myself on the tail of the middle one. I started firing at 500-to-600 yards, 30 degrees angle off, and missed two short bursts. As I swung into trail and closed to point-blank range firing a long burst, I saw many excellent strikes on the fuselage and empennage of the large aircraft and scattered strikes and a small fire on the fighter."[4]

The two-aircraft combination—still intact—went into a steep dive. "As I was at this point overrunning them," Righetti noted, "I did not actually see them crash; but five or ten seconds later I observed a large explosion and spotted considerable burning wreckage."

"Still not realizing just what we were attacking, but feeling that I had destroyed one complete unit, I turned slightly port for another," he said. In a later radio interview he recalled, "The propellers of both planes were spinning ... really an odd sight."[5] It was indeed an unusual scene as no one in the Eighth Air Force had ever encountered the odd contraptions.

"As I closed, and even before I could open fire, I discovered that the 'Buzz-Bomb' was actually an FW-190 fastened atop the heavy twin-engine aircraft. As I was closing to fire, the heavy aircraft seemed to be jettisoned, went into a shallow diving turn to the left, and crashed and burned in a small hamlet."

Righetti pressed after the enemy fighter that only a moment before had been attached to the larger aircraft. Attacking from behind, he set it afire. "Jerry went out of control and crashed straight ahead. At this point I noticed a few tracers too close and coming from behind. I broke sharply left and up into the low cloud."

Richard Gibbs was Righetti's wingman and he wasted no time in knocking down another of the Mistel combinations. He set one of the bigger ships on fire and immediately attacked the fighter when the two aircraft separated. "After a short dive the FW-190 was released. The 190 appeared to be unstable in the air, but it managed to get in violent evasive action during the ensuing combat."[6]

Gibbs saddled up on the enemy fighter and began firing from a range of two hundred yards. He continued to fire bursts until he was nearly on top of the German. "I saw many strikes all over the aircraft and observed parts of the cowling and the canopy fly off. There was also fire in or around the cockpit." Gibbs skidded out to the right to keep from running into the enemy fighter. "As I looked back, I saw where the 190 had crashed into the ground."

Righetti probably didn't realize it, but the group of three Mistels that he and Gibbs shot down were trailed by a line of three more. These were attacked by his number three and four men, Bernard Howes and Patrick Moore. Both of them had actually continued their firing runs on the locomotives and spotted the second group of Mistels after pulling up from their attack. Howes led Moore into a hard left turn in pursuit, and after a short engagement the two of them knocked down a pair of the combinations.

The fighting was over in just a few minutes. When the shooting stopped, Righetti's White Flight claimed five of the six Ju-88s and four of the six fighters. Of these, Righetti claimed two of the Ju-88s, one of the fighters and another fighter as probably destroyed.

It is difficult to reconcile the 55th's air combat claims that day against remaining German records. Fritz Lorbach was a Ju-88 pilot with KG 200 and was the pilot of one of three crews that were ferrying Mistels from Kolberg, in eastern Germany, to a base in Denmark. Because it was a ferry flight rather than an operational sortie, the Ju-88s were flying with crews. Lorbach recalled that he and his comrades were especially wary because the fighters atop the Ju-88s were unarmed. As they approached the airfield at Hagenow—about twenty miles east of Boizenburg—he spotted a flight of fighters that he mistakenly identified as Me-109s.

As it developed, the fighters were American P-51s and they attacked immediately. All three Ju-88s were shot down, including Lorbach's: "The crew of my Ju-88 was not injured even though the left engine was on fire and I had to make an emergency landing in the woods."[7] About half of the men aboard the other Ju-88s perished as did the pilots of the Mistel fighters.

Although there are discrepancies, it is likely that it was Lorbach's flight that Righetti and his men attacked that day. That Righetti and the other pilots described the location of the encounter as the vicinity of Boizenburg rather than Hagenow is minor considering the limited visibility and the fact that American pilots were typically not as familiar with German geography as were their enemy counterparts. Too, Boizenburg and Hagenow were only about twenty miles apart. However, that being said, it is unusual that none of the Americans mentioned the combat taking place in the vicinity of an airfield.

Additionally, the 55th's mission summary report clearly stated that two different formations of three aircraft were spotted: "… observed 6 pick-a-backs (FW 190s straddling Ju 88s) at about 800 feet intently prowling along on a NW heading. Combo's were flying in a cheesey 'V' of 3's in trail." The exact origin of this observation is difficult to determine as Righetti observed that the three Mistels he attacked were in a loose line abreast, whereas Howes declared that the three Mistels he and Moore engaged after firing on the trains were flying in trail. And in a newspaper article that described the attack as the first in which Eighth Air Force fighters encountered the Mistel combinations, Righetti was quoted: "… I spotted five strange-looking contraptions—He-111s with FW-190s perched on top, riding pick-a-back." Based on this article, it is apparent that the mission debriefings occurred later and correctly determined, and recorded, that the bigger ships were Ju-88s rather than He-111s.

Another discrepancy is that the fighters atop the Ju-88s in Lorbach's formation were Me-109s rather than FW-190s. This conflicts with the encounter reports filed by the 55th's men. None of them mentions Me-109s. The discussion is further muddied by Lorbach's declaration that the Mustangs did shoot down an FW-190 over Hagenow that was not associated with the Mistels whatsoever. This information notwithstanding, it was not uncommon for the two German fighter types to be mistaken for each other.

Ultimately, it must be acknowledged that air combat was a whirling maelstrom that was nearly impossible to accurately recreate after the fact. Indeed, the records of air combat between opposing sides very rarely reconciled to a fine degree of accuracy. It should also be considered that many of the German Air Force's records were destroyed or lost and that KG 200 was a secretive unit. It is unlikely that all the details considering this particular engagement will ever be known for certain.

Regardless of how many Mistel combinations were airborne that day, Righetti's gun camera film showed excellent strikes and flames on one combination, and good strikes on two other aircraft. He was consequently awarded credit for two of the Ju-88s and one of the fighters. Other pilots were credited with aerial victories over three other Ju-88s and three FW-190s.

The encounter caused quite a buzz. Aside from the Allied intelligence offices, the public was fascinated by the notion of conjoined combat aircraft. And Righetti was obviously pleased when he wrote home to the family that evening. "Got a special commendation from General Doolittle and my pictures [gun camera film] will make national news-reels on account of targets were pickaback jobs—no one [in the Eighth Air Force] had nailed any before." In fact, just as Righetti said, the Army Pictorial Service released a newsreel, *Air Support on the Western Front*, that featured, among other footage, his gun camera film from the mission.

The criticism of Germany's leadership and its proclivity to chase after dubious concepts in search of a wonder weapon should be tempered by the acknowledgement that the United States also tested similar concepts. For instance, Operation *Aphrodite* was an American effort to steer unmanned, radio-controlled bombers—loaded with high explosives—into German targets. It was a bigger failure than the Mistel effort and claimed the life of Joseph P. Kennedy, the older brother of the future president. On the other hand, whereas the United States had the resources to spare for such experiments, Germany did not. And of course, it should be recalled that the United States was successful in developing and fielding the most effective wonder weapon of the war—the atomic bomb.

Righetti, like most men, had his aircraft embellished to denote how many enemy aircraft he had been credited with destroying. These included aircraft destroyed on the ground, for which the Eighth Air Force gave official credit. That is not to say that these official credits counted toward qualification as an "ace," as this was not an official designation in the USAAF, and the popular notion of an ace was of a pilot that had been credited with five or more *aerial* victories.

Righetti wrote home during this time to describe how the "swastikas on *Katy* look super." To be sure, the kill markings that Righetti mentioned were among the most unique in the Eighth Air Force—certainly no other aircraft in the world carried them. Rather than traditional red, black and white Nazi flags, or simple black swastikas or iron crosses, the markings were made up of a black swastika on a circular field of yellow or light green, with a darker green border. The swastikas were ragged, as if riddled by gunfire. Superimposed over each, was a stylized katydid with wings that spanned the entire marking. The markings were arranged in a single horizontal row along the left side of *Katydid*'s nose.

These were individual artworks rather than decals, or stencil jobs. Each was carefully and painstakingly created. To be sure, the layered nature of the many features required several hours of detailed attention and indicated that the now-unknown artist was particularly dedicated to Righetti, or well-rewarded, or both.

February 11, 1945: "Still stinking weather. So, no mission. Goddam."

During the period following Righetti's assignment to the 55th, the unit seemed to undergo a metamorphosis. Whereas its record since it began combat operations during October 1943 had seldom been stellar in comparison to other fighter groups, it had certainly been satisfactory.

However, the group began to particularly distinguish itself as 1944 gave way to 1945. On February 13, 1945, the 55th's commander, George Crowell, described to his men just how well they had performed the previous month. Aside from excellent maintenance and readiness figures, the 55th "destroyed 157 locomotives, 5 times as many as the next closest in the Wing [66th]." Crowell further noted that, "The 55th Fighter Group placed second among groups in the 66th Wing in total enemy aircraft destroyed, but led the Wing in aircraft destroyed on the ground claiming three times as many destroyed as claimed by the next closest fighter group."[8]

Crowell was in command of the group at this time, and the credit for the unit's successes consequently belonged to him. And certainly the 55th's performance had been on the uptick to some degree during the months following the transition from the P-38 to the P-51. But there is no denying the fact that the pace of improvement accelerated following Righetti's arrival. Indeed, the men of the group emulated his aggressiveness with a spirit that had previously been missing.

And the results were apparent.

"SEEMS LIKE AN EXCELLENT
BREAK FOR ME"

When Righetti left the States for England he did so with the hope—if not the expectation—of commanding a fighter group. Notwithstanding his lack of combat experience, his record as a pilot, an administrator and a leader was excellent. He had paid his dues for several years in the training command and had additionally performed well at the 55th as a pilot, a squadron commander and the deputy group commander. In short, he had done everything that could have been expected of him and he did it well, and by the book, and without stepping on anyone's toes.

And he was finally rewarded for it during mid-February 1945 when the 55th's commanding officer, George Crowell, reached the end of his combat tour. Righetti wrote home upon being notified, but his tone was matter-of-fact. "Guess I've got a little better news today. This afternoon word came through that our group C.O. [Commanding Officer] was being taken off operations and that in a week or ten days I would start functioning permanently as C.O."

"He was *very* different from Righetti," recalled Herman Schonenberg of Crowell. The observation was disputed by no one as Crowell's conservative approach to combat operations stood in marked contrast to Righetti's almost reckless aggressiveness. "It seemed to me that he was pretty much all business," said Frank Birtciel about Righetti. "We were there to engage the enemy and you could just about bet that when he went along, things would pop." Birtciel, who had been with the 55th during its indifferent combat debut in October 1943 said that he "just wished we'd had him in our early days of the P-38."[1]

Still, notwithstanding their different dispositions, there was never evidence of conflict or any kind of a rift between Righetti and Crowell. Righetti's service as one of Crowell's squadron commanders, and later as his deputy, was obviously good enough to earn him command of the group. Before Crowell departed, he handed Righetti a commendation: "It is my very great pleasure to extend to you my appreciation and commendation for the superior manner in which you have performed your duties during the time I have been in command."[2] Decades later, Crowell recalled Righetti, as "charming," and "one you'd like to have as a friend."[3] For his part, Righetti never mentioned Crowell in his letters, but extant photographs show them together in social situations.

"This will make the largest job I've had in the Army so far," Righetti wrote. "A group C.O. has his own station complete. Seems like an excellent break for me." Certainly, this was the most responsibility Righetti had ever been given. Barely six years earlier he had been accountable for nothing more than a dairy truck. And he was correct in noting that "a group C.O. has his own station complete." He was in charge not only of the 55th and the base at Wormingford, but also the various support units that performed heavy maintenance on his aircraft and that provided logistics, security and other support. In total, these units numbered just less than two thousand men.

Ed Giller, the commander of the 343rd Fighter Squadron, had been with the 55th since before it had arrived in England. He was glad for the change of command. "Righetti was an inspiration from the time he arrived. He was a go-getter. And when he took over, the attitude changed even more—he really fired the group up."[4]

Giller also recalled that Righetti didn't try to make wholesale changes to administrative or operational procedures that were proven and working well. And although Righetti appreciated military discipline and demanded it where it was appropriate, he was no martinet. "He enjoyed mixing with the men," Giller said. "He was certainly not a recluse." This casual approach served him well in judging the morale of the unit and in uncovering issues that otherwise might have festered out of sight.

Leedom John was a junior officer who remembered being excited at Righetti's assumption of command. "He was a good leader and had our deepest respect—he *led* us! He didn't tell you how to do it, he showed you by doing it. He was a *good* leader!" Richard Gibbs, who had shot down a Mistel combination with Righetti on February 3, 1945, and later scored two more aerial victories, observed that the group responded positively: "I do think the 55th was the most aggressive and most successful outfit during the last three months of the war."[5]

Righetti officially took command of the 55th on February 22, 1945, and his excitement was still evident a few days later on February 25. "The new job is the best by far I've ever had. Lots of responsibility I know, but really satisfying. Now I'm really slapping Jerry with my own outfit and knocking chunks out of him too. We got 14 enemy aircraft today—7 jets—and although I didn't personally score, they're all my boys now that I have the group."

In fact, the seven Me-262s that Righetti's 55th knocked down that day was the highest single-day jet tally of any fighter group during the war. It was near the airfield at Giebelstadt that the 55th's 38th Fighter Squadron caught six of them, together with a number of FW-190s, in the process of taking off and landing. Millard Anderson was hit by antiaircraft fire as he sprayed rounds at a pair of just-landed FW-190s. He subsequently started for home with his wingman and shortly thereafter spotted an Me-262 flying low and to his left in the opposite direction. "I immediately did a wingover and closed dead astern to about 750 or 800 feet range. As my gunsight had been knocked out, I placed the Me-262 in the center of the front canopy and held the trigger down until hits were observed. The enemy aircraft caught on fire behind the canopy and the wheels fell down. Then the pilot jettisoned the canopy and bailed out."[6]

The mission summary report noted, "All jets sighted were tacked onto and either exploded or crashed." The seventh jet was spotted at three thousand feet over the airfield at Leipheim. "Blow job racked it up trying to set it down on the field, but it was exploded in midair by a determined Mustang attack."

Although Righetti didn't score in the air on that particular mission, he received permission to lead the group on another that same afternoon.

He was quoted in a press release: "I thought that maybe we could catch the Luftwaffe out on a mission," Righetti declared, "but we couldn't find a single plane. We did spot some German soldiers taking physical training exercises near Weisbaden, and I took my group down to strafe them. The Jerries ran into their barracks, so we shot hell out of their buildings."[7]

One of the units at Wormingford for which Righetti was not responsible was the 3rd Scouting Force. Formed during September 1944, about a month before Righetti arrived, the 3rd was one of three scouting forces created late in the war to check weather conditions over targets prior to bombing raids. They were additionally tasked with determining the disposition of enemy antiaircraft and fighter units at specific locations.

The 3rd Scouting Force was equipped with a handful of P-51s and, unlike the other two scouting units, a few B-17s. Although the 55th initially provided pilots to help man the 3rd at least into December 1944, the unit later received its own pilots—usually bomber men who had volunteered after completing their combat tours. The aircraft wore the same markings as the 55th's, except that the rudders sported a red and white checkered pattern, painted on the diagonal. All of the scouting units provided good service and the 3rd excelled not only in executing its primary mission, but in downing 22 Luftwaffe fighters while doing so.

Late in the morning of February 27, the 55th launched 49 P-51s in two groups to escort B-17s from the 3d Air Division to Leipzig. The escort across the target and back out was uneventful and once the bombers were safely on their way home, Righetti took his formation down to look for something to kill. Approaching the deck, the group broke into four-ship flights in order to better maneuver.

Righetti flew as low as he dared. "I came up a valley 10 or 15 feet high," he wrote home, "to keep out of flak, and was really shucking." His rancher's eye noted the nature of the landscape over which his aircraft roared. "The valley sloped upward, was farmed in the bottom and had tall green timber on both sides. There was considerable snow about."

"As I popped over the ridge at the head of the valley and started down the slope on the other side, I was very tickled to see laid out before me a beautiful cavalry post complete with corrals, stables, barracks, haystacks and Heinie soldiers. There were about a dozen of them squatting cowpuncher style around a pretty bonfire in one of the corrals straight ahead." Righetti dipped a wing and flew directly at the fire.

If, as a rancher, he felt any empathy with the German horsemen, he didn't let it get in the way of his war-making duties. "Dropped the pipper on the bonfire and squeezed [the trigger]. Was just a little [too far] out of range to put out just the fire—boyish prank—as I originally intended, so the .50 [caliber] slugs rendered the meeting adjourned and the one German hay hustler still able to navigate dragged himself in front of my wingman."

Righetti and his men wheeled around and shredded the enemy camp with gunfire. "We worked the place over for a few minutes and left with the detachment pretty much written off Adolph's [sic] books—sure did burn pretty." The truth of the matter was that the scene the 55th left behind was anything but pretty. Barracks, paddocks and haystacks burned bright orange against the cold, leaden sky. Horses and wounded men screamed. Loose animals galloped across the frozen, blood-spattered ground, chased by the men who were still able to do so, or who weren't tending their dead or wounded comrades.

Righetti tallied his claims for the day: "2 loco[motive]s destroyed, 2 trucks destroyed, 3 high tension towers severely damaged, 12 goods wagons [boxcars] damaged, one radio tower rendered useless, plus the cavalry post on which I claimed 20-plus Jerry groomsmen, 4 barracks complete with sack artists [napping soldiers] and 40-plus head of cavalry mounts. Tough war. Hope this isn't too ugly."

In fact, it was ugly. And perhaps it was too ugly for the family to consider. But the horse and "Heinie" killing was also necessary. Notwithstanding the stereotypical image of the German army and its blitzkrieg attacks, the truth was that only 20 percent of its units were mechanized. The balance relied on horse transport which was slow, unreliable and manpower-intensive. On the other hand, horses—many horses—were available in Germany and the territories it conquered. The Wehrmacht used nearly three million of them during the war—more than any other nation's army. And they were used to move artillery, ammunition and other war material—stuff with which to kill Allied soldiers. And so, just as trucks and trains were legitimate targets, so were horses. Righetti must have reconciled himself to killing the enemy by that time in his combat career, but this was the first mission during which he had shot up horses. Because he had grown up with them, and learned to love them, it is likely that the casual tone of his letter did not match what he felt.

In fact this notion was buttressed by a radio show broadcast by Ted Malone a couple of months earlier. Malone was a radio celebrity, sponsored by Westinghouse, who specialized in human interest stories for the "folks back home." The focus of his December 6, 1944, show—transmitted via shortwave from England—was the good work of the 4-H Clubs of America which was finishing its national convention in Chicago that evening. Malone featured a couple of former 4-H members, now fighting the Nazis.

"Tell you another fella who'd like to be there tonight too," said Malone. "Lieutenant Colonel Elwyn G. Righetti of San Luis Obispo, California. He's the C.O. of one of our Mustang fighter squadrons. Lives on a cattle ranch back in the States." Malone strengthened Righetti's 4-H connection by noting that, as a member, he "always went to the stock show in South San Francisco."

Malone went on. "The fellas say that in strafing, Colonel Righetti doesn't mind shooting up trains or convoys, but he *always* avoids a team of horses." The truth was that Righetti actively looked for trains and convoys and other legitimate targets. And now, more than two months after the broadcast, his reluctance to shoot horses, which were also legitimate targets, had faded.

Malone kept with the theme of the broadcast and made a declaration that wasn't true but which made the story a bit better. He described how Righetti's aircraft, *Katydid*, "has a big four-leaf clover painted on it. And in each leaf there's a big 'H' painted—4-H." Understandably, considering his audience, Malone did not mention the bare breasts of the katydid caricature that also graced *Katydid's* nose.[8]

The 4-H clover might never have been painted on Righetti's aircraft. In a letter home he described the meeting with Malone during which he promised the broadcaster, "to paint a 4-H insignia on *Katydid*, which I had planned to do anyhow." However, there is no evidence that his P-51 ever sported a clover. It is likely that the exigencies of wartime operations overtook the necessity of decorating the aircraft per Malone's request.

It didn't take long before the leadership at the 66th Fighter Wing tried to rein in their new commander at the 55th Fighter Group. Although Righetti's aggressiveness and guidance in the air were appreciated, the 66th's staff wanted more of his time for administrative activities. "Didn't fly today," he wrote on February 28. The general [Brigadier General Murray Woodbury] says that one out of three [missions] is all I can have, but I think I'll cheat a bit."

Righetti led the 55th again on March 3, 1945. The group was tasked to escort B-17s of the 1st Air Division to the synthetic fuel production plant at Ruhland, north of Dresden, in eastern Germany. No enemy aircraft were encountered and the group broke up and descended from thirty thousand feet to look for targets of opportunity on the return leg. Righetti was at the head of the 338th Fighter Squadron but uncharacteristically was unable to find much worth shooting at. The group's mission summary report shows that the squadron shot up a factory of some sort but the action was literally nothing to write home about as Righetti did not mention it in any of his letters.

Such was not the case with Robert Cox of the 38th Fighter Squadron. On the leg to Ruhland his engine stopped and he jettisoned his drop tanks. After a gut-wrenching moment he coaxed the engine back to life. Still, with a diminished fuel supply and an engine he did not trust, Cox turned for home on his own. In fact, the group experienced an unusually high number of problems that morning as a total of eight of the forty-nine aircraft it sent airborne turned back to Wormingford without completing the mission.

Cox evidently regained confidence in his engine as the route he chose took him toward southern Germany rather than directly back to England. The adventure turned into everything that Righetti could have wished for himself. Motoring along at only two thousand feet, Cox spied "two radar-equipped Dornier 217s over Kitzingen Airfield. One was circling the field at 1,000 feet and the second was just taking off, ninety degrees to my flight path." Kitzingen, to that point in the war, had been an operational training field. When Cox stumbled over it that day it was readying to transition to full-fledged combat operations.

Cox dove after the circling Do-217. "Making a shallow turn to the right I closed to about 300 yards, dead astern, and started firing. After one long burst, strikes were seen on the bomber's fuselage, right engine and right wing. The engine burst into flames and the plane rolled over and went straight in from 500 feet."

The other Dornier turned hard back toward the field. "I then went after the second Dornier," Cox said, "and as I closed to within range and was about to fire, the pilot attempted to turn into the field for a landing. His hurried turn resulted in his wing hitting the ground which sent him cartwheeling down the runway, exploding and burning."

Laid out below Cox were, "fifty-plus aircraft parked wingtip-to-wingtip in front of hangars with others dispersed about the field." He made repeated passes on the neatly arrayed aircraft, setting five Do-217s and a fuel truck ablaze. "On my last pass I had only two flak guns shooting at me and my aim was erratic so it was time to head for home."

After climbing to altitude, Cox spotted a flight of ten Me-109s headed directly for him. "I had no doubt they were being vectored to me by the information supplied from Kitzingen Field. They broke into me, firing as they came. I turned into them upward, passing directly under the lead ship and went into the overcast flying on instruments until well out of the area."[9]

Aside from Cox, the 38th, like the 338th, found little worth molesting and made no claims. However the 55th's third squadron, the 343rd, created plenty of action. Half the squadron dropped down to shoot up train and road traffic in the vicinity of Brux, Czechoslovakia, making claims for 21 locomotives. The other half of the squadron discovered a hodgepodge of approximately 35 aircraft parked on the airfield at Prague/Letnany. The group immediately started strafing and made multiple passes despite heavy antiaircraft fire.

Brookes Liles was hit and flames reached back from his engine. "I was right above him," said squadron mate Marvin Satenstein, "and could see that his aircraft was still under control, but he couldn't get much power out of it." Satenstein followed the stricken aircraft for another minute or so until Liles bellied it into a field. "I watched him get out of his aircraft and just then it caught fire."[10]

Satenstein and a handful of squadron mates—including Bernard Howes—circled Liles. Howes and Liles were very close friends, having gone through flight training together. Howes surprised everyone by announcing that he intended to land and retrieve Liles.

A handful of such rescues had been successfully made during the previous year. The press loved it while Doolittle, the head of the Eighth Air Force, hated it. In fact, he forbade the practice as it was too dangerous and risked losing two men instead of just one. Nevertheless, more than one airman had disobeyed Doolittle's order and Howes readied to do the same in order to save his friend.

After making a pass over the field where Liles had crashed, Howes made another circuit, lowered his landing gear, and set his aircraft, My L'il Honey, down. Liles ran to meet him and the two men shed equipment—to include parachutes—to make enough room inside the already-snug cockpit. Finally, with enemy ground fire growing intense they shoehorned themselves into the little fighter and started their takeoff roll. The aircraft accelerated and Howes made a radio call, "Gang, keep your fingers crossed and we'll make it."

Crossed fingers were not enough and a German bullet blew the throttle from Howes's hand. "The Mustang rose for a little bit," Satenstein said, "but didn't have the speed and settled back on the ground." On making contact the aircraft bounced then cartwheeled and crashed, catching fire as it did so.

Miraculously, the two pilots were not killed. Liles's nose was broken and Howes sustained a blow to the head that gave him a concussion and temporarily blinded him. Their squadron mates circled overhead while Liles dragged Howes away from the burning aircraft. "I buzzed the wreck," said Satenstein. "I saw both Howes and Liles walking to the east towards a large highway. Both looked okay and waved to me as I passed over them." Both men were quickly captured and made POWs. They survived the war and Howes's eyesight returned as his concussion abated.

Although he made no mention of it, it is possible that Righetti had to answer to higher headquarters for the forbidden stunt. Doolittle had given orders against these attempts because he anticipated the sorts of failures that Howes and Liles so aptly showcased. Still, no one anywhere denied that reining in the devotion of the men to each other was a good problem to have. On the other hand, ordering that same sort of loyalty would have been very difficult indeed.

Ultimately, Robert Cox's claims for the two Do-217s destroyed over Kitzingen that day, as well as the five destroyed on the ground, were disallowed. Beginning in 1943, the Eighth Air Force's Fighter Command, or VIII FC, periodically convened Victory Credit Boards, or VCBs. Their purpose was to evaluate the claims of pilots—for both ground and air targets—against available evidence. This evidence typically included the individual pilot's statement, usually in the form of a Pilot's Personal Encounter Report, as well as witness reports and gun camera film. The board members were experienced pilots with the technical expertise necessary to adjudicate the many claims.

This validation of claims by a higher authority provided a level of standardization and sense of fairness among the Eighth's fighter pilots. It helped ensure that the claims of all the pilots were held to the same level of scrutiny regardless of rank or affiliation. This meant that a group commander's claims were evaluated with the same rigor as the lowliest lieutenant's.

Still, the system was imperfect. Gun camera film was notoriously unreliable and could be rendered useless by any number of factors to include camera failure, improper aperture settings, dirty camera ports, airframe vibration, and bad handling and processing. Victorious pilots often waited anxiously for days as the gun camera film necessary to support their claims was developed. More than a few were crushed to learn that the imagery was so poor that nothing could be ascertained.

That the gun camera was so unreliable is evidenced by the paucity of good, clear, gun camera imagery when considered against the enormous numbers of aircraft that were shot down. Certainly, much footage has been lost, destroyed or abandoned but it was never dependable and the Victory Credit Board was often put in a difficult position when presented with fuzzy and indistinct imagery that represented a pilot's claim for victory.

On the other hand, the film sometimes added clarity to claims. More than a month after the event, on December 5, 1944, Righetti wrote of the Me-109 for which he and Cramer shared credit after knocking it down on November 2. "Confirmation came through yesterday on *my* Me-109. Four more and I'll be an ace. Pictures gave me full, instead of shared, credit." In the end he did nothing to try to change the initial finding of shared credit. He was likely satisfied in knowing that he had inflicted the lion's share of the damage, and additionally did not want to run the risk of ruining the good relationship—and friendship—he shared with Cramer.

If the system had a weakness, it was in the witness statements. In the absence of usable gun camera film, total reliance was on the honor and integrity of the men and what they wrote in their witness reports. It assumed that high-ranking officers did not bully or otherwise influence their junior counterparts. It also had to presume that friends did not bolster each other's claims based simply on their relationships. Although it would be naïve to believe that such behaviors did not occur at all, it is generally accepted that they did not to any great degree.

In Cox's case, he was alone and could offer no witness statements. At the top of his encounter report there was a handwritten notation, "film all white," which indicated that his gun camera film showed nothing and consequently failed to support his account. At the bottom of the encounter report there was another handwritten note: "Colonel Righetti will call General Woodbury on this claim." Across the page, there was one more scrawl: "Group officials believe pilot's story okay."[11]

The notion that Righetti would approach the wing commander to support the claims of one of his pilots was consistent with his personality. "He always took up for the pilots," recalled Carroll Henry. "Especially the ones he liked. He would chew somebody to pieces if he felt like it … he chewed on a few I guess." Of course it is unlikely that Righetti tore into General Woodbury, but it is quite probable that he pled Cox's case to him. Ultimately, however, Cox's claims were disallowed.[12] He was only one of many pilots whose achievements were never officially recognized for the valid reason that they simply could not be proved.

On March 3, 1945, the same day that Howes botched his rescue of Liles, and the same day that Cox shot down the Do-217s, the United States Strategic Air Forces in Europe—headed by Carl Spaatz—recognized Righetti and the 55th with a news release. "Lt. Col Elwyn G. Righetti's train-busting 55th Fighter Group has cost the Germans more than half a thousand locomotives since the first of the year in strafing sweeps over the enemy rail network. Pilots of the 55th, one of the 'hottest' train-busting units in the Eighth Air Force, Saturday shot up 23 [actually, 21] locomotives in Czechoslovakia, increasing the total to 534 immobilized since January 1."[13]

Although he preferred flying over staff work, Righetti readily acknowledged that there were aspects about the non-flying duties of his new command that were rewarding. He was called to an Eighth Air Force planning conference on March 6 and admitted that he felt "very important planning the war as well as fighting it. Felt very proud when introduced to General Doolittle to have him say, 'I've heard a lot of you, Righetti.'"

In the same letter he reported that he had, "a new *Katydid*. It's fresh from the factory with all the latest Hun headaches [improvements]. It's a beauty—the original *Katydid* was war weary." Righetti's regular crew chief, Millard "Doak" Easton, remembered both the original *Katydid* and the later aircraft, Serial Number 44-72227. "When Righetti came along he got an old airplane, well broken in and noisy from wear. He liked it and remarked on how noisy it was." However, it was only a few months before *Katydid* reached the mark of 350 combat hours—the point at which the P-51s were removed from combat duty.

When replacement aircraft arrived, they weren't immediately put into service. Instead, they were assigned to a pilot whose ground crew was responsible for ensuring the ship was compliant with the latest technical orders. Easton remembered that the process typically consumed three days, and that it took a similar period for him to prepare Righetti's new *Katydid*. "I had a new P-51 all ready for him," he recalled. Righetti was excited about his new ship and immediately took it for a test hop. "When he came back," Easton recalled, "he said, 'You know, this one is too damned quiet!'"

Righetti was appropriately businesslike with Easton and the rest of his ground crew. "I never saw him except when he was going to fly, and then, not for long." For his part, that was fine with Easton who had already been through several pilots since the group had been flying P-38s back in the States. "I never tried to get too close as it's hard to get over sending a man out and have him not come back."

Happily for Easton and the rest of the crew, Righetti didn't waste their time with petty maintenance gripes or ambiguous complaints. "He never gave me any tough write-ups," said Easton. "But he told me if the engine was even a slight bit rough." Righetti's sensitivity in this regard was hardly unique. "Once over the North Sea," Frank Birtciel said, "every pilot I knew became very sensitive to every little rumble or tick or pop the engine made."[14]

Righetti closed the letter about his new aircraft with a declaration that was especially curious. "Something I never thought of before. Don't ever worry about me. I'll get home okay." It is obvious he meant to reassure the family. But it was nevertheless an odd statement to make as it stood in stark contrast to the several references he had already made to the grim possibility that he might not survive his combat tour. Nevertheless, his positive attitude persisted at least until the next day when after explaining that the Luftwaffe rarely rose to contest the 55th any longer, he wrote, "It all boils down to this—my chances of getting home now are 80% or 90%, at least."

"I HIT THE DECK"

Although the majority of the Luftwaffe's flyers during early 1945 were markedly inexperienced when compared to their Allied counterparts, the March 18 encounter of Thomas Kiernan of the 338th Fighter Squadron showed that the Germans were not totally bereft of skilled pilots. On that morning while the 338th flew on a southwest heading just slightly north of Giessen, Germany, bogies—unidentified aircraft— were spotted through a gap in the clouds. Kiernan led his Red Flight down to investigate. The squadron's Yellow Flight accompanied him.

"The first plane I saw as we reached their altitude was a Spit[fire], so I called them in as friendly. Immediately thereafter I saw an FW-190 and then saw five more 190s and two 109s in a rat race with the Spitfire." The FW-190s were "long-nosed" FW-190Ds, powered by the inline, liquid-cooled Junkers Jumo 213 rather than the BMW 801, air-cooled radial engine that powered earlier variants. Kiernan immediately pitched into the fight and called the rest of the squadron down to assist.

"I got on the tail of a 190 but couldn't get a shot at him because of his extremely sharp maneuvers," said Kiernan. "He tried rolls, quick turns and practically split-essed from 1,000 feet." Kiernan and the German continued their one-on-one duel for several minutes before Kiernan was able to score. "We finally got into a tight turn right on the treetops, and I got in a high deflection burst, observing one or two strikes on his left wing."

The enemy flyer turned hard back under Kiernan. "I put my nose almost straight down and fired two short bursts from directly above him and saw good strikes on the rear of his canopy and in his fuselage near the tail. He went right on into the ground from this half-roll in a vertical dive."

Kiernan commented on the skill of the vanquished German. "This Jerry was very aggressive and skillful at evasive action. At no time did he present anything but a high deflection shot. He did not try to run, although he was at all times close to clouds, which he could have used for evasion."[1]

Archie Dargan was Yellow Flight's number four man. Unlike Kiernan's opponent, his adversary did in fact try to take advantage of the clouds. As he entered the fight Dargan spotted one of the long-nosed FW-190Ds closing on his tail. He turned hard into the German who then turned his attention to another pilot from Yellow Flight. Dargan chased him and the enemy pilot rolled violently and dived before pulling straight up and climbing into the cloud layer. "He spun out of the clouds," Dargan said, "recovered, and then repeated the procedure. I did not try to follow him in the clouds, but caught him each time as he came out." Dargan finally got in three short bursts of gunfire which set the enemy aircraft on fire and into the ground with its pilot still aboard.

As Dargan climbed back to altitude he spotted another FW-190D diving on him, head-on. "He did not fire," Dargan said. "I fired a quarter-second burst and noticed that only one gun in my right wing was still firing." Dargan noted no effects from his gunfire and turned to engage the enemy pilot. "The enemy aircraft constantly reversed his turn and did barrel rolls, but finally leveled out, and as he did I got in a half-second burst from dead astern, observing a few strikes. Almost [as soon] as I started getting strikes the pilot jettisoned his canopy and bailed from about 4,000 feet."[2]

It was encounters such as Kiernan's and Dargan's—multiplied many times by many pilots across many fighter groups over a period of many months—that inexorably ground the Luftwaffe into impotency.

New pilots continued to arrive at the 55th during the late winter and early spring of 1945, even as the Allies pushed the Nazis deeper and deeper into Germany. Few questioned how the war would end, but everyone understood that the fighting would have to continue until that end was reached. And the newcomers were expected to do their share—whatever it might be.

The attitudes of Righetti and his old hands toward the newly joined pilots were probably consistent with the theme of a speech that General George Patton, the commander of the Third Army, gave to one of his unblooded divisions in early March 1945. "You, the American soldier, are the greatest soldier in the world," Patton declared. "You are part of an army that has done the greatest thing in the world. You are fighting for the greatest country in the world. And now the fight is won and almost over, so you can't help but be goddamn heroes."

"You men are lucky, very lucky," he continued. "Now, when you go back home, and in later years when your descendants ask you, 'Grandpop, what did you do in the Second World War?' you won't have to say, 'Well, sonny, I shoveled shit in Alabama.'" Through the speech, Patton exhorted the men to be unmercifully aggressive toward the Germans regardless of the fact that the fighting was almost finished. And he closed with an unabashed reminder: "Shoot and keep shooting. Attack quickly and decisively. Take care of yourself. Never trust a German."[3]

For the most part, the 55th's men did "shoot and keep shooting." But it came at a cost. Of the fifteen groups in the Eighth Air Force's Fighter Command, the 55th lost more aircraft than all but two, and both of those units had been in combat longer. The 55th was also near the bottom of the heap in terms of enemy aircraft destroyed when compared to the number of aircraft it lost. It is impossible to pin that poor performance on any one factor with certainty, although part of it was likely attributable to the problematic P-38 which the 55th operated during the first part of its combat career from October 1943 to July 1944. Moreover, the group's leadership had not always been of the highest caliber.

Another important factor was the emphasis the group put on strafing, especially during Righetti's time with the 55th. Down low, the aircraft were within the effective range of every antiaircraft weapon the Germans fielded. In fact, even light infantry guns achieved some success against strafing fighters. Still, the 55th wasn't unique in its attacks against enemy airfields as several other units also racked up considerable strafing scores—and losses.

Moreover, the P-51 was especially susceptible to gunfire. Its inline engine's heat was carried away by a mixture of water and glycol that was cooled as it passed through an air-cooled radiator. This radiator and the coolant, or "header," tank was not protected or redundant. Neither was the circuit of lines than ran between the engine and the radiator. Consequently, a punctured header tank or a severed coolant line guaranteed engine failure. The only variable was the period of time it took before the engine overheated and seized completely.

In fact, many Missing Air Crew Reports (MACR) included a variation of the same statement: "I caught sight of his aircraft and could see a stream of coolant coming from the underside." This statement was invariably followed by something similar to: "He called over the radio that his engine had quit and that he was bailing out."

The P-51 was not unique in its vulnerability to ground fire. In fact, almost all aircraft powered by liquid-cooled engines were similarly susceptible; the RAF's excellent Spitfire was an example, as was the P-38. An exception was the Red Air Force's Il-2 Sturmovik which was very heavily armored. That the P-51 had such a poor reputation as a ground strafer was due in part to the fact that it was so often compared to its contemporary, the P-47. The big and heavily gunned "Jug" was powered by the air-cooled Pratt & Whitney R-2800 radial engine that was spectacularly rugged, and capable of absorbing extreme levels of punishment.

The 55th was sent on two missions on March 21, 1945. The first was to Hopsten, a Luftwaffe airfield approximately twenty miles from Germany's border with the Netherlands, east of the Rhine. Although it wasn't an important base early in the war, it hosted more units and grew increasingly critical during 1944 and 1945 as the Allied strategic bombing campaign intensified. Consequently, with the British scheduled to cross the Rhine from the Netherlands on March 23, its neutralization was essential.

Righetti led 58 P-51s out of Wormingford on that date. Unusually, 33 of the aircraft were loaded with a single Mk29 five hundred-pound cluster bomb. These bombs were in turn loaded with ninety four-pound fragmentation bombs designed to scatter across the target area when the main bomb body broke apart at a predetermined altitude. The Mk29—a virtual copy of a German design—was intended to be used against "soft" targets such as troops, trucks, and aircraft on the ground.

Notwithstanding the curious bomb load that many of the aircraft carried, the 55th was still tasked with escorting 1st Air Division B-17s to Hopsten. As it developed, the bombers were unmolested and Righetti pulled the group aside as the big aircraft dumped their loads on the airfield. "Bombing results by the heavies were perfect and obliterated the airdrome, practically all bombs either dropping on the runways or the built up installations."

The 55th's bombs were icing on the cake. Before the smoke from the B-17 raid had time to settle, Righetti led the 38th Fighter Squadron down on the gun emplacements that protected Hopsten's east side. "After dropping my frag," said Righetti, "I hit the deck on the south side of the field and did two complete turns around the perimeter track at zero altitude."[4] He spotted only two FW-190s. For his trouble, even though the antiaircraft gunners had just endured a raid by heavy bombers, Righetti's aircraft was hit in the tail by a 37-millimeter cannon round. As close as he was to the ground, he nevertheless maintained control of *Katydid*.

Righetti's wingman, June Stallings, was not so fortunate. A relative newcomer—having only joined the group less than a month earlier—he was caught in a stream of antiaircraft fire, knocked down and killed. Anxious to suppress the enemy guns, Righetti radioed their locations to the 343rd Fighter Squadron which was still orbiting overhead. "I called in the gun positions, and Tudor Squadron frag bombed them."

"I pulled up and out while this bombing was in progress," Righetti said, "and determined that my aircraft was in satisfactory condition for an attack upon the FW-190s which I had previously spotted." He indulged himself with an inventive attack. "I then approached from northeast to southwest and fired a two-second burst at 400-to-300 yards, deck level, through a small shed behind which the grounded fighter was sitting. I observed good strikes and a small explosion and left the FW-190 burning brightly."

Righetti set up for an attack on the other enemy fighter. "I broke into the smoke of the burning hangar, then turned right and returned out of the sun for a fast diving pass at the only remaining undamaged aircraft that I could locate." He had no need for trick shooting on this pass and fired his guns from a range of eight hundred yards. "This FW-190 burst into flames and continued burning throughout the next ten to fifteen minutes."

Aside from the two aircraft Righetti set afire, only four others were discovered. These were flamed by pilots of the 343rd. The scarcity of aircraft at Hopsten caught the group by surprise as photoreconnaissance just two days earlier had uncovered nearly 80 aircraft. "It is believed that the Heinies had wind of this attack and moved out in advance," noted the mission summary report.

But whereas enemy aircraft were scarce, the antiaircraft fire—despite the bombing raid—was concentrated and intense as noted in the mission summary report. "Flak positions encountered were of a mound type built up about 8 feet above the ground," recounted the mission summary report. "At the top they are about 14 feet in diameter with a pit 6–8 feet across for the gun, and the rest, protective revetment. Frag bombs were relatively ineffective as only one direct hit was seen, and on the succeeding passes the Heinies were back on the guns. Dive strafing also seemed to have only momentary effects."

"After 15 minutes of agitating the target," the mission summary report noted, "a box of big friends [bombers] of the fourth force called in over "C" [channel] requesting to bomb our target. We moved over and all their bombs burst perfectly on the East–West runway." After this interlude the 55th went back to work. Righetti, in particular, was determined to find more aircraft: "Group leader cased the airdrome at deck level for half an hour, but search only revealed that enemy aircraft were conspicuous by their absence."

With no more aircraft on which to direct their guns, the group's pilots shot up everything else on the airfield—refueling points, antiaircraft guns, outbuildings, and the main hangar that was already ablaze. But the "shoot 'em up" wasn't one-sided. Aside from June Stallings, Dudley Amoss was also caught by antiaircraft fire. "Our flight, in taking evasive action, became split up and my aircraft was hit. I called my leader [Righetti] and notified him of my trouble and said I was taking a course of 240 for friendly territory." Amoss cleared the area to the west while the rest of the 55th continued its rampage.

Hopsten, notwithstanding its very active antiaircraft gunners, was put out of commission for the short term. The bombers had cratered its runways and many of its buildings were afire. The 55th had shot up what aircraft its pilots could find as well as everything else that presented itself as a worthwhile target. After nearly half an hour of strafing, there remained little that was worth the risk of being shot down. "Flak continued intense," said Righetti, "and since this airdrome could not be further considered in the big dividend class, I called my boys together and we set course for home."

After being hit early during the action at Hopsten that day, Dudley Amoss headed west. The smoke that filled his cockpit seeped through his goggles and burned his eyes. "I had been flying for about six minutes on this course at 1,000 feet," he said, "when I spotted five FW-190s at two o'clock below me at tree top level. Since my aircraft, though still pouring smoke into the cockpit, was behaving fairly well, I decided to attack."[5]

The enemy aircraft passed under Amoss in a loose vee formation. "Pulling around to the left, I got on the tail of the trailing FW-190 on the right, and at 200 yards gave him a short burst. He immediately exploded in midair."

Amoss continued up the right leg of the vee formation and lined up on the next enemy fighter. "Almost as soon as I opened fire, the Jerry skidded off to the right and mushed right down into the trees. For some reason, the other three 190s still hadn't spotted me, so I headed after the leader. As I squeezed the trigger he started violent evasive action and I'm not certain whether I scored any hits on him or not.

At any rate he suddenly did a snap to the right and went straight in and exploded."

Amoss's engine finally failed a few minutes later. He weaved through a copse of trees before setting the aircraft down in an open field. German civilians were on the scene almost immediately and threatened him as he climbed from the cockpit. Amoss reached for his pistol and there ensued a short standoff until a Luftwaffe officer arrived, made him a prisoner, and spirited him away to safety.

It is interesting to note that after being liberated from Stalag Luft I at the end of the war, Amoss filed an encounter report together with a sworn statement.[6] Suprisingly, the Victory Credit Board allowed his claim for the destruction of three FW-190s.[7] This was done despite the fact that there were no eyewitness statements and certainly no gun camera film evidence. This stands in marked contrast to the disallowal of the claims made by Robert Cox for the destruction of seven Do-217s on March 3, for which he likewise had no witnesses or gun camera film.

Why Amoss's claims were allowed can only be guessed at. It might have been an unofficial concession to compensate him for his time as a POW. Or, postwar, the Victory Credit Board might simply have been ready to close up shop and honoring Amoss's claim might have been the most expeditious means to resolve the case. Regardless, awarding him credit for downing three enemy aircraft, despite the fact that he had no witnesses or gun camera film, was unusual. As a result, because he had earlier downed a trainer as well as an Me-262, he achieved ace status.

Righetti lost his wingman, June Stallings, on March 21. He had lost another wingman, Ken Griffith, a few months earlier on December 24. In the make-believe world of perfect fighter piloting there was sometimes a stigma attached to a flight leader who lost a wingman. In this fanciful construct, the flight leader was supposed to nurture, protect and mentor his wingman while introducing him to the harsh realities of combat in measured doses. Ultimately, the carefully coddled wingman was supposed to evolve into a topnotch teammate with whom the flight leader could sweep the skies clear of the enemy.

Although there were examples of combat pairings in the USAAF that were deadly effective, the reality was that these were rare. In truth, although most men regularly flew with a handful of other pilots, the demands of wartime operations didn't allow the same pilots to fly together on every mission. Illness, rest requirements, aircraft availability, reassignment and combat losses were only some of the factors at play.

In Righetti's case, as the group commander, he flew with each of the three squadrons rather than exclusively with one. Consequently, there was no reasonable way for him to fly with the same wingman on every sortie. In fact, he often flew with wingmen with whom he never flew again. Certainly there were no opportunities for him to spend extended periods mentoring anyone. However, he did fly with some men more than once—Carroll Henry being an example. "He was the greatest pilot I ever flew with," said Henry. "I just liked flying with him."

Further, the notion that a flight leader could protect a wingman from every danger was flawed. Certainly, especially dangerous situations might be avoided. However, the nature of their work was such that the men were often required to operate in those especially dangerous situations; it was their job. The loss of June Stallings at Hopsten offers a good example. The group's mission was to bomb and strafe the airfield, and Righetti led the men in doing just that. There was no way that he could have done so while keeping Stallings safe from enemy fire.

Moreover, wingmen were generally younger and inexperienced. Accordingly, no matter how much mentoring they received, they often made mistakes that were deadly. Also, their primary job was to protect their flight leader, especially from threats originating from the rear. It was a task that sometimes put them in unfavorable positions, and unfavorable positions often produced unhappy results. Finally, although skill and guile might be used by a flight leader to ensure that he and his wingman prevailed over enemy pilots, skill and guile were of little value against bad luck. In particular, there was little a flight leader could do to protect his wingman against mechanical failure, or an unlucky flak burst. Frank Birtciel, who flew two combat tours, recollected that,

"Strafing and flak evasion was mostly just 'outhouse luck' luck as far as getting hit."

Ultimately, the reality was that half the pilots on every mission were wingmen. Therefore, wingmen were regularly shot down. Holding their flight leaders accountable—without cause—made no sense at all and generally did not happen. Certainly no one with any credibility attached any blame to Righetti for the wingmen he lost.

Tom Welch was the 55th's intelligence officer and a friend of Righetti's. As the intelligence officer he did not fly but rather was responsible for briefing the group's pilots on enemy activities and capabilities both in general and for specific missions. He was also responsible for creating the group's mission summary reports after the pilots returned to Wormingford. Welch, like Righetti, had a big, fun-loving personality and a good sense of humor.

He was also, like many men of the time, an unabashed admirer of Damon Runyon. Runyon started his career as a reporter and sportswriter and became especially well known for his short stories, a few of which formed the basis for the classic play, *Guys and Dolls*. Runyon's stories featured colorful characters such as thugs, and down-and-outers and men-done-wrong. These colorful characters had equally colorful names such as, Bookie Bob, Harry the Horse, Izzy Cheesecake and Spanish John, and always talked in the present tense, rarely using contractions. Their "wise-guy" patter was characterized by a type of slang and street-savvy smartness that was widely imitated as it wended its way into the American vernacular.

It was during mid-March 1945 that Welch started crafting the narratives for the group's mission summary reports in a Runyonesque style that stood in stark contrast to the cryptic feel that was typical of official documents of that sort. He debuted his new style in the mission summary report for the second mission of March 21, a pure fighter sweep. With no bombers to escort, Righetti was free to take the 55th hunting however he wanted. It was a fantastic opportunity ruined by the fact that the group could find little that was worthy of attention. He led the group through and around the area between Wurzburg and Giebelstadt with no luck as recorded by the mission summary report "with apologies to Damon Runyan [sic]":

> We are charging along thru the lesser Reich, all rodded up, looking for some live ones with a little less than somewhat of our usual success. As we are chugging across Giebelstadt we are not seeing anything of Jerries, but a bunch of flak passers pre-flighting their roscoes. However, we are not having any truck with these Heinies, and are tossing them the chill as we have already agitated a few too many of this particular type Heinie this morning and they are no kind of Heinie to be going around in the company of, expecially if they are all sored up at you.

And then, something caught the group's attention. "We are thinking we have been slipped the phonus bolonus, when who are we seeing near Ochenfurt but some of Der Fuehrer's young 'uns playing with some pull jobs or gliders." Righetti and the 55th had found a glider school.

Glider clubs were popular in Germany following World War I when the restrictions imposed by the Versailles Treaty—particularly against anything resembling military aircraft—were so onerous. Glider training continued to be important to the Luftwaffe in various degrees before and during the war and was especially popular with the Hitler Youth. However, regardless of whether or not a budding pilot was trained on gliders it still took well more than a year to be made ready for combat. Consequently, it was curious that glider training was still being conducted when the war was quite obviously nearing its end, and Allied fighters were everywhere. That being said, it is quite possible that the students the 55th had discovered that day were being prepared to pilot one of Germany's wonder weapons.

In fact, the Heinkel He-162 Volksjäger, or People's Fighter, was nearing operational status. A very simple design powered by a single jet engine, it was constructed of wood and other readily available materials, and was intended to be quickly manufactured in enormous numbers by semi-skilled and unskilled labor. Göring, who essentially considered the He-162 to be disposable, pushed to have it introduced into combat as quickly as possible.

The popular notion was that the new jet was to be flown by pilots with a minimum of training, many of whom would be drawn from the Hitler Youth. The bulk of their training was to be conducted with gliders which were also readily manufactured and could be operated with little or no fuel. In the event, the idea was absurd as the He-162, although reputedly a fine flying aircraft, demanded more skill than a hastily trained glider pilot could bring to the cockpit.

Righetti and the rest of the 55th didn't know or care about any of this. Rather, they dove on the gliders where they were parked on the side of a hill. "It must have been a preflight school of some kind," recalled Leedom John of the 338th Fighter Squadron, "because there were young men in a number of groups gathered around gliders. They did not know we were there until we hit them on the first pass, still gathered around the gliders."

The terrified youngsters scattered as the 55th wheeled around for another firing run. The group's pilots fired on everything—the fleeing students, their abandoned gliders and the airfield's hangar. "On the second pass," said Leedom John, "they were running up the hill toward a woods but a lot of them never made it, as they were easy targets right out in the open with no cover. I'll remember it until the day I die." For his part, although he shot up several of the unpowered crates and presumably sprayed the students, Righetti's recollection was less dramatic as he barely mentioned the episode when he wrote home a few days later.

"I'M PRETTY MUCH TIRED"

The Luftwaffe's units were continuously chased from their airfields as the Allies thrust deeper into Germany during the last few weeks of the war. As the various German staffs, and support personnel and flyers retreated, they sent large numbers of serviceable aircraft into the heart of the Reich. They also took their antiaircraft weapons with them. Consequently, the shrinking numbers of airfields still under Nazi control were packed with aircraft and the guns necessary to defend them. Attacking the airfields—always a dangerous job—became even more so. So, it was reasonable for the pilots, some from the 55th, to question whether or not it was necessary to make these risky attacks given the obvious fact that Germany was going to lose the war.

No one knew for sure. On the one hand, assuming enough fuel was set aside, there was absolutely no reason to believe that Germany wouldn't or couldn't mount another version of the massive surprise attack—*Bodenplatte*—that achieved limited success a few months earlier on New Year's Day. Although that effort had failed to achieve its most ambitious objectives, Germany had little to lose by trying again. Certainly there were enough aircraft available and probably, with careful planning, adequate fuel. By scraping the very bottom of the pilot barrel to round up every airman available—to include the wounded—it might have been possible to launch something even bigger than *Bodenplatte*.

On the other hand, no one on either side believed that such an attack, even if it caused great damage, would change the outcome of the war.

The Allies could have absorbed any punishment that Germany was able to deliver at that point. Still, there was nothing to argue against the idea that a large, desperate, last-ditch effort might cause many military and civilian casualties.

Consequently, if the 55th—and every other fighter unit—lost a dozen, or even twenty or more pilots during a concerted campaign of airfield attacks, who was to say that those men and machines were more valuable than the hundreds or even thousands of lives that might be lost in a massive German air strike that hit London neighborhoods, or Parisian rail stations, or Antwerp dockyards? The answer was unknowable and Righetti intended to engage the Germans until he was called off, or until they surrendered or were utterly destroyed.

And he intended to do so, because it was his job. When distilled, his orders were to use the 55th to escort the Eighth's heavy bombers, and to help destroy the Luftwaffe in particular and the German war machine in general. His orders were not to keep his men from being killed. Had that been the case there would have been no need for the group to ever leave Wormingford. Certainly, he was not expected to be reckless with the lives of his men, but neither was he to avoid tough targets. And to his credit—and theirs—his men always followed him, as Herman Schonenberg said: "I don't think the colonel [Righetti] really ever worried about us pilots following him."

Still, there was grumbling. "There was some talk about [how] the price we were paying was not worth the aircraft on the ground, and we were paying a pretty hefty price," said Paul Reeves. But if the enemy does not come up to meet you, then you best go get him in the bushes." Another pilot recalled, "At the latter part of the war we didn't have to take unnecessary chances for a few ground kills. That's how I looked at it. Most of us did as directed and a lot of pilots paid dearly." For his part, Roy Cooper, a young lieutenant, noted that he considered it "an honor" to fly as Righetti's wingman, "even though I came home with a few hits [to his aircraft] during these missions."[1]

John Cunnick was a young lieutenant who liked Righetti. "I think he was a little crazy," he said. "He was very competitive. It was rumored that he and John Landers had a thing going to see who could get the most targets." Landers was a former 55th pilot who, at that time, commanded the 78th Fighter Group.

Although interesting, there is no substantive evidence to support such a supposition. However, it is virtually certain that Righetti and Landers knew each other. In fact, Landers left the 55th for another fighter group just as Righetti arrived. Moreover, they both became group commanders on the same day; Landers relieved Righetti's old friend Fred Gray at the 78th on the same day that Righetti relieved Crowell at the 55th. Those similarities notwithstanding, Landers had been flying combat since early in the war and had scored six aerial victories against the Japanese by the end of 1942 during the time that Righetti was still yoked to the training command. Since that time, while flying both P-38s and P-51s, Landers had scored eight more.

However, in terms of strafing victories, the two men were neck and neck. Landers made a play to put it away when he scored a single-sortie record of eight strafing victories in early April. The story was carried by the 3d Air Division's magazine, *Strikes*. And it was a story that Righetti likely saw. So, the idea of an "ace race" between the two men is not totally without merit.

In fact, it is given some weight by Jack Ilfrey who was a colorful ace and squadron commander with combat experience dating from the early years of the war in North Africa. "I met Righetti—he was hell bent for leather," Ilfrey said. Although he knew Righetti only casually, he was very close to Landers, having attended Texas A&M with him as well as flight training. Indeed the two shared Stateside assignments after their first combat tours. Ilfrey insisted that the competition between Righetti and Landers was real, although it was based on nothing more than his familiarity with the two men. "That was no rumor—it was an absolute fact. Those were two very gung ho pilots. Unofficially I was rooting for Landers, but officially I sided with other squadron and group commanders [who believed] that they were taking too many risks and losing too many planes and pilots. But believe me, that was the ultimate thrill. When you think about it, we actually had a license to kill."[2]

Certainly Righetti was aggressive, if not, "a little crazy." And he was, outwardly at least, supremely self-confident. It was part of his nature and it was what was necessary to perform his duties. In fact, even his enemy counterparts recognized the need for audacious action by men who already lived at the very edge of recklessness. The great German ace Walter Krupinski, who was credited with 197 aerial victories, spoke of the need for these qualities. "I would not want to fly in combat with a pilot who did not have a healthy ego, and a good sense of self-respect. Call us a little narcissistic perhaps, but if you don't have that kind of arrogance in the cockpit, you will die. That is what makes you aggressive, and active aggression is most of what is needed to achieve victory over your opponent."[3]

It was in Righetti's nature to look after his family, especially his younger brother Maurice. Since before the time Maurice had gone into the service, Elwyn had readily shared his knowledge and advice, and had mentioned more than once that he was anxious for the two of them to serve together, although Maurice had been directed into bombers. Nevertheless, Righetti campaigned intensively over a period of several months to get his brother to England and into the Eighth Air Force.

"A bit of news," he wrote. "I thought you all might like to know that Junior will be under my wing before you all read this. I called his replacement pool here in the UK just now and though he hasn't arrived yet, he is expected momentarily. The second he hits there, certain wheels will start rolling, assigning him to my division. I'll let him fly enough of his bomb missions to decide whether or not it's the place for him, then take whatever steps I feel are best for all concerned. I can have him in fighters immediately if I want him, but hardly think it fair. I'll keep you posted day-to-day."

As it developed, the plans that Righetti had so carefully crafted for his younger brother went unrealized. Maurice was assigned to a B-29 unit in India. "We were at first sorry to know that Maurice is in India," wrote sister Betty, "especially since you counted on him being in England; but you know you can't be his keeper, or even help him much in the really tight spots, and it might hinder you."

Betty was much like her brother—concerned and anxious about everyone in the family. And strong-willed. "So, since he's in the good ship [B-29] he is, we're glad he's having new experiences and a life of his own. If he'll only get his head out, and appreciate his opportunities, Pop and Mom will be a lot happier. They feel badly only because Maurice still seems so unhappy and unresigned [sic] at the Army's way of doing things." In fact, Maurice had excelled. And if he was "unhappy and unresigned" at the Army's way of doing things, he was no different than the many millions of uniformed men who often felt similarly.

Betty's advice to Righetti was good. Aside from his wife and young child, Righetti was additionally responsible for the nearly two thousand men of the 55th and its support elements, as well as his own person. Trying to take care of his brother and control what the USAAF was doing with him—or wasn't—was distracting and counterproductive, if not hurtful.

Betty was a proud aunt and bragged fondly about Righetti's daughter in the same letter. "Kyle's the sweetest, most affectionate, smart little devil—she's certainly a composite of her parents." Betty, who inherited more than her share of the Righetti family's strong-mindedness, also confessed to upsetting his wife, Cathryn, who was back at the ranch from San Antonio. "And Kyle's mama is quite a gal too. Generally, we get along pretty well. But she got pretty sore the other nite at me. Guess she ought to have been sore. I wouldn't appreciate the crack I made about her relatives if she'd made it about mine. Otherwise we live in peace and amity. Mom is out taking care of Grampaw, and Katy and I are concocting all sorts of strange and delightful dishes to serve as meals to a sometimes startled Pop and Ernie."

Ultimately, Righetti reconciled himself to Maurice's unexpected assignment, despite the fact that it upset his plans. "Everything's rosy except that Junior's coming here was a false steer. Ain't too bad though. I've had three letters from him in the last four days and he seems very happy. He ought to be, he has one of the best deals in the Air Corps."

Early April was uneventful for Righetti and the 55th. No missions were flown on April 1, and nothing remarkable occurred during the escort missions that were flown during the next five days. They were bone-numbingly cold, high-altitude penetrations deep into Germany. The five hours or more that the men spent in the unpressurized cockpits of their P-51s dulled their senses despite the fact that they wore oxygen masks. And although alertness was an imperative, the discipline to remain so was difficult to maintain when the enemy so seldom made an appearance. In fact, many of the men, particularly the later arrivals, had never even seen an enemy aircraft aloft; at the rate the war was drawing to a close that might remain the case. A poorly composed poem at the end of the group's mission summary report for April 6 captured their collective attitude at the absence of their German foes:

> Der Luftwaffie is in a mighty blue mood,
> They've run out of everything, including altitude,
> In fact those Heinies are so weak in the knees,
> They won't even come up and shoot the breeze.

It is likely that many more "Heinie" fliers would have liked to have "come up and shoot the breeze," than was actually the case. However, the Luftwaffe was strangled for fuel. It is true that the majority of the Luftwaffe's pilots at that time were green and ill-trained, but they were still capable of flying. Only the lack of fuel kept them from flying more, as indicated by the recollection of a German pilot and aircraft maintenance officer: "Getting fuel for the fighters was not so much a logistics operation, more of an intelligence battle. We would send tankers on circuitous journeys, picking up 5,000 litres in one place, 2,500 litres at another; sometimes it might take as long as a week to collect the twenty tons of fuel needed for a single fighter operation."[4]

Another German pilot confirmed that fuel, rather than aircraft, was the critical shortcoming during the chaotic closing weeks of the war when it was easier to get new aircraft rather than repair those that were damaged: "We simply went to the depot nearby, where they had hundreds of brand-new [Me-]109s—G-10s, G-14s and even the very latest K models [these were variants of the Me-109]. There was no proper organization anymore. The depot staff just said, 'There are the aircraft, take what you want and go away.' But getting fuel—that was more difficult."[5]

Of the five missions the 55th flew from April 2 to April 6, Righetti went on only one, an unexceptional bomber escort to Kiel on April 3. By that time it was clear to him that the war was winding down and would possibly be finished before he reached the magic number of three hundred combat hours required to complete his overseas tour. "War looks very fine from this angle at this time," he wrote. "Reckon its termination is now pretty much the governing factor of my return home."

He was also, as a group commander, keen to be promoted although he professed indifference. "Still no eagles here [promotion to colonel], so I sweat, sweat, sweat—not that it makes any particular difference with me, Kay, but I did want to raise your allotment and will the day I get mine raised. Also I have a new battle jacket with eagles embroidered on it and sure want to wear it." And he was weary. "I'm pretty much tired and have nothing to say, so I'll ring off—see you all soon."

Although the April 3 mission had been uneventful for Righetti and the rest of the group, it was far from that for Frank Birtciel, one of the 55th's original cadre. "We were specifically briefed that there was to be no strafing on the mission. The front lines were very fluid at that point and no one was sure exactly where Patton's army was. They didn't want us to accidentally shoot up our own units."[6]

"Gene Ryan was leading the 343rd that day and I was leading Yellow Flight," said Birtciel. "The rendezvous and escort with the bombers went fine. It was uneventful and pretty much a milk run." On the return leg Ryan dragged the squadron across Holland and over the North Sea. "I started to notice brown spots on my canopy as we got to a point about a third of the way across the water," said Birtciel. "I wasn't sure where it was coming from and so I flew up and looked over the aircraft flying in front of me." Birtciel saw nothing obvious on the other P-51s and came to the uncomfortable conclusion that the mysterious brown spots were coming from his own aircraft. Engine trouble over the North Sea was a nightmare that dogged every pilot of the Eighth Air Force.

"And then," said Birtciel, "it was as if someone threw a white sheet over my canopy. I couldn't see anything." Part of the engine's coolant system—the header engine tank which sat just behind the propeller hub—had blown. The mixture of ethylene glycol and water that streamed back over the windscreen and canopy blocked Birtciel's vision.

"I called out Mayday three times," said Birtciel, "and immediately turned back toward land. My first priority was to get away from the water." He had good reason to be concerned; Air/Sea Rescue, or ASR, had improved dramatically since the early days of the war, but the North Sea in early April was still numbingly cold and his chances of surviving a bailout over land were dramatically better than they would have been had he jumped out over the water.

"The other three pilots in Yellow Flight escorted me back toward the coast while the coolant mixture slowly dissipated from my windscreen and canopy," recalled Birtciel. "In the meantime I had to figure out where to go—what to do. The Germans still held Ostend, but there was a highway that ran out of Ostend to Brussels and I planned to follow that to an airfield I had landed at a few months earlier when I had also had engine trouble."

Birtciel coaxed his aircraft back across the coast south of Ostend while the engine—robbed of cooling—chewed itself apart. "Pieces of pistons and rings and other bits flew out the exhaust stacks. It was as if there was a small volcano on each side of the nose." It was becoming apparent to Birtciel that his odds of making it to Brussels were quickly diminishing.

"I was a little worried about losing that airplane, the *Millie G*," he remembered. "It was brand new and had been assigned to our squadron commander, Ed Giller. I was flying it on its first mission and I was a little concerned that I might get into some hot water if I didn't bring it back." In fact, Birtciel was flying a brand-new *Millie G* because Giller's previous *Millie G* had been shot down just a couple of weeks earlier while flown by another pilot. It was a disturbing trend. In fact, Giller was assigned four different P-51s with the *Millie G* name.

Birtciel's anxiety about losing Giller's new aircraft quickly became secondary to his own survival when the engine fire burned a hole through the firewall next to his left foot. The cockpit quickly became uninhabitable. "I released my harness and radio cords and oxygen and such," said Birtciel, "and opened the canopy. But when I stood up to jump out I was jerked back by my G-suit hose. I had forgotten to disconnect it." While Birtciel—still partly out of the cockpit—wrestled with the hose, the aircraft fell into a spin from about four thousand feet.

"When I finally got myself free I went over the right side of the aircraft and my feet were smashed against the horizontal stabilizer which started me tumbling head-over-heels. I threw my arms out to stop the tumbling but the only thing that happened was that my gloves filled with air and were torn off."

Plummeting earthward, Birtciel saw his aircraft hit the ground and burst into flames. "It was a pretty big explosion," he recalled. "There was still plenty of gas on board." But as spectacular as the explosion might have been, Birtciel had little time to dwell on it. "By that time the ground was really rushing up and I pulled the ripcord. It took a little time for the pilot chute to open and pull out the main chute, but I was in a bit of a hurry so I pulled the ripcord again. It came right out of its harness and the parachute opened just as it was supposed to."

It was a close thing. The parachute opened with a hard crack and snapped Birtciel's fall to something that was survivable only a few seconds before he would have slammed to his death. "I floated down through some telephone wires," he said, "and hit the ground hard. It was like a movie with a segment missing. I only remembered the parachute opening. The next thing I recalled, I was lying on my back with a bunch of Belgians standing over me."

Birtciel had landed at the edge of a recently tilled field. "There was a pair of men who tried to help me off of the ground, but I couldn't get up. I looked down at my feet but my legs ended at my knees. I thought for a moment that my lower legs had been chopped off when I had hit the airplane." But the reality was that he had sunk deeply into the soft earth. Had the ground not been so well-turned, his legs—and more—would have been badly shattered by the fall.

"They helped pulled me out of the soil and I was able to stand on my own. As it was," said Birtciel, "Except for some bruises I was uninjured. When I got my bearings I saw that the Belgian women were wasting no time cutting my parachute to pieces—the material was valuable. And there was a crowd of people standing around the burning airplane.

Ammunition was cooking off and I shouted at them to get away, but they either didn't understand or didn't care. Anyway, they didn't move. The rest of my flight was circling overhead and I waved at them to let them know I was alright. Then, they headed to England."

Although the location where Birtciel came down was in Allied hands, it was dangerous enough that the RAF men who arrived in a jeep to retrieve him urged him to hurry aboard. "They took me to a building that had been converted to a hospital and looked me over," remembered Birtciel. "The doctor said that I was okay but would be very sore during the next few days. He sure wasn't wrong."

As a precaution against Birtciel being a German spy, an RAF officer was assigned to escort him. "He was with me full time," said Birtciel. "They finally took me to an airfield northeast of Brussels and flew me to London. Once we got there the 55th sent one of the pilots down from Wormingford and he confirmed that I was who I said I was."

Birtciel was anxious to return to duty and finish his combat tour. "When I got back to the base, the flight surgeon asked me if I had been knocked unconscious at any time when I bailed out. I couldn't remember being unconscious because I was unconscious, so I told him, no. I flew my next mission on April 7."

Righetti, his time and energy again consumed by his administrative duties, missed the mission of April 7. It is virtually certain that he wished he hadn't as it delivered the sort of excitement that at least some of the men had been craving. Although the 55th's pilots did not know it, the day marked the desperate launch of a last-ditch Luftwaffe attempt to knock the Allied air offensive back on its heels.

Hans-Joachim "Hajo" Hermann was a veteran German bomber pilot, and one of fewer than two hundred recipients of the Knight's Cross with Swords. He first saw combat during the Spanish Civil War and following the start of World War II flew more than three hundred bomber missions on multiple fronts, to include action during the Battle of Britain. Later, during the autumn of 1943 while Righetti was training pilots and Kyle was teething and Cathryn was sewing chair covers, Hermann achieved notoriety as the creator of the Wild Boar night fighter tactics that so badly savaged the RAF's bombers. Flying night fighters during this period he was credited with nine aerial victories. Now, during the closing months of the war, he was a colonel and commanded 9. Flieger-Division (J), headquartered in Prague.

An ardent patriot, Hermann was a leading advocate of the Rammjäger concept—the use of fighters to ram American bombers. He rationalized it with a memorandum, *Mathematical Justification for Suicide Missions*, which essentially declared that good results could be obtained using less fuel and neophyte pilots, while experiencing only a marginally higher fatality rate than was then the norm with traditional fighter tactics.[7] To his mind, the concept wasn't actually suicidal as the pilots were intended to smash into the more fragile sections of their targets and then abandon their aircraft, assuming they survived.

The notion, although desperate, was not totally devoid of logic. The problem for the Luftwaffe was that, aside from all the other talent that was required to fly a frontline fighter, the aerial gunnery skills necessary to shoot down another aircraft were quite complex and required extensive training. On the other hand, simply crashing a fighter into a large aircraft that was flying a steady course required much less skill. And the physics of mass and force virtually guaranteed that the targeted aircraft would suffer mortal damage.

So, by early 1945, with Germany critically short of skilled pilots, the idea of neophyte pilots smashing themselves into American bomber streams made some rational sense even if the moral case was not compelling. Hermann planned to solicit volunteers from the ranks of green pilots who had recently completed training, or whose training had been forestalled by the chaos that marked the closing phases of the war. In fact, neither Hitler nor Reichsmarschall Göring, Hitler's deputy and the head of the Luftwaffe, liked the idea. Despite assurances that the Rammjäger pilots would not technically be committing suicide, the likelihood that they would be killed was believed to be quite high.

Still, Hermann campaigned enthusiastically for men, and aircraft, and permission to use them as a Rammjäger shock force. He reasoned that if a massive number of bombers were knocked down, the Americans might curtail operations long enough for the Luftwaffe to field a meaningful number of Me-262s and other advanced fighters. He outlined his thinking in a memorandum to Göring: "The time until Me-262 operations can be expanded must be bridged; the time is also approaching by which the conventional fighter force, which, as is known, has only a slight prospect of success, will be completely exhausted and grounded."

Hermann also underscored the need for a single crushing blow against the Americans: "We need to achieve success of such numerical significance that the enemy will change both the frequency of his attacks and his methods. We need the consequences that only success can bring."[8]

However, there was the pesky reality that simply receiving and setting aside the fifteen hundred aircraft he wanted, as well as the necessary pilots, mechanics, administrative support and fuel, was not a foregone conclusion. Apart from the Allied bombing raids, roving bands of fighter aircraft—such as Righetti often led—made it ever more difficult to move anything during the day by rail, air, road, or river. Such an undertaking would demand virtually every resource the Luftwaffe could muster.

Nevertheless, with the situation essentially hopeless and with nothing worthwhile to lose, Göring finally gave Hermann permission to put the plan in motion. In the call for volunteers that he issued on March 8, Göring declared: "The fateful battle for the Reich, our people and our Homeland has reached a critical stage. Almost the whole world is against us. They have sworn to destroy us in battle and in their blind hate, to wipe us out. With one final effort we must stem this threatening wave."[9]

The message went out mostly to training organizations, but also to a few frontline units. No particulars were given and the men were told only that they would be volunteering for a mission of great importance—one that had the potential to change the course of the war. They were also told that their chances of survival would be slim. Notwithstanding the paucity of details and the likelihood that their probable reward would be death, the response exceeded Hermann's expectations. More than two thousand men, including veteran flyers, put themselves forward. In fact, there were more volunteers than could be used and many of the combat veterans were refused as they were considered more valuable in their conventional units.

192 • Vanished Hero

The men volunteered for roughly the same reasons. Aside from the fact that they came to manhood during a time of war and ultra-nationalistic fervor, many of their families, or parts of their families, had been displaced or killed by the Allied bombing. Then, there were those whose training had been sidelined by the lack of fuel. They saw the call as an opportunity to finally get into combat; it was their chance to make a difference. Further, like young men everywhere, some volunteered simply because their friends did. Finally, because so little was divulged about the nature of the special mission, some of the young men certainly must have believed they were going to be put at the controls of a new wonder weapon.

The first of about 250 volunteers began reporting to the airbase at Stendal, about fifty miles west of Berlin, on March 24. By this time, Hermann had received the unhappy news that rather than 1,500 fighters, he could expect to receive no more than 350. It wasn't nearly the number of aircraft he needed to strike the sort of catastrophic blow he envisioned. Still, he pressed ahead with the plan, hoping that an initial success with the smaller number of fighters might serve as the proof he needed to get the enormous formations of aircraft he really wanted.

The following day, March 25, Hermann shared the details of the planned mission with the assembled volunteers, now officially organized as Schulungslehrgang Elbe, or Training Course Elbe. It was a cover name and the group was more informally known as Sonderkommando Elbe, or Special Command Elbe. They had been selected largely because they had at least a few hours' experience flying the Me-109. The plan was for them to fly Me-109s that had been stripped of weapons and armor in order to make them as light, fast and maneuverable as possible. For self-defense, the aircraft were to retain only a single MG131 machine gun armed with a few dozen rounds of ammunition.[10] The volunteers, covered by fighters from conventional units, were to ram the American bombers and then jump clear of the wreckage. They were also told at this meeting—and reminded during the subsequent days—that they were free to change their minds at any time.

One of the men recorded his disenchantment upon learning the truth: "I knew with absolute certainty that we had lost the war. There was no wonder weapon. There was no atom bomb. We would simply be sent to the slaughter. And only to prolong the rule of the Third Reich's big boys by minutes."[11] It was a sad, scornful cynicism that must certainly have been shared by some of his comrades. The magnificent Third Reich—with all its spectacular technological and military achievements—was reduced to sending youngsters to smash themselves into the seemingly endless streams of American bombers. Still, the number of volunteers who changed their minds was essentially nil.

During the rest of March and into April the men were invited to various political lectures and classes, as well as propaganda films. None of them were mandatory as Hermann was worried that the volunteers might quit rather than endure the shrill nattering of the Nazi party flacks sent to Stendal by Goebbels' propaganda mill. One of the men remembered that he and the majority of his colleagues bristled at the veiled attempts to fortify their dedication to the Nazi cause. "We volunteered willingly for a risky mission and didn't need any further mental treatment."[12]

There was no flight training for the special operation as there simply wasn't enough fuel to support it. And curiously, there were no detailed technical discussions as to how the ramming ought to be done. There were, however, presentations made by combat veterans who had made and obviously survived ramming attacks. It was generally agreed that the bombers ought to be attacked from behind, and that the most vulnerable points were the tail section, the cockpit and the wings behind the engines. There was also quite a bit of debate as to whether or not the canopy ought to be jettisoned before hitting the bombers in order to increase the odds of successfully jumping from the aircraft. The canopy did offer some protection but the aircraft would twist and bend as it struck a bomber and there was a real risk that the canopy might jam in place and trap the pilot; no consensus was reached on this point.

During late March, a group of volunteers was sent to a pair of bases near Prague, Gbell and Kletzan. Not long afterward, during the night of April 4, the remaining men of Sonderkommando Elbe at Stendal were divided into five groups. One of these was kept at Stendal while the other four were dispersed by road to other airfields in the region.

Sachau and Gardelegen were located about fifteen miles southwest of Stendal, while Mortitz and Delitzsch were about fifty miles south. The operation, codenamed *Werwolf*, was scheduled for April 6, less than a month following Göring's initial call for volunteers.

But there weren't enough aircraft available on April 6 and the operation was postponed until April 7. Even on that day the promised number of 350 fighters was not delivered. Only about two hundred Me-109s had been staged by mid-morning and these were still not entirely ready. In fact, the group at Stendal started the day with no aircraft whatsoever. Ground crews at all the airfields raced to remove armor, guns and other equipment while simultaneously fueling them and otherwise preparing them for the unprecedented operation.

However, not all the aircraft were configured as planned, and some simply required too much work to be made operational in time. Consequently, the Sonderkommando Elbe organizations at the different airfields were in a frenzied state of disarray as available aircraft were reviewed against pilot rosters, and choices were made as to who would fly that day. Ultimately, aircraft were assigned, plans were modified and reviewed, and formations began to take off.

More than 1,300 American bombers with nearly 850 fighter escorts motored toward an array of targets in central and northern Germany. Righetti's 55th was in the mix although he was stuck at Wormingford catching up on the myriad ground duties required of a fighter group commander. Meanwhile, as noon approached, just under two hundred Rammjäger pilots of Sonderkommando Elbe were airborne and moving toward the planned staging areas over Magdeburg and Dömitz. The scattered formations of Me-109s were a pitiful shadow of the colossal force Hermann originally envisioned.

As it developed, other German Air Force fighter units were also airborne that day but the coordination with Sonderkommando Elbe was poor to nonexistent and the appearance of both at the same place and time was due more to happenstance than to meticulous planning. Even had there been a carefully orchestrated plan, it would have been difficult to execute as the radio transmitters of the ramming aircraft had been removed; the young flyers were unable to talk to anyone. The receivers were tuned to a channel on which martial music was broadcast as well as directive orders of a general nature. Moreover, propaganda and Nazi slogans were read by a female: "Think of our dead wives and children who lie buried under the ruins of our towns," and "Deutschland über alles." Rather than bolstering the morale of the pilots, this Nazi flim-flammery upset many of them.[13]

The poor training of the young German pilots quickly manifested itself as many of them became lost or were unable to join with their flight leaders. Moreover, some encountered cloudy conditions and icing from which they failed to escape. At least one pilot simply bailed out from his ice-crusted fighter. Additionally, many of the pilots experienced mechanical issues and returned to base or bailed out. Finally, the fighters based near Prague were ordered back to their airfields as it became apparent that they would not have enough fuel to find and engage the Americans.

Regardless, something more than a hundred Rammjäger pilots in groups of various sizes made contact with the American formations at different locations. The 55th's mission summary report recorded the group's encounter with the Rammjägers in the vicinity of Celle, "where the first Me-109 snuffled down from 3 o'clock for a short jab at Vinegrove 1-8 [the 493rd Bomb Group], but was snared and scragged [shot down] before he got a crack at the 17's. From then on enemy aircraft played acey-ducey with the force, sending about 10 Me's [Me-109s] down singly to stool out the escort and make them drop tanks."

The notion that the young German pilots were trying to compel their American counterparts to drop their external fuel tanks in order to foreshorten their range was invented by the 55th's pilots. The pilots of Sonderkommando Elbe cared about the American fighters only inasmuch as they did not want to be shot down. "We put the sneeze on the first 6 jokers thru pranging them down at 10,000 feet," the report continued. "Blows [Me-262s] stayed high and aloof, just snuffling along and tossing a gander at the proceedings below ... The enemy aircraft were at all times readied up for attack, were loose and elusive, and in no respect raw hands at the way they used cloud cover."

That the German pilots dodged the 55th's attacks by ducking into the clouds was a basic survival tactic rather than an indicator of any great experience. Although it is possible, perhaps likely, that the 55th encountered Me-109s from other units, there is little doubt that many of the fighters it engaged were from Sonderkommando Elbe. The mission summary report noted, "1 [B-17] down at Gifhorn ... rammed by 1 of 3 attacking Me-109s." Another less successful ramming was described: "1 heavy [B-17] collided with 109. Enemy aircraft destroyed but heavy turned for home minus wing tip and one engine." Frank Birtciel recalled: "A 109 attacked in a dive [of] about 30 degrees and hit the B-17 just short of the radio man's gun and just ahead of the waist guns. Could not tell if it was deliberate or not, but did not look like a firing pass."

It is apparent from the report that some of the Me-109s made diving passes against the B-17s, but did not ram them. Certainly, these aircraft could have been from other units, but it should also be considered that some of the men from Sonderkommando Elbe must have had second thoughts, or simply could not overcome the powerful and reflexive instinct to avoid a collision; the basic human predisposition toward survival was powerful.

Regardless of whether or not they followed through with their ramming missions, many of the Rammjägers were destroyed by the American escort fighters—six of them by the 55th's 38th Fighter Squadron. The German pilots' lack of training and experience is underscored by the fact that nearly all of them were shot down without putting up much of a fight. An excerpt from John Cunnick's encounter report was typical:

> Our flight dropped tanks and attacked and during the fight I lost our first element and my wingman. I climbed back up to our [assigned bomber] box in hopes of finding them and had just reached the bomber level when I saw another Me-109 come diving thru the formation. I went after him and as he pulled out of his dive at 10,000 feet, I tacked on behind him dead astern at 100 yards. After a short burst, during which I saw my strikes converge on his wing roots and canopy, the pilot bailed out.

The only loss the 55th suffered was Harold Konantz who was mistakenly fired on by gunners aboard the escorted bombers when he closed to ascertain that they were those that the group was assigned to escort. His engine failed several minutes later compelling him to bail out. He was captured immediately and made a POW.

Konantz's older brother, Walter, had just finished his combat tour with the 55th and Harold was flying his aircraft that day. Walter recalled his younger brother's experience: "When he was finally taken to a Luftwaffe base for interrogation he was asked his name and upon answering the Luftwaffe officer shuffled through some papers, picked out one and studied it, then told him, 'We thought you had finished your tour and were on the way home.' He had some very up-to-date data on me!"[14]

Hans Joachim Hermann's hopes for a victory of unprecedented magnitude went so wholly unrealized that the Americans didn't even understand they had been targeted with a special operation; the ramming attacks were initially thought to be unintentional collisions. Of the approximately two hundred Sonderkommando Elbe pilots that eventually took off that morning, only a small percentage made ramming attacks. In fact, of the dozen or so bombers that were actually hit, the USAAF acknowledged only eight losses. Ultimately, the entire effort was a waste of men and resources—more than fifty aircraft and three dozen pilots.

Klaus Hahn was one of the young Rammjäger pilots who succeeded that day. He recalled, "The feeling was that you were likely flying your last flight today and that you wouldn't return from it. You'll probably be dead. That thought was a part of it," he said, "and you had to accept it and you had to deal with it."[15] It was to be Hahn's first combat mission.

However, it seemed that the odds were against Hahn when his aircraft developed engine trouble soon after taking off from the airfield at Sachau. He was unable to keep up with the other three aircraft that made up his flight. His flight leader dropped back to check on him but, unable to communicate, soon left Hahn on his own; the other three aircraft climbed away and were quickly out of sight. Alone, Hahn considered his options. "To return to base and land was out of the question," he said. "That would have appeared to be cowardice, so I climbed slowly up to 10,000 meters and then even higher and waited for things to start happening. I must admit, it was an uncomfortable feeling to be flying all alone up there. My plane began running normal. I suspect that the starter gear had gotten stuck and then later freed itself."[16]

It was some time before he saw any other aircraft, but he finally spotted a four-ship of fighters winging toward him. "I almost shouted for joy as, suddenly, four single-motor aircraft approached me. For me there was no doubt—these were Me-109s, because they were flying in the standard *schwarm* formation. This was the greatest mistake of my life. As I came closer to them I recognized them as Mustangs. There was no escape—I had to engage in combat."

The P-51s immediately began shredding Hahn's aircraft with .50 caliber machine gun rounds. His canopy and instrument panel were hit and his face was cut by shards of glass. "I started taking hits from my left rear. My arm fell off the throttle. I felt warmth on my neck and splintered pieces of the dashboard flew into my face. I did not feel any pain and in an instant I was determined to get out of there. I did a half roll to fall out of the plane."

"What actually happened was quite different," he said. "I got a big shock. I looked up at my left hand that was pushing against the canopy. To be more exact, what remained of my hand slapped against the windshield. It was a clump of bloody meat mixed with a tattered leather glove."

His aircraft trailing smoke, Hahn spotted a formation of B-17s directly below him. Badly wounded and seriously shaken by his encounter with the American fighters, he still had the presence of mind—and sense of purpose—to push his fighter down toward the bombers. "I did not dive straight at my target," he recorded, "but a little from the side. I pulled my machine out of the dive as steeply as I could and charged at the side of the bomber. With the high speed that I had built up in the power dive, I approached the bomber very rapidly. What actually happened during the actual ramming, I cannot tell from my own observations."[17]

In fact, Hahn had no recollection of his impact with the B-17. His next memory was of spinning through the sky. "How I escaped from my 'Beule' I have no idea." Beule translates as "bulge" and referred to the many protruding fairings that covered the various equipment and ammunition bays that were added to later models of the Me-109. "It will be an eternal question for me, how I succeeded in escaping. I have no idea how I got rid of the canopy, how I unbuckled by seat harness and such, since my left arm was useless. I came to my senses later on and found myself spinning down. One of my first thoughts was to fall as far as possible then deploy the parachute. I estimate I deployed my parachute at about a thousand meters." The shock of the parachute's opening knocked Hahn unconscious. And once he hit the ground he found that he was unable to move. "Later I learned that both of my femurs were knocked out of their hip sockets, apparently from the impact of landing. Then the pain set in."

"Two German soldiers were the first to find me," Hahn said. "It is an unpleasant memory. They stole everything from my cargo leg pockets and disappeared with the comment that I was a goner. Then came the local inhabitants, all older men and women and my memory of that is a pleasant one. The inhabitants who found me stopped an Army ambulance that just happened to be driving by. It drove me to several different hospitals that refused to admit me but finally I and an Army Lieutenant Colonel who had suffered a shot to the head were accepted into the German Army hospital at Munster-Lager." Hahn's left arm was eventually amputated, but after a painful and protracted recuperation period he made an otherwise full recovery.

The aircraft that Hahn had hit was most probably flown by Budd Wentz of the 487th Bomb Group. "Suddenly," Wentz said, "while on route to the IP [Initial Point], we received a terrific jolt and bang. I tightened up on the wheel to prevent it from swerving. The waist gunner reported over the intercom that our plane had been hit in the tail by an Me-109 diving down from four o'clock high."[18]

The rudder of Wentz's B-17 was torn completely away and parts of the vertical stabilizer and both horizontal stabilizers were also shredded or otherwise ripped off. Consequently, he found that adding or pulling power to the engines on one side or the other was the only means by which he could exercise even minimal control over the aircraft. After coaxing the shuddering aircraft westward he spotted an airfield to the north and expertly brought the ship down without crashing.

The airfield—Wernershöhe—was dotted with Me-262s and Wentz and his crew were certain they were about to be made POWs. He was startled then, to see American troops running toward his aircraft as he shut the engines down. An officer stood up in his jeep and shouted, "What the hell are you doing? You aren't supposed to land here!" The airfield had been captured just hours earlier.

Wentz and his crew were astounded to discover several captured B-17s at Wernershöhe that had been maintained in working order. Since soon after the Americans started flying against the Nazis in 1942, the Germans had scavenged wrecked aircraft and in some cases returned them to flying condition. These aircraft were used for training and, occasionally, clandestine missions. Exhibiting remarkable resourcefulness, Wentz and his men used a jeep generator for electrical power and started the engines of one of the captured bombers. "Then we took off and flew back to our air base [Lavenham] in England," Wentz said.

"DON'T BE A FOOL"

Although the main body of the Luftwaffe had been rendered impotent, the speedy, jet-powered Me-262s had proved themselves virtually
invulnerable to Allied piston-powered fighters. Essentially, the jet pilots
went where they wanted and did what they wanted so long as they had
adequate fuel. When confronted, they simply raced out of harm's way.
For the most part they were vulnerable only around their bases when
they were still accelerating after takeoff, or when they were compelled
to slow to landing speed. To protect them, the Luftwaffe guarded the
bases with concentrated antiaircraft batteries and protective umbrellas of
traditional fighters.

Although the reality was that the Me-262s were still being operated
in relatively few numbers, there was no denying the truth that the
jets could pose a very real threat to the Allied strategic bombing
campaign if they became more numerous before the war ended. This
was articulated in a report, *Allied Air Supremacy and German Jet Planes*,
which declared, "Maintenance of Allied Air Supremacy over Europe
in 1945 is confronted by a serious threat. This threat menaces both
continuance of our Strategic bombardment and the superiority, both
offensively and defensively, of the fighter bomber cover under which
our troops fight. This threat is the opposition of a large and increasing
German jet plane fighter force ..."[1] Consequently, the USAAF's leadership directed heavy bomber attacks against the Luftwaffe's Me-262
bases.

One of these raids was directed against the airfield at Oberweisenfeld near Munich on April 9, 1945. The 55th was assigned to protect bombers of the 3d Air Division through the target area and back out. Approaching the target, Righetti directed the 338th Fighter Squadron to stay with the bombers while he took the 38th and the 343rd to patrol south of Munich. In the vicinity of Ingolstadt, four Me-262s approached the bomber stream and the 338th moved to block them. Although the P-51s were unable to stop the German fighters from diving through the bombers, none of the ships were hit and the jets did not return for another attack.

At the same time, Ed Giller—leading the 343rd Fighter Squadron—spotted a single Me-262 descending through twenty thousand feet in a gentle turn with two P-51s from another fighter group in hot pursuit. The German jet was outdistancing the two American fighters, but Giller had an altitude advantage and released his external fuel tanks before diving down to join the chase. Close behind him were Red Flight and the other three pilots of his own White Flight. He closed the distance to 1,500 yards but was unable to get any closer. "I followed him for ten minutes with the 262 doing a very gentle turn to the left and losing altitude. We were now over the southern edge of Munich with the German jet at 1,000 feet and me still at 7,000 feet."

The Me-262 pilot made for the airfield at Munich/Reim. Giller was wary of the antiaircraft fire he knew was ready to cover the German jet, but still pressed his attack as the enemy pilot slowed to landing speed. "Going balls out, I caught him at fifty feet just over the perimeter track. He was going west to east about 100 yards to the right of the runway. I fired several bursts and observed strikes on the left wing root and fuselage."

Still moving at 450 miles per hour, Giller blasted past the Me-262. "Looking back, I watched him crash-land on the field 100 yards to the right of the runway in a large cloud of dust and flying pieces. He didn't burn, which I assume was due to the fact he was out of fuel."[2] Red Flight and the rest of White Flight streaked after Giller, low across the airfield which was rippled by streams of antiaircraft fire. As they did so, they flamed an Me-410 on the ground.

Giller led the other pilots up to three thousand feet where they orbited south of the airfield. Righetti described the subsequent action in the group's mission summary report. "Very shortly thereafter Tudor Leader [Giller] spotted an He-111 being towed south on the main autobahn just south of Munich. He dropped down, and upon investigation of the enemy aircraft's destination, he sighted many beautifully hidden aircraft of all types, including jets, parked on the autobahn's shoulders and backed into the woods about six miles south of Munich and surrounding Munich/Brunnthal Landing Ground."

The aircraft that Giller discovered numbered a hundred or more and were well camouflaged with nets, brush and other vegetation. Giller called Righetti and asked for permission to attack which was readily granted. As Giller and his accompanying flights went to work, Righetti immediately directed the 338th to continue escorting the bombers, while he kept the 38th and the remainder of the 343rd to provide top cover for the strafers.

Noted ace Franz Stigler recalled how the "Ami Jabos," or American fighters, made operations from many of the Luftwaffe's fighter bases so dangerous that the Germans were compelled to turn their autobahns into makeshift airfields. "In many respects, this was an improvement over our regular bases," he noted. "It [the autobahn] was long, its concrete strips were numerous, and during the day, two to three fighters could be hidden under its many underpasses. Furthermore, the surrounding woods made for ideal field maintenance. They usually lined the auto-bahn for miles and we soon found ourselves sharing these woodland hideouts with night fighters and even large, four-engine bombers such as the FW-200 Condor."

"Since normal civilian automobile traffic had long since ended," Stigler said, "the highways were virtually empty. Ammunition, fuel and supplies could be quickly brought to us from nearby towns along the excellent network." Stigler recalled that the autobahns were "par-ticularly handy" for inexperienced pilots. "They could be seen for miles from the air, they were mainly long, straight roadbeds and there were enough of them throughout Germany to insure [sic] that a pilot running low on fuel, or, with a damaged aircraft, could find a safe, if temporary, haven."[3]

Righetti's 55th set to work making mayhem of the "haven" that Giller had just discovered. Giller alone destroyed four aircraft to include the He-111 that initially gave the hideout away. "It was sitting on the north side of the woods. I put in a short burst and received in return a nice explosion and fire on the right wing root and engine nacelle."[4]

When Giller and his flights finished their work, Righetti dived down with the rest of the group. On his first pass he set an Me-262 afire. On his second pass he flamed two, twin-engine aircraft. He destroyed two more Me-262s on his third firing run: "One immediately exploded and as I closed on the second, it caught on fire." He made several more passes, firing bursts as he spied new targets. "Although I scored hits on several, since it was impossible for me to determine the extent of damage, I make no claims."

The action quickly grew frenzied as pilots made simultaneous passes from multiple directions. Tom Welch exercised his wise-guy patter in the mission summary report:

> From then on, we are playing the hokus pokus, with Mustangs wild, and what with a few finesses and criss crosses, almost everyone is making their bid. There is only one flak passer who is slipping in a burst of 20 [millimeter antiaircraft fire] every then and now, between doing a little of the hooch kooch, and the shimmy around the slugs that are dropping in on him. Now, of course, he is being of no bother to anyone but himself, and we are leaving the area with very little flak damage, and 55 of the jobs up in smoke and flames and fire.

With his ammunition nearly depleted, Righetti hauled *Katydid* through a turn back toward the autobahn, leveled the aircraft's wings and started one more strafing run. "On my final pass I attacked two enemy aircraft, a long-nose FW-190 and an unidentified twin-engine aircraft parked at the northeast end of the field, on a head-on pass from west to east. The FW-190 caught on fire and I therefore declare it as destroyed, while the unidentified, twin-engine, enemy aircraft suffered considerable damage."[5] Righetti's bag for the day was six aircraft, three of them Me-262s.

In the mission summary report he characterized the group's work that day as "the finest mass of burning destruction ever seen by the undersigned." In fact, the 55th's pilots were eventually awarded credit for an ironic total of 55 enemy aircraft destroyed. Righetti also offered the following observation, perhaps in order to preempt any skeptics. "Each pilot fired most of his ammunition, and there were so many targets that it is sincerely felt that personal claims are accurate and very conservative. There were no less than one hundred aircraft in the immediate area, and flak was limited to three or four light, inaccurate guns."

To add personal context—and even more credibility—he declared, "I made eight-to-ten passes and had one or more aircraft as targets each time; and each of the approximately 35 aircraft [pilots] involved had the same opportunity." Finally, the claims of each pilot included signed, corroborating witness statements from other pilots.

Righetti's letter home that night reflected his excitement at his group's success. "Flew uneventfully yesterday but had good hunch on mission to Munich today, so led again. No interception of bombers [by enemy aircraft] so dropped down and found the woods full of them. My group got 56. I got six destroyed and two damaged—total now twenty. Three were jets for which I get special credit."

That Righetti declared a total of 56 enemy aircraft destroyed by the group rather than the 55 that were later credited officially and recorded in the mission summary report, indicated that the claims had not yet been vetted by the Victory Credit Board. It also showed—with a discrepancy of only one—how carefully Righetti's men managed their claims. Righetti also declared that he was due special acknowledgment for the Me-262s he had destroyed. Certainly the Eighth's leadership made the jets a top priority, but they were still counted the same as any other destroyed aircraft.

Righetti knew that his letter had a certain raggedness to it. His weariness after a very long day and more than five months of combat during the coldest months of the year showed. "If this whole letter seems slightly garbled, it's just that I've had a busy day. I'll do better tomorrow when my head clears—love to all."

The Righetti family knew that men like Elwyn were dying over Europe but there was no way for them or anyone else that wasn't a participant to understand it. They simply prayed for him and continued their life on the ranch. This was underscored in a letter from Pop which he scratched out on the kitchen table of the old ranch house on April 2.

> Not much to tell you. Been fixing or rebuilding fences and farming for Sudan [grass] at the Lewis place. Was to a Holstein cow meeting and learned how a good cow should look. Well, we only have one that would score 10%. The rest, zero or under. The cattle are getting fat. Dairy still doing fine. Hogs getting ready for L.A. [market in Los Angeles]. Even the fatted calf is getting better and better. Your gals are fine. The family is going to the swim club dance April 7th....

Sister Betty likewise kept Righetti abreast of doings on the ranch. "We're certainly enjoying having your two girls here. Some days they're both darlings. Some days just one is. Some days neither is. Aren't we all? Hurry home and kick a few holes in their heads...." It is evident from Betty's words that although the two young women enjoyed living together and helping Righetti's mother run the house, Cathryn's strong will occasionally clashed with her new family's equally willful disposition.

But Betty also reassured her brother with a note of fondness and admiration for his little family: "You'd be so proud of your daughter. She's the smartest little gal. So's your wife. She refuses to go to S.F. [San Francisco] with Jennebell Leach and me. Says she's tired of going places sans escort. She's waiting 'till you get home to take her out."

"We're all fine here, tho' saddened by FDR's sudden death. He was a very great man, I think." Her feelings were shared by a majority of Americans and it would be some time before the Righettis and the rest of the nation got used to the notion of a leader other than Roosevelt.

Betty's letter also included an admonition that certainly must have echoed the feelings of every other Righetti in San Luis Obispo. Although they were exceedingly proud of his considerable combat accomplishments, they knew he had achieved them at considerable risk. "We're sweating out these [last] weeks of your tour. And for gosh sakes, Bud, don't be a fool. You've tempted fate enough. Don't stick your neck out beyond your 300 hours. We're expecting you home and we'd like to see you stay home when you get here. So that's enough sisterly advice for now."

Certainly, as the war was nearly over, the Righettis must have felt that their prayers for Elwyn's safe return were on the verge of being answered. In fact, on April 16, shortly after Betty wrote her letter, Carl Spaatz, the head of the United States Strategic Air Forces in Europe, declared that there was no need to continue the strategic air war—there were no more worthwhile strategic targets. "The advances of the Ground Forces have brought to a close the strategic air war waged by the United States Strategic Air Forces and the Royal Air Force Bomber Command. It has been won with a decisiveness becoming increasingly evident as our armies overrun Germany."[6] From that point, the American heavy bombers were to be used only as necessary to speed the Allied ground advance. Consequently, the need for the Eighth's fighter groups—the 55th among them—to escort the bombers was quickly diminishing.

Indeed, the German armies were in retreat everywhere and the Reich's industry was essentially rubbled. The Luftwaffe was likewise gasping its last and its pilots were increasingly fatalistic as indicated by Hermann Buchner, an Me-262 pilot with JG 7 based at Parchim in northern Germany:

> Parts of our airfield were badly destroyed, the accommodation was unusable and the landing strip was being repaired by the engineers again and again, a feat that required their maximum effort ... Our sanctuary was the mess at Parchim, where all the pilots would gather together, all who were still with us from the party. Talks were given, battles fought, and we tried to make the best of the defeat. Photographs of our fallen comrades hung on the walls and the young pilots had already put nails in, so that their pictures could be hung there. In spite of all this, the mood was not bad—we would pull through.[7]

Another German pilot similarly noted the futility of the Luftwaffe's fight. However, his observation did not end on the same hopeful note.

> We were losing pilots all the time, and had to get used to seeing new faces and hearing new names. So now, I can hardly recall a single name—things were all

mixed up. Almost every day new pilots came up from the reinforcement units, or the schools, full of hope and optimism. The quartermasters were reluctant to find billets for any more pilots; they hated to see these young men take [to] the air when the grim routine of bringing back their remains had to be so often repeated.[8]

For his part, Righetti was conflicted about his role in continuing the fight. And it was apparent that he was homesick: "Want to come home so very badly now," he wrote, "but sure don't want to leave 'till we get this little chore wound up right."

As the leader of the 55th he felt that he was personally making a real difference. "Thought you all might be pleased to know that word from *very* high headquarters gives my group credit for being the largest single factor responsible for Patton's successful drive. We nailed rail transport to such an extent that movement of anything via train was impossible for the 3 weeks prior to his start—over 400 locomotives, etc. You don't want me home when I can do stuff like that here." He was not just writing of his own flying and scoring, but of the results his men had achieved since he had started flying combat.

Although it might have been an exaggeration to say that the 55th was the "largest single factor responsible for Patton's successful drive," that information was obviously passed to Righetti by someone. Certainly, the 55th—his group—was a standout among the many air combat units that made it nearly impossible for the Germans to move anything by road or rail during the daylight hours. And no one could argue that Patton's advance was not made immeasurably easier by the great host of aircraft that swept the battlefield ahead and above his army.

The 55th was sent to harry the Germans once again on April 16; the day that Spaatz declared the end of the strategic air war. It was also the same day that two of Wormingford's Red Cross workers considered birthday plans for Righetti. He would turn thirty the next day and, as the Red Cross was charged with improving the morale of the men, the ladies considered what they might do. Jan Houston Monaghan approached her friend Nelle Huse, "Tomorrow is Colonel Righetti's birthday. Let's invite him for a really nice tea." Huse considered the idea for a moment before replying, "We have too much to do this week, Jan. We don't have time for that tomorrow. We'll do something special for him next week."[9]

The group's assignment that day was not much different than the sorts of missions it had been flying for months. The men were charged with freelancing, or sweeping, through the Salzburg area in support of B-24s from the Eighth's 2nd Air Division. Righetti led fifty-nine aircraft out of Wormingford just before noon.

As had been typical during the previous few months, the Luftwaffe failed to challenge the 55th in the air. The German flyers were too few and spread too thin to oppose every one of the massive American bombing missions in any meaningful way. Accordingly, once the group cleared its area of responsibility, Righetti turned the 338th and the 343rd loose to hunt on their own while he led the 38th down to low altitude to see what mischief he could create.

It would have greatly displeased Betty. The letter in which she had cautioned Righetti against being "a fool" was still on its way as he coasted across the German countryside. Considering his demonstrated aggressiveness to that point, it is not likely that the letter would have made any difference. And Betty, who had spent most of her life with her brother, probably knew this before she ever put pen to paper. Still, it had cost her nothing to plead with him to mind his personal well-being.

Indeed, Righetti's actions that day were exactly opposite what his family would have wished. With the 38th Fighter Squadron in trail, he poked along the autobahn between Salzburg and Munich looking for something worth shooting at. As it developed, there was plenty that merited such attention. "At approximately 1430 we were in the vicinity of Rosenheim, did a 180-degree turn and started up the autobahn leading to Munich. On our starboard [right] side we saw Bod [Bad] Aibling Airdrome with numerous aircraft dispersed on [the] north and south sides of the field."[10] Righetti took White and Red Flights—four aircraft each—down for an attack on the airfield and left Yellow and Blue Flights to provide top cover.

John Kavanaugh, the element leader, or number three man, in White Flight recorded that Righetti led two firing passes and, "then called over the radio and said that the squadron should leave the field as he didn't think the planes parked there had gas in them."[11] Without fuel, aircraft typically didn't burn when attacked, and although they might be damaged beyond any hope of reasonable repair, it was difficult to make that determination from the cockpit of a speeding fighter. The planes they had hit, and that had failed to burn, were Si-204 twin-engine trainers. That the Luftwaffe wasn't keeping precious fuel in their trainers when there was not enough for their combat aircraft was not a surprise.

Righetti led the squadron further northwest following the highway toward Munich. Intense antiaircraft fire and a dearth of worthwhile targets compelled him to bypass the airfield at Holzkirchen after making just one pass without firing a shot. The fact that Righetti, always spoiling for a fight, decided to leave the airfield unmolested was an indication not only of the intensity of the antiaircraft fire but also of the fact that he did possess at least a small scrap of "risk versus reward" sensibility.

In fact, after bypassing Holzkirchen, Righetti took the 38th back to Brunnthal, southeast of Munich. It was the "honey hole" where the group had scored so well on April 9. He took the squadron down for several passes, flying through intense antiaircraft fire. Notwithstanding the intensity of that fire, however, Righetti destroyed three He-111s and two Ju-88s. Together with an Si-204 he shot up at Bad Aibling, it gave him a total of six aircraft destroyed for the day. Altogether, Righetti and the 38th's pilots destroyed seventeen aircraft before Righetti brought them back to Wormingford.

Ed Giller was leading the 343rd Fighter Squadron and found himself over Brunnthal just as Righetti and the 38th were finishing their work. He led the 343rd against a pocket of well-camouflaged enemy aircraft. "Of course," he recalled, "one of the rules is that you don't fly around and around and make multiple passes—[a rule] which I was ignoring."[12]

Nevertheless, when the hunting was good, commonsense had little chance of prevailing over aggressiveness, and Giller flamed an He-111, a Ju-52 and an Me-109. But it cost him. "All of a sudden," Giller said, "there was an enormous explosion and a feeling of a hammer hitting my shoulder." A 20-millimeter cannon shell smashed into the cockpit and exploded near his head. The majority of the blast was focused away from him, however a large chunk of the shell punched through the nylon webbing of his shoulder harness, cut through his clothes, punctured his chest and subsequently skidded across his ribcage under the skin before punching out near his armpit and rolling down his shirtsleeve.

Instinctively, Giller shoved the throttle forward, pulled back on the control stick and pointed his ship home. At the same time, he called to his wingman, Robert Welch, "I'm hit, we're going west." Frank Birtciel recalled that, notwithstanding the fact that Giller was in extremis, Welch was overly excited about the number of aircraft the Germans had hidden along the autobahn, and was reluctant to leave the excellent shooting behind. "Welch wanted to get some more airplanes but Giller repeated his call to head home, and said that he was losing blood."

The group's mission summary report—in decidedly unofficial terms—recounted the broader action, squadron-by-squadron. The review of the 38th Fighter Squadron's performance included the following description:

> Dropped down a little lower in the fast traffic lane and drove right up the autobahn into Brunnthal L/G [Landing Ground], where we found 40–50 mixed types up and down the road. Worked this over, destroying 12, as the intense flak belched, blistered, exhaled, emitted and sputtered from every direction. Even the trees were barking. A stone's throw up north (they were throwing those too) we found Neubiberg and skimmed across snagging a Ju-52 and a U/I [unidentified] T/E [twin-engine aircraft].

The report noted that the enemy flak was "intense and very, very, very accurate, indeed." The author was undoubtedly Tom Welch, the 55th's much-liked and capable intelligence officer. Still, the tone of this particular report is remarkably callous when it is considered that the group lost four men in the day's actions.

Donald Best of the group's 38th Fighter Squadron had been flying combat less than a month. He went down at Brunnthal. His element leader, John Kavanaugh, lost sight of him during the several firing runs. "During the above action, I heard Lt. Best say that he had been hit and was going to have to bail out. I pulled up and looked around but could not locate him. Our group leader [Righetti] told Best to head for friendly territory and to stay with the plane as long as he could. Lt. Best said that he would. That was the last we heard of him."[13]

John Cunnick was part of Kavanaugh's flight and didn't believe that Best was hit by enemy guns. "I think he picked up friendly ricochet fire during a strafing pass. He disappeared into the trees and I couldn't find him."

Patrick Moore was with the 343rd Fighter Squadron which hit Brunnthal and the nearby autobahn shortly after the 38th departed. Moore tipped up on a wing, presumably to get a good look at the airfield below. "The plane started a split S," reported squadron mate Walter Strauch. "Lt. Moore tried to roll and pull out at the same time and succeeded in doing both but as he leveled out he hit the ground and exploded."[14]

Vernon Tally of the group's 338th Fighter Squadron was hit by flak and joined with squadron mate Leedom John who had also been hit and was headed for Wormingford. Either because he was confused or in shock, or because his aircraft was too badly damaged to keep up, Tally drifted away from John. Later, John spotted a distant aircraft and circled back to discover it was Tally. The two joined again and were almost immediately attacked by a four-ship of P-47s which fortunately held their fire. However, John lost sight of Tally during the mix-up and the two never joined again. As it developed, Tally eventually crashed in friendly territory, was knocked unconscious and hospitalized. The 55th was not notified that he had been recovered, and filed a Missing Air Crew Report several days later.

Chester E. Coggeshall, Jr., of the 343rd Fighter Squadron, was flying the last flight of his second combat tour, having started flying P-38s with the 55th in January of 1944. Despite the fact he had been in combat for more than a year, he had never seen an enemy aircraft airborne. Walter Strauch, who had seen Patrick Moore hit the ground and explode, also reported on Coggeshall's demise: "... and when we pulled up to about 1,000 feet I noticed Red leader, Capt. Coggeshall, making a very gentle turn to the left and losing altitude. I immediately started over toward him and noticed his airplane was covered with oil and about this time he made a fast belly landing, dug a wing in, and cartwheeled."[15]

Coggeshall's aircraft came down in the small village of Sillersdorf, where it smashed into a small brick building. Incredibly, he survived, although he was injured. He was immediately captured by a band of local gendarmerie and military men who put him on a stretcher, loaded him into an armored vehicle and moved him about 3 miles to the town of Freilassing. There, a German sergeant ordered the men to move Coggeshall into the dispensary for first aid but their way was physically blocked by August Kobus, who said, "This pig needs no aid."

Kobus was the town's *burgomeister* and *ortsgruppenleiter*—the mayor and local ranking Nazi official. Neither position carried any military rank or authority, but as the German government crumbled, many men in Kobus's position grabbed power when and where they could. Kobus declared that he had been directed by his political superior to "finish" Coggeshall. He ordered the German military personnel to follow him, then climbed onto his bicycle and led the armored car into a wooded area.

Coggeshall was unloaded from the armored car. Kobus shot him once in the head with a .32 caliber pistol. The American airman shrieked and moaned. Kobus shot him again and killed him.[16]

Coggeshall had been murdered even before the 55th landed back at Wormingford.

Ed Giller, still bleeding, pressed westward. "I had a light suit on," said Giller, "and I put my hand inside my shirt and my finger goes into my chest and comes out covered with blood." Worried that he might faint due to loss of blood, Giller called out, "We're gonna head for the lines and if I'm beginning to run out of blood, I'm going to belly in." As it developed, his condition stabilized and after briefly considering landing on the continent for medical care, Giller pressed on to Wormingford. "I landed using just my right hand—throttle, stick and wheels."

After Giller got himself safely on the ground the squadron flight surgeon supervised his movement into a waiting ambulance. There followed several weeks of recovery. "The worst part was that for two weeks I got a penicillin shot every four hours. That got pretty tiresome."

The 55th's three squadrons recorded 52 enemy aircraft destroyed on April 16, 1945. Of that total, Righetti claimed six. However, the frenetic pace continued to fatigue him. Whereas flying was the only job for the majority of his pilots, he had a considerable administrative workload and was often called away to meetings at other bases. Combined with the considerable stress of leading his men—sometimes to their deaths—it all wore him down. He said as much in the letter he wrote to Cathryn after midnight: "Dearest Darling, Only a short note again because tonite Pappy's kinda pooped." In the letter he described how he stayed up late because he wanted to write to her on his birthday—April 17. He also wrote with some excitement about his imminent promotion to colonel. And he wrote of the time they planned to spend together upon his return from the fighting. "Need it worse every day, but still holding out as always."

Finally, he noted the hurt the group sustained during the strafing attacks on Brunnthal that day. "Lost 3 very good friends again today. Don't ever let anyone tell you that the final stages of the European war were easy." He signed off to his wife as "Rig" and, "with all the love there is."

German civilians and officials did not murder Allied flyers whenever they found them. Most downed airmen were not killed and there were many instances when those who were injured were given aid and succor until they were moved to where they could be given professional medical care. There were other instances of kindness as well.

Bert McDowell of the 55th's 338th Fighter Squadron was shot down late in the war. He recalled being under guard awaiting train transport following his capture. "While sitting in the tiny station, a small boy of about eight, who was with his mother, kept staring at me. Finally, he walked over to me, pulled out a cheese sandwich from a brown paper bag and offered it to me. I said 'Dunker' (thank you, one of the few German words I knew). I almost cried, I was so overwhelmed by this gesture of generosity and friendliness to a prisoner of war."[17]

"ONE MORE PASS"

In light of the fact that Spaatz had declared an end to the strategic air war on April 16, and had stated that "our Strategic Air Forces must operate with our Tactical Air Forces in close cooperation with our armies," there must have been a tactical imperative to attack Dresden the following day. Regardless of whether there was or not, the 55th and the Eighth's other fighter groups took the heavy bombers deep into Germany on a mission that looked no different from any of the hundreds that had earlier combined to help bring Germany to its knees. Then, having hit their targets, the bombers headed back to England and the 55th's pilots dropped down to shoot up whatever targets they might find.

The group's 343rd Fighter Squadron arrived over the airfield at Kamenz, about 25 miles northeast of Dresden. Based there were elements of Schlachtgeschwader 77, or SG 77. SG 77 was a ground–attack unit that operated heavily armed and armored FW-190s. At that time, loaded with bombs and antitank rockets, its pilots were engaged in operations against Red Army units advancing from the east.

Robert Welch and Philip Erby spotted a pair of SG 77 FW-190s that had just gotten airborne out of Kamenz. Welch led Erby on a diving attack. "I took the one on the left, and he [Erby] took the one on the right. They were flying line abreast at 3,000 feet. We came down on them from 9,000 feet and attacked, from dead astern." The German pilots did not react and apparently never spotted their attackers.

"We both knocked them down at about the same time," said Welch. "I watched his 190 crash, just south of mine, in a woods near a lake. It exploded and burned upon crashing."

Welch and Erby paid for their aggressiveness. "Suddenly I was hit by flak," Welch recorded, "so I called Lieutenant Erby and told him I was heading for Russian lines." Erby responded that he had also been hit and asked Welch to wait for him. In the haze, the two pilots had lost sight of each other. Welch decided to turn back toward the American lines and radioed his intentions to Erby who agreed to do the same. "He called about four minutes later and said he was going to bail out," Welch said. "He never called again and I could not raise him after repeated attempts."[1]

Richard Gibbs and his wingman followed Welch and Erby, but broke away as antiaircraft fire from the airfield intensified. As Gibbs felt his way around Kamenz—clear of the deadly guns—he caught sight of two more FW-190s just taking off to the west. He waited until the two German pilots were well clear of the airfield and then dived after one of the FW-190s, opening fire at a range of five hundred yards. "I was on his tail and closed all the way to 40 yards, firing all the time. The 190 burst into flames and did a half roll into the trees. We were both at 100 to 200 feet when he dove to the ground."

With oil from the downed enemy aircraft smeared across his windscreen, Gibbs pulled up and away. "I started doing climbing turns looking around for something else to latch onto." Spying another FW-190 crossing above him, Gibbs raised the nose of his P-51 and sprayed the enemy aircraft with his six machine guns. Noting hits on the German aircraft's wings, he turned hard behind it and fired several more bursts, "hitting him along the fuselage. The FW-190 continued in his dive and I passed him up at 1,000 feet, noting holes in the tail, and the canopy gone, with the pilot looking over at me. By the time he hit the ground he was smoking badly. The pilot tried to belly land, but was not very successful."[2]

The four aircraft that Gibbs, Welch and Erby knocked down were among the nine total aerial victories the 343rd claimed that day against SG 77. Still, the action around Kamenz that day was costly. Aside from

Erby, George Apple and Daniel Langelier were shot down and killed by antiaircraft fire. Neither Erby's remains, nor Langelier's, were ever recovered.

Righetti and Carroll Henry—with the 338th overhead—found the enemy at Riesa. And that is where Righetti's *Katydid* was caught by the enemy antiaircraft fire.

Immediately after being hit, Righetti called that he was losing oil pressure. Carroll Henry watched antiaircraft rounds streak past Righetti's *Katydid*. "I saw a burst," he said, "and I saw the plane losing coolant." Henry called over the radio and warned Righetti that his aircraft was streaming the water and glycol mixture that was so critical to keeping the engine operating within its temperature limits. It was the P-51's Achilles heel. Oil system aside, without coolant the engine overheated and seized—often within just a minute or so.

Righetti reefed *Katydid* into a hard, climbing turn as soon as he was hit. Once he was satisfied that he did not need to immediately bail out, he checked his engine gauges and saw nothing good. Nevertheless, there wasn't much he could do about it and he glanced away to check for enemy fighters.

Righetti's reputation as an extraordinarily aggressive pilot was well known, but his subsequent actions, especially considering the reality that his engine was about to quit, and the additional fact that he was still under fire from the antiaircraft guns that were positioned around the airfield, were almost farcical. "I have enough ammo for one more pass," he called.[3] Instead of limping away toward relative safety, Righetti hauled his aircraft around through several more hard turns, dropped down to the deck and shot up another aircraft.

Although certainly too caught up in the moment to consider it, so much of what he had written home to Cathryn and his family—and much of what they had written to him—became suddenly, terribly and dreadfully real and relevant. *I'm going off to war now, Mom ... Words can't express what a really wonderful game this is ... Don't be a fool, Bud ... If I get home ... I love you more than I ever have before ... you don't get knocked off until your number comes up … Hope this isn't too ugly … I wonder too, occasionally, if I'm changing a little …*

Henry tried to follow Righetti, as he recorded in the Missing Air Crew Report, or MACR: "I called him, telling him that I was tacking on. He acknowledged, saying that he was heading out on 270 degrees [west]. I was about 3,000 feet and overran him due to excess speed gained while letting down. He was at six o'clock [behind] to me and I rolled out on 270 degrees."[4]

Henry pulled his throttle back and made several turns as he tried to regain sight of his commander. It was no good—Righetti was nowhere to be seen. Likewise, no one in the 338th orbiting overhead was able to track his aircraft through the haze.

It was only a short time later that the engine gave up. Righetti opted to crash land rather than bail out, and he pointed *Katydid* toward an open space in the Saxony countryside. He left his landing gear tucked in the wings. If he landed on rough ground with his wheels extended there was a good chance they might snag on something and send the aircraft somersaulting.

The silver fighter touched down and the shriek of its metal underside ripping across the ground drowned out every other sound. It decelerated violently and Righetti's face smashed into the gunsight; he had forgotten to lock his safety harness. An instant or two later, *Katydid* heaved to a stop. Aside from his heavy breathing there was no sound but a faint ticking as the hot metal of the dead engine cooled and contracted.

Still seeing stars, Righetti called over the radio. "Tell the family I'm okay. Broke my nose on landing. It's been a hell of a lot of fun working with you, gang. Be seeing you a little later."[5]

"YOUR LITTLE DAUGHTER IS SURE GETTING CUTER"

Ray Sharp, the rotund little smartass, orbited high overhead with the rest of the 338th. It was Sharp who, several months earlier, had told Righetti to fetch coal for the junior officers. Now, with Righetti down in enemy territory, he broke radio discipline to take one last dig: "Tough luck, Colonel!"

Poor weather in England and low fuel compelled most of the 55th to land at bases on the continent that afternoon. Nevertheless, there was melancholy and angst among the group's men upon learning that Righetti had gone down. "We felt that we'd had a little wind taken out of our sails," said Ed Giller.[1] Frank Stich, who shared the same birthday as Righetti, was left holding the bottle of champagne they had planned to finish upon Righetti's return. The two Red Cross workers, Jan Houston Monaghan and Nelle Huse, wondered if Righetti would have been safe and sound that very moment if they had followed through on the idea to host a birthday tea for him.

"When I found out what happened to Colonel Righetti," said Don Downes, "I felt really badly." Downes was the crew chief who had fled Wormingford in the wake of his run-in with Righetti prior to the mission. "He was a strong-minded man, but he was fair."

"We had all seen a number of our buddies go down," recalled Carroll Henry, "but never before had I seen such a sad and downhearted bunch of fellows because of the loss of our best buddy and commanding officer."[2]

Still, Righetti had made a successful crash landing, and the end of the war was near at hand. There were real expectations that he would be back at Wormingford within weeks.

Tom Welch included a tribute to him in the group's mission summary report. It is obvious that he had no idea that Righetti had been shot down on his thirtieth birthday:

> We're going to miss you, Colonel. All twenty-nine years of your bursting energy and vitality, your eagerness and courage, your initiative and leadership that moulded [sic] us into a deadly fightin' machine, whipping the Hun at every turn. We're going to miss your cheerfulness, your decisiveness, and your understanding of human nature. You spelled aggressiveness whenever and wherever you flew, and made us into one of the eagerest gangs of eager beavers.

Arthur Thorsen recalled that Welch, "Voiced the feeling of every man in the group."[3] Third Air Division's magazine, *Strikes*, reproduced Welch's tribute to Righetti in its edition of April 21, only four days after he had gone down.

And then, nothing happened. The 55th flew its last mission four days later on April 21. As expected, the war ended early the next month on May 8, 1945. And with the battle for Okinawa still raging in the Ryukus, and the invasion of Japan anticipated for late that year, the group started training for operations in the Pacific. Although attention was focused elsewhere at that point, Righetti's record of 27 enemy aircraft destroyed on the ground stood as the highest tally in the Eighth Air Force.

And still, there was no word of him.

In fact, all through the remainder of that spring there was no information on Righetti or his whereabouts. This seemed particularly odd since, on the day he had gone down, the American lines were only about forty miles to the west while the Red Army was roughly the same distance to the east. Both forces closed on the area rapidly, and met at the Elbe River a week later on April 25.

The area within which Righetti was presumed to have put his aircraft down was later occupied by the Soviets. In as much as it is implicit that invading armies create chaos, the Red Army was in a class of its own. No nation had been so brutalized by Germany as had the Soviet Union and its soldiers exacted retribution whenever, wherever and however they could. Armed lawlessness was the norm as the Soviets raced into the Reich, and many Germans were unable to protect their personal property. Indeed, the best that most could hope for was to go unmolested as robbery, rape and capricious killings were commonplace, and resistance virtually guaranteed a bullet. The following story from Riesa stands as an example:

> After the Russian army arrived they went into the houses and plundered and did many other terrible things. Most of the Russian soldiers were drunk. On one farm the Russians found an automobile, quite a rare thing then, and they wanted to take it. But there had been no gasoline for a long time and therefore they couldn't start it. The Russians gave the farmer five minutes to get the car started and if he couldn't they wanted to shoot him. Of course the car wouldn't start. Only because the farmer's wife and children stood in front of the farmer and wouldn't move, the Russians let him live, but then burned down his farm.[4]

When it is considered that the Soviets lost tens of millions of lives in the fighting, and were otherwise busy exacting retribution on the German populace, the imperative to investigate the fates of a few downed American airmen was not strong. There is no indication that they spent any time doing so, at least not in the case of Righetti. And although the United States was already spending significant resources to discover the whereabouts of its servicemen—both living and dead— elsewhere, it was exceedingly difficult to do so in areas controlled by the Red Army.

Lorraine worked at the Pentagon and was the first of the Righettis to learn that her brother had been shot down. "I was on duty one morning at my desk when another soldier came by and said he had read a brief article in the *Washington Post* that an Elwyn Righetti had gone down and was missing in action. I called home and Elwyn's wife Katie answered the phone. I told her what I had heard but I didn't talk to Mom or Dad."[5]

The War Department sent a telegram to Cathryn on May 3, 1945, just more than two weeks after Righetti went down. It informed her that he was missing and little else. The family feared the worst, but held tenaciously to the hope that Righetti was alive. Everyone on the ranch watched for the arrival of the telegram that would bring news of his safety, and there was always someone within reach of the telephone. Day after day, Ernie noted in his diary, "No word of Elwyn."

No one talked of the possibility that he might be dead—doing so might just make it so. It was a nearly a month later when a letter received from the Air Staff, dated May 31, 1945, outlined the information that Carroll Henry had provided in the 55th's mission summary report for April 17, 1945.[6]

For a month or so the family continued to write letters to Righetti just as regularly as when he was still flying out of Wormingford. Mom, who wrote to "Dearest Elwyn, our Hero," was the most devoted. She stayed away from the dramatic and histrionic, and instead wrote of day-to-day doings. "Your little daughter is sure getting cuter every day, and so sweet too. This evening as she was ready for bed she came out to the back porch where I was busy at something and said, 'Grandma, I want to kiss you good nite.' She looked so sweet and clean and adorable as Kaki [Cathryn] had just bathed her. She is sure growing like a weed."

During the first couple of months following Righetti's disappearance, the family's hopes were not unreasonable. Europe was in a state of frenzied pandemonium at the close of the war, and for months afterward, as new governments came to power, old governments collapsed and borders were redrawn. Diplomatic relationships were still being established or patched, and the rift between the United States and the Soviet Union that would eventually grow into the Cold War was evident and growing. Moreover, refugees clogged cities that were unable to care for them, and disease and hunger were endemic. That there was no word from Righetti in such a scenario could be rationalized by loved ones desperate not to believe the worst.

This was especially true when words of encouragement came from other sources. Major Tom Welch, Righetti's good friend, and the 55th's intelligence officer, was still in England. He made it clear to Elwyn's mother and the rest of the family during July 1945 that finding Righetti was of primary importance to him. "I regret that at this time that I have no positive information concerning Rig's whereabouts, however, rest assured that I am, to the best of my ability, trying to track him down.

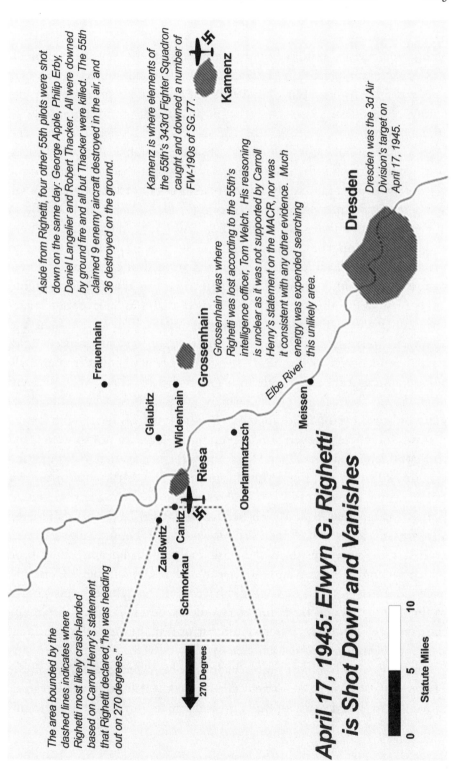

April 17, 1945: Elwyn G. Righetti
is Shot Down and Vanishes

The area bounded by the dashed lines indicates where Righetti most likely crash-landed based on Carroll Henry's statement that Righetti declared, "he was heading out on 270 degrees."

Aside from Righetti, four other 55th pilots were shot down on the same day: George Apple, Philip Erby, Daniel Langelier and Robert Thacker. All were downed by ground fire and all but Thacker were killed. The 55th claimed 9 enemy aircraft destroyed in the air, and 36 destroyed on the ground.

Kamenz is where elements of the 55th's 343rd Fighter Squadron caught and downed a number of FW-190s of SG.77.

Grossenhain was where Righetti was lost according to the 55th's intelligence officer, Tom Welch. His reasoning is unclear as it was not supported by Carroll Henry's statement on the MACR, nor was it consistent with any other evidence. Much energy was expended searching this unlikely area.

Dresden was the 3d Air Division's target on April 17, 1945.

Kamenz
Frauenhain
Glaubitz
Wildenhain
Grossenhain
Dresden
Elbe River
Meissen
Oberlammatzsch
Riesa
Canitz
Zaußwitz
Schmorkau
270 Degrees

0 5 10
Statute Miles

Things in general are still in a very confused state over on the continent, and you can appreciate the difficulties that are encountered."[7]

It was clear in his letter that Welch understood, to some degree, the family's fretfulness. "I am fully cognizant of the continuous state of anxiety which you, Kate [Cathryn], and the others are suffering, and I wish that I could give you some positive assurance that would ease your minds. Lacking that, however, may I suggest that you think of me as your own personal family representative over here, at your disposal, and searchingly and thoroughly carrying out the one task that fills all our minds, namely that of locating Rig." Welch's fondness for Righetti and, by extension, the Righetti family, is what likely compelled him to make an incredibly imprudent statement, even though he surely knew better: "I am confident, and I want you to be too, that Rig is all right."

He shared his theory that he believed that Righetti crashed near Grossenhain, a small town about fifteen miles north of Dresden and about ten miles east of Riesa. This information was inconsistent with what was recorded in the 55th's mission summary report immediately after Righetti went down. He also raised the possibility that Righetti might be under treatment in a German or Soviet hospital and unable to get word to the proper authorities. Welch closed his letter with a note that was too cheery—even condescending. "Please try not to worry, and feel confident that I will send you any information that I dig up, and as soon as I dig it up. Keep your heads high, and as they say in the Air Forces, your 'thumbs up.'"

It is curious that Tom Welch believed Righetti could have still been alive months after he had been shot down. Welch knew Righetti as well or better than anyone from the 55th Fighter Group and understood his considerable energy and single-minded resourcefulness. Certainly, hospitalized or not, Righetti would have made his whereabouts known to the authorities and his family very quickly. After all, notwithstanding the very real confusion, discord and turmoil in Europe, the continent had not degenerated into total chaos.

Any hope that Righetti simply hadn't yet been processed through the Prisoner of War, or POW, system faded quickly. Although the Germans moved or marched many of them great distances during the last months of the war, American POWs were accounted for fairly quickly and accurately. Accordingly, Welch's theory was little more than a thin weave of hopefulness and naiveté, and not nearly substantial enough to justify his belief that Righetti was alive and simply had not been located.

Nothing continued to happen while the Righettis waited and clung to Welch's reassurances. In fact, it seemed that the only time the government or anyone else took action was when the family asked, pleaded, or cajoled. For example, sister Lorraine wrote to the Associated Press to ask about a source quoted in an article that described the mission on which Righetti disappeared. "It has been four months since he was shot down, and to this day all we have had to go on is the usual 'Missing in Action' message from the War Department. We have contacted men in his group, but they have been unable to give us any help."[8]

The exasperation and hurt in Lorraine's voice continued: "I would like to get to the source of that story to see if I might get a lead as to what became of him. Is there any way you can help me? I should appreciate anything you can tell me." To its credit, the Associated Press answered her three days later, but gave her nothing new other than the name and address of the article's author.

At that point, four months after his disappearance, the Righettis must have known that Righetti was dead even if they didn't articulate it to each other. It is likely that Cathryn, his wife, was the most grounded and realistic, as most of the requests for help and information came from Righetti's mother, his sister Lorraine, or his brother Maurice. Still, the family persisted. A letter from Mom Righetti reached General Dwight D. Eisenhower's desk in Europe. He, or his staff, replied with boilerplate indicating that he fully understood "your mental distress in failing to hear news of your son," and indicating that a "full investigation" would be undertaken. Although not so flagrant, it seemed that Eisenhower—or someone on his staff—suffered from the same need to please as Tom Welch as the letter closed with, "I sincerely hope we will be able to send you some reassuring news."[9]

The tone of the next letter that Tom Welch wrote at the same time was in stark contrast to his earlier, almost breezy note. "I have been unable to dig up a clue as to Rig's whereabouts. I'm worried and very uneasy now. I can't understand it. One has to first beg people to go after any information like we want, for some reason or other."[10]

Welch wrote that a field team might be formed to travel into Soviet-controlled territory near Dresden. "They assured me they could do this for me. Although it may take time, I am confident they will. I have assured myself that I am going to remain here until we find out something definite." It is implicit in the letter, although not explicitly stated, that Welch hoped to find out what happened to Righetti, rather than actually finding Righetti alive and well. He no longer believed Righetti was alive.

Mom Righetti went so far as to write to President Truman. She received a reply from the War Department that was little more than soft words. "Your desire for additional details regarding the disappearance of Colonel Righetti is most understandable, and I regret that so much sorrow has come to you."[11] Still, the letter did note that there had been considerable progress in resolving the cases of men gone missing in action: "I wish to advise that on 31 October 1945 there were 12,485 of our men listed as missing in the European Area, and that number had been reduced to 3,868 as of 13 December 1945." This was indeed encouraging news, but it did nothing for the Righettis.

The family started to grasp at straws. Lorraine asked various headquarters if it were possible that her brother might be hospitalized somewhere with amnesia. The family also asked if he was being held in secrecy—for his own protection—to do work for the ongoing war crimes trials at Nuremburg. Both notions were irrational, and the questions led nowhere.

Carroll Henry, Righetti's last wingman, corresponded with the family and suggested they contact the 55th Fighter Group directly which, at that time, was based at Kaufbeuren, Germany. In response to Lorraine's queries, Jack Hayes, the commanding officer—Righetti's position when he was shot down—was frank and sympathetic in his reply to her: "I have delayed writing you because, for a long time, we hoped to be able to send one of our officers into Russian-occupied Germany, where Colonel Righetti went down, for the purpose of searching the area and making inquiries of the local inhabitants who might remember the incident and give an account of the Colonel's fate."[12]

Hayes's story was typical for any organization that tried to cooperate with the Soviets. "However, it has proven impossible to secure permission to do this. It is practically impossible to gain admittance to Russian territory, whatever the pretext."

And then Hayes wrote what the family surely must have been thinking for some time. "The passing of time has diminished our hopes for Colonel Righetti's return. At first we had great hopes but now there seems only the remotest possibility that he may come back. In fairness to your feelings and that you may not be deceived by false hope, I cannot sincerely believe that he has survived."

In an effort to salve any hurt that his forthright assessment might have caused, Hayes recalled Righetti's legacy. "His loss was a hard blow to us both as individuals and as an organization. He not only was an extremely competent officer, but possessed a degree of courage that marked him way above most men." It is especially striking in a "small world" sort of way that Colonel Hayes was one of the four students who made up Righetti's very first class. He had described them in a letter home: "Cobeaga, Hayes, Stockett and Pound—two of them poor, and two of them worse."

Further correspondence yielded no new information. Elwyn Righetti was simply gone. The family was gratified when they learned that he had been promoted to the rank of colonel and been awarded the Distinguished Service Cross during 1945 while he was still classified as Missing in Action. Still, neither was adequate solace for their loss.

Finally, the War Department wrote Pop and Mom Righetti to inform them that their son was presumed dead "per Public Law 490, 77th Congress." In a letter dated April 18, 1946, which referenced "exhaustive investigation" that was likely never performed, the War Department declared: "In view of the fact that twelve months have now expired without the receipt of evidence to support a continued presumption of survival, the War Department must terminate such absence by a presumptive finding of death." In fairness to the government, the law allowed the military to "close the books" on missing servicemen for purposes of pay, allowances and insurance.

Late that year, Mom Righetti received a letter outlining information that existed in no official files. The veracity of this information is unproven, yet it has become part of the Righetti legend. Fred Gray, a colonel by then, had been friends with Righetti and Cathryn dating back to their time together in the training command at San Antonio. Gray had been Righetti's boss and preceded him to England where he eventually took command of the 78th Fighter Group. He had helped Righetti get posted to the 55th Fighter Group soon after his arrival.

Gray described what he discovered through unofficial back channels. His description of the strafing attack on April 17, 1945, aligned reasonably well with the account in the group's mission summary report, which was based on the narrative provided by Carroll Henry, Righetti's wingman. However, Gray's version diverged from that in the mission summary report beginning at the point when Righetti reported that he had crash landed and was fine. Gray's story had an additional element: "He [Carroll Henry] started on out and about ten minutes later, according to the boys at Rig's group, heard him [Righetti] say something about the farmers coming out after him. That, as far as I've been able to learn, is the last that has been heard of him."[13]

Gray additionally described how he visited the USAAF's personnel section in the Pentagon to talk with a friend who was also a friend of Righetti's. "He told me, unofficially, that he had heard that the people whose duty it is to locate missing persons had finally got a confession from one of the Nazis that the civilians had killed Rig when they got to him. He further stated that he had information to the effect that those civilians had been rounded up, five of them already had been hanged and two more were being tried at the time."

Fred Gray might have believed that repeating this hearsay was the right thing to do, but it did not stand up under even cursory review. First, Carroll Henry was the last one to see and communicate with Righetti and he described no such communication about "farmers coming out after him." This would have been perhaps the most important element of the event and certainly would have merited mention. Moreover, there was no reason for Henry to hide such a communication. In later letters he exchanged with the Righettis, Henry was obviously sympathetic and very concerned about Elwyn's fate, yet he made no mention of hostile farmers.

However, if he had actually received such a radio transmission from Righetti and shared it with the debriefing officers, there would have been no reason for the USAAF to suppress it. It was widely known that downed Allied airmen were sometimes caught and lynched, or otherwise murdered, by German civilians and occasionally by military personnel. And at that very time—1946—there were Germans being held, tried, found guilty and executed for just such actions.

One example was the trial convened on June 18, 1946. Franz Linehart and his son, Markus Linehart, were tried for the murder of three American airmen from the 484th Bomb Group who parachuted from their stricken B-24 bomber during a strike against Graz on March 4, 1945, the month before Righetti was shot down. Two of the Americans were captured and brought to a road where it intersected with a railroad.[14] There, a crowd gathered while the two flyers, Harold Brocious and Levi Morrow, were guarded by a pair of policemen. The policemen left when Nazi party officials and associated hangers-on—including the Lineharts—arrived and began to incite the crowd. An official stripped one of the airmen of his personal belongings while Franz Linehart beat another.

A German soldier appeared and tried to stop the abuse but was brushed aside. Franz Linehart's son, Markus, then stepped forward and ordered Brocious and Morrow to their knees. When they complied he shot them both in the back of the head with a pistol. A third captured flyer, wounded and much abused, was taken to the jail house at Strassgang where he was further tormented. A short time later he was taken to where Brocious and Morrow had been murdered. Upon seeing their bodies he begged for his life, showing photos of his family. He was given no mercy and was forced to his knees and likewise shot in the back of the head and killed, presumably by Markus Linehart. Both Lineharts were congratulated at a celebration that evening.

Ultimately, Markus Linehart was found guilty and hanged on November 26, 1946. His father, Franz Linehart was sentenced to prison. When it is considered that trials like this were conducted, it made no sense that the authorities—if they had known—would have covered up the fact that Righetti had been similarly killed.

Further, Righetti had gone down in territory later controlled by the Soviets. Although it is known that three small U.S. teams were allowed to search the area for missing Americans during 1946, they reported nothing regarding Righetti. And the American teams certainly had no authority to mete out justice on the spot. So Gray's statement that "the people whose duty it is to locate missing persons had finally got a confession from one of the Nazis that the civilians had killed Rig when they got to him," could not have been true. That is, it could not have been true unless it had been the Soviets that had found and hanged Righetti's murderers. However, had that been the case, the Soviets certainly would have crowed about the justice they had levied to avenge his death.

In fact, Soviet soldiers shot and killed four men, a woman and her ten-year-old daughter on April 24, 1945, after reaching Riesa. The men were older and established in the town—the mayor, the station master, the head of the local farming agency and a blacksmith's helper. They also served as air raid wardens. Just as was the case with the mother and her daughter, the reasons why these men were killed has been lost.[15]

Elwyn Righetti notched accomplishments so quickly during his relatively short time with the 55th Fighter Group that the USAAF's award processes simply could not keep up. However, the end of the war slowed the input of recommendations for decorations and by 1947 there was, quite literally, a stack of medals for him.

The Army could not hold them for a man that "per Public Law 490, 77th Congress," was presumed dead. Consequently, a parade was scheduled for November 6, 1947, at Fort Ord, California, more than one hundred miles north of the ranch. The awards were to be presented to the Righetti family and it developed to be an event worthy of the war hero that Righetti was. San Luis Obispo's newspaper, *The Tribune*, described the ceremony under a banner that read, "Highest Honors Accorded Col. Righetti." The 12th Infantry Regiment passed six companies in review, preparatory to the award of the Distinguished Service Cross and the Silver Star, as well as clusters to his Distinguished Flying Cross and his Air Medal.

Righetti's wife, Cathryn, who just a few short years earlier had set up house with him with such delighted excitement, who made him meals, who sewed his clothes and nursed his ills and loved him, and who had given him a child, watched from the side as the medals were presented to little Kyle. Righetti's family and friends stood nearby.

The citation for the Distinguished Service Cross—second only to the Medal of Honor—reminded them of how he was lost. It read, in part: "After destroying eight parked aircraft in five daring low level attacks, Colonel Righetti's aircraft was hit. With coolant liquid violently streaming from his badly damaged aircraft, Colonel Righetti, knowing that he would be unable to reach friendly territory, calmly and deliberately attacked the airdrome again. Using all his remaining ammunition in this attack, he destroyed his ninth aircraft, then crash landed his crippled plane in enemy territory."

Certainly more than one family member must have regretted the bravery that won Elwyn such high distinction.

The Tribune noted, "Army officials did their utmost to make the occasion a pleasant and dignified one for members of Col. Righetti's family, all of whom were dinner guests of General [Jens] Doe at the Ft. Ord officer's club, following the ceremony."

It wasn't until 1948 that the Army, under Soviet escort, conducted two searches for Righetti. The first occurred on June 21, 1948, and visited Riesa, Schmorkau, and Grossenhain. The visit to Riesa was centered on a search for two enlisted men and had no connection to Righetti, although the town's police chief, Max Gross, did offer that a plane had crashed to the southwest of Riesa. This tip was not investigated further.[16]

Unfortunately, the focus of the search for Righetti was centered on the town of Grossenhain. This was because Tom Welch—the 55th's intelligence officer—mistakenly mentioned it as the likely crash site in a letter to Righetti's family. In fact, Righetti was shot down while strafing aircraft at Riesa, about ten miles to the west of Grossenhain and about twenty miles northwest of Dresden. It is known that the Righettis shared Welch's letter with the authorities and from that point Grossenhain took on a life of its own. Welch's conjecture was foolish and without foundation—and curious. Nevertheless, it caused the Army to follow a false lead that it would continue to chase in later years.

From the report, it appears that the team did, or was allowed to do, nothing more than visit the town's cemetery. There, they found no record of Righetti. The team did note that there were a number of unmarked graves and that it was possible that Righetti "might be one of the unknowns." However, the odds were evidently not compelling enough to arrange a disinterment.

The visit to Schmorkau on July 15, 1948, made more sense. It was a village only about five miles west of Riesa (it is assumed that this was the point of interest rather than the larger town of the same name located approximately fifteen miles *northeast* of Dresden). However, the rigor of the search effort there, as recorded in the report, was wholly unimpressive. The investigating officer could find no one in authority. He finally cornered the *bürgermeister's* wife, Frau Bruch, who told him, "that no American was ever buried here." The officer then attempted to find the area's vicar in a nearby town, but he likewise was not available. That town's *bürgermeister* asserted that his office held all the vicar's records, "and he was sure that no American deceased were recorded."[17]

These pitiful efforts at both Grossenhain and Schmorkau were remarkable not only for their absolute lack of rigor, but because Grossenhain was in the wrong area. A simple review of Righetti's Missing Air Crew Report would have kept the team focused in the proper area. The report included Carroll Henry's recollection that Righetti headed west after strafing the Riesa airfield. Instead, the disinterested and incompetent pantomime of a search for Righetti appears to have been nothing but an exercise in "box checking." To be sure, what the report narratives described could not—by any stretch—be called a comprehensive search.

The Righetti family, as did every family, deserved better. Ultimately, even the Army recognized that the search efforts had been unsatisfactory. In a letter dated May 5, 1953, the Army's quartermaster general cited the MACR report and noted that the investigations at Grossenhain and Schmorkau were performed poorly. The letter declared that the search effort "is not considered adequate." Notwithstanding that obvious truth, nothing more was done. The mortuary detachment simply replied that, "the case will remain in suspense, pending further action desired by your office."[18]

Except for Mom Righetti—who rationally knew that her son was dead but emotionally could not let go—the family gradually adjusted to the notion that Elwyn was gone. Lives had to be lived and his loss was managed by the family members as each was able. Cathryn's situation was perhaps the most difficult. She was a young, beautiful woman with a child and a husband that she was mostly certain was gone. She needed to move on, but doing so while living with her husband's family surely was not easy. Righetti had not only been loved at home, he had been lionized. And it is possible that some of the family felt she still belonged to him.

But she did manage to move on. In fact, she made the acquaintance of Colonel Robert Mailheau at the Fort Ord presentation ceremony during which Righetti's medals were presented to her daughter, Kyle. Mailheau had escaped the Bataan Death March in the Philippines in 1942 and spent the rest of the war waging guerilla warfare against the Japanese. He and Cathryn developed a mutual affection and were married on May 14, 1948.

"I FELT BAD"

Although the Righettis exchanged occasional letters with the government and a few of Elwyn's former comrades during the decades that followed his disappearance, there is no evidence that there was any serious official effort made to discover what happened to him. The difficulties associated with getting permission to enter communist East Germany, not to mention actually operating there, were overwhelming. This, together with the lack of any tangible leads, made the notion of renewing the search unrealistic. In the meantime, many of the residents of Riesa and the surrounding area who had survived the war—and the subsequent brutal Soviet occupation—moved away, or died or went on with their lives. To the extent that they could, they forgot much of those dark times.

Few go through life without encountering a certain something that tickles their fancy. Those tickles sometimes develop into pleasant diversions such as woodworking or coin collecting or bird watching. Occasionally, stronger interests or infatuations are developed that cause a certain level of discomfiture as they consume energy and attention and time, often to no good end. Rarely, those fixations become soul—and body—destroying addictions. Familiar examples include drugs, alcohol, and food.

Tony Meldahl's fascination with the Righetti story, if not quite an addiction, was almost certainly an obsession. An Army veteran who served in Germany during the 1970s, he was fluent in German and taught it in the classroom following his military service. He was also a rabid researcher who had worked with the late Iris Chang, author of *The Rape of Nanking: The Forgotten Holocaust of World War II*.

Meldahl recalled the spark that ignited his passion for the story: "I saw a reprint of a wartime article on Righetti. I never wanted to write this story and I knew nothing about World War II air warfare. I was just surprised that practically nothing had been written on him and I felt bad that his story might never be told."

Researching Righetti was a project that consumed Meldahl to varying degrees for more than twenty years. It is impossible to know what about the Righetti story was so compelling to him, but it is reasonable to believe that he was incredulous that such a famous fighter ace—and there is no denying Righetti's celebrity during the last few weeks of the war—could so wholly and utterly disappear. It was a mystery that he was driven to solve.

Meldahl embarked on that effort almost immediately after reading the article. He scoured the publicly available records to learn whatever he could and additionally contacted Righetti's family. Mom and Pop had long since passed away, but he did get in touch with Elwyn's siblings. He also corresponded with Righetti's comrades from the 55th. Importantly, he reached across the Atlantic to contact a journalist who lived in the town of Riesa, near where Righetti was shot down. That journalist, Rudolf Daum, had flown sport gliders as a young man during the early years of the war and still had a keen interest in aviation. When Meldahl contacted him, Daum's interest in Righetti was excited and he readily agreed to help however he was able.

By the late spring of 1993 the two men had created a plan for a comprehensive publicity campaign in Riesa and the surrounding communities. Their objective was to determine—definitively—what happened to Righetti and, if possible, find his grave. Not only would it solve the mystery, but it would bring some measure of closure to the family. Both Meldahl and Daum believed that someone in Riesa or the surrounding communities had to know something, notwithstanding the fact that nearly fifty years had passed since Righetti had gone down.

Meldahl meticulously outlined to Daum the circumstances and specifics of Righetti's last flight. In particular, Meldahl made certain that the material from which Daum would create newspaper copy was consistent with the wartime statement of Carroll Henry, Righetti's wingman on April 17, 1945. Moreover, Meldahl plotted on a map an area to the west of Riesa where it was most likely that Righetti had gone down. This was based on Henry's recollection that Righetti had declared he was headed west after making his last strafing run at the airfield at Riesa. Meldahl's plot additionally took into account the distance that the P-51 could have traveled from the airfield during the brief period before Righetti called over the radio that he had crash-landed his aircraft and was not badly hurt. Narrowing the search area was imperative to the effort's chances of success.

Whereas Meldahl contributed facts and analysis from the United States, Daum was actually on the scene, albeit long after the event. And as a reporter for a regional newspaper—with backing from his editors—he had a powerful tool with which to jump-start the search. He started using that tool with vigor during June and July of 1993.

During that period Daum wrote five different articles. He used different angles for each and described how Meldahl, an *"Amerikanischen historiker,"* was trying to determine the fate of a famous American fighter pilot. In each of the articles Daum briefly outlined Righetti's story, laid out the associated facts and described the progress made to that point. In one of the articles he made an overt attempt to relate Righetti to a famous German fighter pilot when he colorfully described him as the "Richthofen of the Strafers." Manfred von Richthofen had been the Red Baron of World War I fame.

Aside from Daum's newspaper articles, handbills were posted across the region. A local printing shop donated two thousand brightly colored sheets that described the search. The handbills were specifically directed at the citizens of towns and villages that fell within the area that Meldahl plotted.

Importantly, a promise was made that, "Your clues, upon your request, will be treated with utmost confidentiality."[1] This was considered an imperative as the fall of the Berlin Wall had only just occurred two years earlier during 1991. People were still wary of speaking out. They had lived for many decades—first under the Nazis, and then, the communists—knowing that it was in their best interest to keep secrets to themselves. Seldom did good things come from speaking with the authorities, and certainly a person did not work with outsiders. Indeed, the wives of two respondents approached Daum privately after he interviewed their husbands. They asked that their husbands not be identified by name in whatever story he might write.

The responses to the campaign were encouraging if not overwhelming. As with any broad investigation, much information was collected that was not relevant. For instance, many people reported on the demise of one or more American bombers. And more than one respondent asked why there was a search being made for an American pilot. Most of the population believed that the Americans played only a minor part in the war and certainly had little to do with the fight against the Germans. Such a grotesque misunderstanding of history was due to the fact that the children educated after the war were taught that Nazi Germany's defeat was solely the work of the Soviets and the Red Army. The effort was also unusual because similar searches for missing German servicemen—and there were untold thousands—were rarely ever made.

Nevertheless, there were some interesting leads. Werner Struck was seventeen years old at the close of the war and had just been released from his duties with an antiaircraft unit on April 17, 1945, so that he could go home to plant potatoes.[2] He was cycling near Frauenhain, about ten miles northeast of Riesa, when he spotted an aircraft circling a few thousand feet above the countryside. His antiaircraft training helped him to immediately identify the fighter as a P-51. The aircraft was afire and its pilot jumped clear and opened his parachute. Struck pedaled furiously in the direction of the descending figure.

Karl Augusten was a 34-year-old German soldier who had been wounded and was convalescing in the area.[3] He, like Struck, was on a bicycle when he spotted the American. He arrived on the scene to find the enemy pilot already out of his parachute harness and gesticulating animatedly with a pair of Polish POWs that had been impressed as farm laborers. Augusten noted that the lower part of the American's trousers were burned away and he looked as if he were wearing shorts. His face was red, as if it was burned.

Struck arrived soon after Augusten. His recollection of the flyer's burned trousers matched Augusten's account. Struck recalled that the pilot was tall and athletic and he saw hair underneath the pilot's helmet that he described as dark blonde. It wasn't long before two Luftwaffe officers arrived in a *Kübelwagen*. The American raised his hands and surrendered his pistol. Struck noted that one of the Luftwaffe officers translated and that the American seemed to make a good impression as he asked for something to drink and to be taken to the hospital. The American was soon afterward taken away in the direction of Grossenhain, about eight miles to the south. Augusten recalled that he was allowed to keep the flyer's parachute.

Hildegard Wachtel told of an American flyer, badly burned, taken to a farmhouse at Wildenhain, just west of Grossenhain. There he was given something to drink. The farm wife tore linen into strips and dressed his wounds. There was also a *Schutzstaffel*, or SS, man there who had a hook in place of his left hand. His name was Rahn and he shooed curious onlookers away.[4]

An additional eyewitness account of the American flyer came from ten-year-old Wilfried Treppe. He recalled that, just a few days before the Russians occupied the town, the authorities took a "big, strong blonde man" through Grossenhain. The man's trousers were burned.[5]

This scorched American flyer, in all likelihood, was not Righetti but rather Robert K. Thacker of the 55th's 338th Fighter Squadron. Frederick Wirth's statement on the MACR noted that the 338th made a pass over Riesa at about 4,500 feet and then returned to scrutinize it further. "At an altitude of 4,500 feet three bursts of flak (heavy) exploded right under Lt. Thacker's plane and immediately he began streaming black smoke. He veered off to the northwest and I followed him, attempting to get tight on his wing for a good visual check on his plane."[6]

Wirth was unable to catch Thacker before the latter bailed out. "I circled as his chute opened and he floated to the ground. He landed safely and gathered up his chute and ran for the woods. His aircraft hit the ground and exploded." Once Thacker reached the ground, Wirth's account is not exactly consistent with those of Augusten and Struck, but it is close.

And although Thacker's aircraft certainly threw up a considerable quantity of earth when it struck the ground, it probably did not explode. Of the more than twenty tips received, two witnesses described an aircraft with its nose buried in the ground at an angle and its tail pointed skyward at the end of a crumpled but intact fuselage. Both wings were bent but not broken. Hildegard Wachtel went with her sister to the crash site and crawled into the aircraft's cockpit two different times. She recalled that there were papers scattered around the cockpit and that the aircraft was hauled away within a day or two.

Although the different accounts place Thacker not too far from Riesa where Righetti likely went down, Thacker had bailed out whereas Righetti had crash-landed *Katydid*. This is obvious because he made a radio call after he reached the ground; he would have had no radio with which to communicate had he parachuted. Thacker likewise matched the description provided by the Germans; he was tall, fit and blonde. As it developed, Thacker was eventually moved to Stalag Luft VIIA and was back in American hands on May 2, just two weeks later.

Of all the accounts that came of Daum and Meldahl's campaign, only a couple offered promise of being pertinent to Righetti. Klaus Neidhardt recalled an American fighter crashing during this time between Koblen and Wolkish in, or near, the Koblen River.[7] The pilot was supposedly arrested by a group of Hitler Youth and kept overnight at the fire station in nearby Oberlommatzsch. This was about five miles southeast of Riesa, toward Dresden. The next day the pilot was supposed to have been taken to Meissen, about halfway between Riesa and Dresden. Neidhardt noted that the pilot was "dark" which might have been consistent with Righetti's olive complexion. Unfortunately, Neidhardt was unable to offer any more information.

Werner Schäfer from Großrügeln, Germany, was a teenager who saw a "one-motor" aircraft make an emergency landing during this time at Zaußwitz on the road between Stehle and Borna only about three miles northwest of the Riesa airfield.[8] The pilot was long gone by the time he reached the aircraft but he clambered over it with his friends and, naturally, as any teenage boy might, attempted to fire the guns. He had no success. Schäfer declared that a flight of P-38s later bombed the aircraft. Reiner Proschwitz remembered the same aircraft and noted that it came to rest close to a small train station.[9] Of all the many leads, especially because of its location, it seems that this one is most consistent with Righetti's actions as described by his wingman, Carroll Henry.

That there were so many accounts of Thacker, but virtually nothing of Righetti is not totally surprising. Thacker parachuted from his aircraft and was obviously seen by many people as he slowly drifted down. On the other hand, Righetti presumably flew at treetop level until he finally bellied his aircraft onto the ground. Consequently, at a lower altitude—and assuming he did not go down in a populated area—he would not have been so easily spotted by as many people.

As much effort as Rudolf Daum, Tony Meldahl and others put into the search for Righetti, they ultimately did not succeed in resolving the mystery or in finding his remains. Notwithstanding their careful analysis and the information they did manage to collect, they were still amateurs without any sort of relevant training, credentials, or the authority or backing of an official agency or organization. Still, there was no denying their commitment to solve the mystery for the Righetti family even though they had no obligation to do so.

Whether or not the United States government was, or is, equally committed is difficult to ascertain. Various organizations were active in collecting and identifying the remains of missing servicemen during the years following World War II. Likewise, similar activities were conducted following subsequent conflicts. However such efforts weren't put under the umbrella of a single command until January 2015 when, in the pall of ineptitude and venality, the Joint POW/MIA Accounting Command, also known as JPAC, was merged with the Defense Prisoner of War/Missing Personnel Office, or DPMO, and elements of the Air Force's Life Sciences Lab. The newly created organization is the Defense POW/MIA Accounting Agency, or DPAA.

Of the three organizations, JPAC had been the most visible. Although it focused during much of its early existence on recovering the remains of servicemen lost during the Vietnam War, JPAC also sent teams elsewhere around the world to look for those who disappeared in other conflicts. The mission was obviously important and quite public as evidenced by occasional high-profile news stories that described how the government located and brought home to grateful families the remains of their lost sons.

However, despite JPAC's successes, there was much that was rotten within the organization. Its mission was unique and each case that it sought to resolve was similarly unique with its own peculiar geographic, cultural, environmental, diplomatic and legal considerations. For instance the recovery of a pilot who had smashed his aircraft into Vietnam's Annamese mountain range was quite different from the investigation of remains discovered in a Belgian barn lot.

When it is considered that JPAC fielded eighteen teams of a dozen or more personnel—not including locals often hired on location—the opportunities for mismanagement, waste and fraud were manifold. This was particularly true because JPAC's commanders typically had little experience outside the organization with leading such an effort; there was literally nowhere else in the world to get it. Additional stress came from heartbreaking inquiries by family members, many of them aging, who were desperate for closure. Often included with those inquiries were leads and information that consumed resources but regularly proved to be of little value. Thin budgets were additionally problematic as there was no end of leads to investigate, but not enough resources to chase them all.

And prioritizing when, where and for whom to search was also difficult. For instance, evidence might indicate a high percentage of success for an effort to recover the remains of a particular serviceman. But if that serviceman had no living relatives, was it worth retrieving him rather than investigating the less-promising case of another serviceman whose family was vigorously represented by an influential congressman?

JPAC struggled with these issues and more, including disinterested oversight, fragmented organizational structures, and multiple and confusing chains of command. The organization's efficiency faltered as the average time to resolve a set of remains once it was recovered slipped from four years during the 1990s to eleven years a decade later. Rather than embracing new technologies, JPAC clung to outdated methods for everything from the cataloguing of remains to forensic practices.

It all came to a head during 2012 when the Pentagon completed—and initially suppressed—an internal report. The findings were stunning. JPAC was described as mismanaged, "acutely dysfunctional" and at risk of "total failure." The organization was criticized for staging sham ceremonies that misled the public and the families of missing servicemen into believing that flag-draped caskets, supposedly flown in from overseas locations, held the remains of their loved ones when such was sometimes not the case.

Moreover, the overseas conduct of some team members was under investigation. Many of the missions sent into the field were characterized as unfocused, unproductive and little more than "military tourism." There was a backlog of hundreds of sets of recovered remains and little hope of identifying even two hundred sets per year. During the previous five years, more than half-a-billion dollars had been spent, yet the yearly average of remains identified was only 72.[10]

The level of effort expended by the government to find Righetti following the fall of the Berlin Wall in 1991 is unknown. JPAC typically did not communicate with the families of service members for whom it was searching as it did not want to create false hopes. Certainly, none of the Righettis were ever told that a search was conducted specifically to look for Elwyn. However, in his Individual Deceased Personnel File (IDPF) there is a cryptic scribble on a copy of a report dated January 30, 1951. The report was generated by a board formed to determine the recoverability of various sets of remains. The board determined that Righetti's remains were not recoverable. The scribble, dated February 23, 1992, more than forty years after the report was generated, read: "It seems to me that either the graves registration detachment didn't try very hard or someone wasn't cooperating." The note was unsigned. Whether or not it was related to any sort of official investigation during 1992 is unknown.[11]

Nothing noteworthy happened for nearly fifteen years. And then, on August 23, 2007, Manfred Mueller of *Saechsische Zeitung* wrote an article about a search being conducted by JPAC. The subtitle noted that, "A team of the MIA search service of the US armed forces puts the Canitz Cemetery under the looking glass."[12] Canitz is a small town adjacent to Riesa to the west.

Mueller interviewed one of the JPAC team members, Lieutenant Frank Huffman, who he described as somewhat reticent to share information. "We are looking for the crewmembers of three aircraft, a bomber and two fighters which were shot down over Saxony and Brandenburg." Characteristically, Huffman would not disclose the names of the men for which the team was searching.

In contrast to the American officer's reluctance to make known the specifics of his mission, Mueller told him about the 1993 search that Tony Meldahl and Rudolf Daum had undertaken. "When confronted with the information about Daum, Lieutenant Huffman became interested and began to investigate. There now was no doubt—the Americans were hunting for the remains of Lieutenant Colonel Elwyn Guido Righetti." In fact the JPAC team might well have been looking for Righetti, but he was probably only one of many MIA servicemen for whom they were searching. Several American fliers had gone unaccounted for in the area, to include Daniel Langelier and Philip Erby. Both men were pilots with the 55th's 343rd Fighter Squadron. And both were shot down during the same mission as Righetti.

"According to information from JPAC," Mueller wrote, "Elwyn Righetti was buried in some area around Riesa. The Americans discovered the grave of an unnamed soldier in the village cemetery. However, is this who they are searching for? It could also be a Russian, or, much more likely, a German soldier." Mueller's question remains unanswered, and it is doubtful that the JPAC team discovered anything related to Righetti.

JPAC was back in the area two years later and a reporter from *Saechsische Zeitung* was again there to ask questions. Sandro Rahrisch wrote an article published on April 15, 2009. It was headlined: *Americans are Looking for a Missing Pilot*. His subtitle noted that, "A US military team continues to gather clues about a military pilot who disappeared. Now they are in Grossenhain."[13]

Again, if the JPAC team was looking for Righetti, they were in the wrong location. Tom Welch's imprudent 1945 letter to the family had done damage he never could have imagined. Rahrisch's article went far afield and described JPAC's interest in an aircraft wreck supposedly located in a lake near Kamenz. It also mistakenly associated Righetti with a P-51 pilot that, "survived by jumping out of his plane and using his parachute, and then he was taken prisoner by Luftwaffe officers." This parachuting pilot was almost certainly Thacker. Again, there is no indication that this JPAC team learned anything relevant to Righetti.

However, it is apparent that the government maintained an interest in finding Righetti. On November 17, 2010, a historian with DPMO e-mailed a German researcher who had been caught up in the search. The e-mail declared that a DPMO person was meeting with Ernie Righetti that following weekend. The family learned nothing from the meeting, however both Ernie and Doris contributed DNA samples. Whether these were intended to be matched against a set of remains that had already been recovered, or to be available in the event that promising remains were found, is unknown.

At this point, with the information available, it is impossible to know with certainty what happened to Righetti. Certainly, the popular notion that he was murdered by a mob of German civilians or by local government officials is plausible although there is absolutely no direct evidence to support it. If such was the case, it is remarkable that despite all the searching—and decades after the fact—no one has come forward with a confession, an eyewitness account or even second- or third-hand hearsay. Such crimes, especially if committed by more than one or two people are very difficult to keep secret. This is particularly so when such knowledge can be used to gain leverage or power in local politics or village vendettas.

It might have been additionally difficult for civilians to kill Righetti because he carried a sidearm. He always wore a .45 caliber pistol when he flew and declared more than once that he would use it if he had to.

"We all knew we would be probably be killed if captured by civilians rather than the military," Russell Haworth said. Righetti's crew chief, Millard "Doak" Easton, recalled, "He showed me the .45 and said, "If they get me, I'll take some of them too."

Certainly, making such a declaration is one thing, whereas actually following through is quite another. It is possible that Righetti surrendered to a large and well-armed mob of German civilians only to be subsequently lynched. But again, it is unlikely that such a crowd could have kept the secret.

Perhaps more likely is that Righetti was picked up, spirited away and murdered by SS or other military personnel. As already noted, Thacker came into contact with the SS, so there is no question that there were units in the area. And, although Thacker wasn't murdered, the SS certainly had a history of killing downed Allied flyers. William Cullerton of the 355th Fighter Group actually survived such an encounter. He was shot down on April 8, 1945, while strafing the airfield at Ansbach. He evaded for two days until April 10, when the wooded area in which he was hiding was hit by an American artillery barrage:

> I saw wood penetrating wood—shards of wood shot through a tree trunk ... I ran up a little mound and when I went down the berm there were about fifteen German soldiers in SS uniforms. They all turned and aimed their guns at me. So I surrendered. They told me, "You stand here." And I was standing in one spot about ten yards away from them and they were having a little meeting—they were deciding what to do with me. And a guy came over and disarmed me. He had my .45 [pistol]. Then he said, "For you the war is over," and that son-of-a-bitch pressed my pistol against my stomach and shot me with my own gun. I flew through the air, spun around and fell down.[14]

Cullerton was left for dead. Nevertheless, despite the round that passed through his body—badly damaging his liver—he survived and was dragged from the woods a couple of days later. After a period of indifferent medical care he escaped back into the forest when it was rumored that the Germans were readying to kill their Allied patients. Ultimately, he was rescued by an American armored unit.

Another possibility is that Righetti was caught up and killed in a prisoner hunt. On the same day he was shot down, a group of concentration camp prisoners marched into Glaubitz, just east of Riesa. They halted to rest at the town's sporting field when the area came under air attack. One report stated that they were strafed by American fighters. In the ensuing confusion the guards took cover and many of the prisoners fled to the nearby Glaubitzer Forest. Once the threat of air attack passed, the escaped prisoners were hunted down, executed and buried in a mass grave in the forest.[15]

Although Righetti went down to the west of Riesa, and Glaubitz was to the east of Riesa, the distance between the two could have been as little as three or four miles. If he had in fact evaded to the cover of the forest at Glaubitz, it is quite possible that he could have been caught up in the hunt. It follows then that he might have been captured and executed, or killed while trying to avoid capture.

Beyond these options the speculation grows increasingly diaphanous. Perhaps Righetti hid for a few days and was later killed by a farmer while asking for or stealing food. Or, because the area was full of refugees fleeing the advancing Soviets he might have been robbed and killed for who he was, or what he carried and wore—a pistol, good boots and warm clothing. Or he might have been shot or killed while trying to cross the lines to the west or the east. Certainly, an artillery barrage could have rendered him into unidentifiable bits.

Another possibility that must be considered puts all the different analyses and speculation into total disarray. That possibility is that Carroll Henry and the rest of the 338th misidentified the airfield that Righetti had attacked. A close examination of the group's mission summary report shows that there was a great deal of uncertainty about where the 55th actually made its attacks on April 17. For instance, the report does not identify Kamenz by name, but instead declares, "At about the same time [as Righetti's attack on Riesa] south of Dresden, 5 FW 190's were sighted taking off from and [sic] A/F [airfield] all bombed up. Some dropped their bombs, some dropped in with their bombs."[16] In fact, Kamenz was not "south of Dresden," but instead was about 25 miles northeast of Dresden. The report includes several similar mistakes, although it does declare that Righetti did attack the airfield at Riesa.

On the other hand, the group's historical data summary for April 1945 declared that Righetti was Missing in Action, "2 miles west of Grossenhaim [sic] airdrome, Germany."[17] This was an error as Riesa is approximately ten miles west of Grossenhain and Righetti was last seen flying to the west from Riesa. Moreover, the first page of the Missing Air Crew Report incorrectly noted the location as thirty miles south of Dresden, while the accompanying hand-drawn map—part of the same report—showed the location at Riesa, northwest of Dresden.[18]

Such confusion was not unusual at all. The Eighth's fighter pilots flew to all corners of the continent from one day to the next and did not become intimately familiar with the landscapes below them. In fact, getting lost was not unheard of, and some fighters never returned to their bases but rather ran out of fuel over the North Sea. Indeed, even bombers with navigators lost their way; neutral Switzerland was mistakenly bombed so often that George Marshall, the Army's chief of staff, sent Carl Spaatz on a special delegation to apologize to the Swiss government.

Still, there is no way of knowing the truth and the Riesa airfield remains the most obvious candidate for the airfield that Righetti strafed.

A final option must be deliberated when reviewing Righetti's possible fate. Although the Soviets denied any knowledge of him, it is an understatement to declare that they were not always forthright. Nor has Russia been upfront since the fall of the Berlin Wall. In fact, it is possible that Righetti bellied his aircraft onto the road at Zaußwitz as described by Werner Schäfer. After making his last radio call, he could have escaped to the countryside and hidden for the next several days. He had the woodcraft and the physical stamina to do so.

Subsequently, when the Soviets rolled into the area several days later, it would have been logical for Righetti to believe that he was safe. He might have approached a Red Army unit and identified himself as a ranking American pilot. Had that been the case, he would have been passed up the chain of command until reaching someone of authority. Once it was understood who he was—and that there was no record of his fate on either the German or American side—the Soviets might have held him.

Forever.

However, anecdotal accounts aside, there is little real evidence that the Soviets kept Americans after World War II. But the issue is not entirely settled and the *Comprehensive Report of the U.S. Side of the U.S–Russia Joint Commission of POW/MIAs*, dated June 17, 1996, declared: "There are a number of ongoing issues of concern to the U.S. side of the WW II W[working] G[roup] and the Commission. They deal primarily with details on the fates of individual American servicemen. Requests for additional information from the Russian side have been made. Research to clarify details related to the fates of these servicemen continues in U.S. archives."[19]

The report additionally states: "It remains to be determined whether any American prisoners of war liberated in 1945 by Soviet forces were not returned to US military control but were held in Soviet prisons. There were individuals known to have been POWs of the Germans who did not return to U.S. military control after VE Day. Military authorities expended considerable effort, including inquiries to the Soviets, in determining what might have happened to these men."[20] Further, the commission was perplexed by the nature of at least one bit of evidence: "One intriguing aspect of this case [another serviceman—NOT Righetti], however, is that the Soviet era documents we received from the Russian archives refer to American POWs in Soviet camps during 1946 and 1947 in a seemingly matter of fact way."[21]

California Senator William Knowland queried the Army at the behest of Mom Righetti. The reply from the Adjutant General of the Army, Major General Edward Witsell, dated April 11, 1946, indicated that there were ongoing efforts to return American soldiers from Soviet-held territory during that period. "The United States Military Mission to the Union of Soviet Socialist Republics, in cooperation with the Russian government, has been making every effort to effect the return of our soldiers from Russian-held territory as soon as their presence becomes known."[22]

Notwithstanding these statements, there is little information in the public domain that indicates the Soviets purposely kept large numbers of men who had formerly been held in German POW camps. That this is so is borne out by the fact that the government was not inundated after the war by inquiries from families wanting to know where their POWs were.

In fact, as described in a letter to Righetti's mother, the American Embassy in Moscow—as directed by no less a figure than Eisenhower— "asked the Soviet authorities to try to find your son. On November 30, 1945, however, they informed us that their search had proved fruitless and that they could find no record of him in the Soviet Union."[23]

However, as unlikely as the possibility seems, it is difficult to argue that the Soviets could not have held men whose disposition was unknown— as was the case with Righetti—against their will. In the pandemonium of the Red Army's advance through Europe, and away from prying eyes, it would not have been difficult to secret Allied personnel away to locations where they could be exploited for their military or technical knowledge. Once that was done it would have been easy to dump them into the labor gulags where they could be worked in anonymity until they died. It is an unsettling topic as even a quick scan of the literature raises disturbing and unanswered questions.

Indeed, the government is still investigating various possibilities in the context of what role they might have played in the disappearance of American servicemen: "In the course of eight field investigations, spanning almost ten years, no such information was discovered. DPAA [Defense POW/MIA Accounting Agency] continues to have JCSD [Joint Commission Support Directorate] researchers working in former Soviet archives look for any materials pertaining to possible American losses, including Col[onel] Righetti."[24]

Congress, which itself is no model of sagacity or efficiency, directed the aforementioned consolidation of JPAC and DPMO with elements of the Air Force's Life Sciences Lab. Notwithstanding the hard work of certain individuals within them, the organizations had proved themselves unequal to their tasks. The new organization is the Defense POW/MIA Accounting Agency, or DPAA. It is curious that Congress believed that combining three nonperforming organizations would produce a fully functioning agency, but few will argue against the notion that Congress is a great manufacturer of incomprehensibilities.

My experience with the DPAA was mixed, but ultimately satisfactory. After I provided information on the possible burial site of a missing American—not related to the Righetti case—the DPAA thanked me for reaching out. When I asked about Righetti, the organization acknowledged that his case was well known and that the government was eager to locate his remains. I explained my interest and requested material related to recent recovery efforts.

The initial response was enthusiastic and encouraging, but—without going into stultifying detail—there followed a long period with little progress. Certainly, I understood there were priorities more important than my request. However, after several months my frustration exceeded a certain threshold and I reluctantly contacted the head of the DPAA directly. Lieutenant General (Retired) Michael Linnington responded immediately and we shared an agreeable telephone conversation during which he described how the organization was, in fact, very energized to execute its mission. The activities he described and the statistics he cited were heartening.

General Linnington also apologized for the delays associated with my request and followed up with the Office of the Secretary of Defense for Public Affairs which was holding the information that the DPAA had generated in response to my request. Presumably in reaction to General Linnington's keen interest, approval for release of that information was expedited. It was finally received two days prior to the contracted delivery date of the manuscript for this book.

I provide this recap not only to illustrate my own "woe-is-me" difficulties, but also to highlight how families like the Righettis are simply worn down over the decades by the government's seeming indifference. Indeed, one disgruntled wag declares that the mantra of DPAA's management is, "Delay, deny, and wait for the families to die." Tellingly, when I first met the family and declared my intent to engage with the various relevant government agencies, that declaration was met with a note of skepticism, if not outright derision: "We're not going to get our hopes up again."

In fact, the material I received from the DPAA duplicated much of what I had already discovered. Nevertheless, there was value in knowing that the government's investigations produced results that nearly mirrored my own; it indicated that there was no cache of publicly accessible documents that I had failed to uncover. What the DPAA did not have were the interviews conducted with local residents by Rudolf Daum during his collaboration with Tony Meldahl in 1993. This was material that Tony had earlier offered to share, however that offer went unacknowledged by the government.

The information the DPAA most recently forwarded showed that the government reinvigorated its efforts to find Righetti's remains more than a decade ago, and remains committed to the present day:

> Between 2002 and 2007, the Department of Defense conducted new analyses of information related to Col[onel] Righetti's case. Multiple agencies—the Joint POW/MIA Accounting Command (JPAC) and the Central Identification Laboratory (CIL), Defense POW/Missing Personnel Office (DPMO) and the U.S. Joint Commission Support Directorate (JCSD, within DPMO), all charged with accounting for American service members still missing from past conflicts, sent investigative teams to Germany in 2007, 2008, 2009, and 2010, to investigate potential information concerning the circumstances of Col[onel] Righetti's loss.[25]

Indeed, another investigation was performed by the DPAA just as this manuscript neared completion. Sadly, as with those completed during the previous decades, nothing noteworthy was discovered during this particular search. "As of this most recent investigative mission in February 2016, DPAA has not discovered any definitive details regarding the circumstances of [the] death of Col[onel] Righetti. DPAA is in contact with local researchers, however, who can often be instrumental in such cases, and will continue to follow up on all possible leads in the case."[26]

The disturbing certainty is that there remain more than 73,000 American MIA cases from World War II and that there is little chance that even a tiny percentage of them will ever be resolved. Admittedly, the majority of them were lost at sea and are not recoverable. And, notwithstanding the evident incompetence and lassitude of the various government agencies that have been charged with finding and bringing home the nation's dead, landscapes have literally changed, as have governments and their willingness to assist in recovery efforts. Perhaps most important is the sad and inescapable reality that most of those persons who could have provided worthwhile information are now dead.

Despite the fact that the details surrounding the ultimate fates of the nation's World War II MIA servicemen and women remain unknown, it is good that they are honored and remembered. Cynics might make a logical case that there is little value in recovering bone shards, teeth and rotting relics at great expense, only to return them to families who have little memory, or even knowledge, of those to whom they once belonged. But such thinking fails to consider the spiritual obligation to these men who were once vital and beloved sons and brothers and fathers. They went into the fight believing that if they perished, their nation would bring them home or, failing that, preserve their legacy.

This book, hopefully, is a small part of that preservation.

EPILOGUE

The car started down the drive. Elwyn Righetti's sister Elizabeth, past her ninetieth birthday, turned and walked back toward the house. She didn't watch the car leave, nor did she wave good-bye to her visitors. "I waved Elwyn down the drive in 1944. He didn't come back. I've never since waved anyone down the drive."

The house and barn and silo and much of the ranch as it was during Elwyn Righetti's childhood are still extant. The family has grown and many descendants remain in the area. Consistent with the changing character of the area, the one-room schoolhouse—the Independence Grammar School—where Elwyn and his siblings matriculated, is now a wine-tasting room.

Mom and Pop stayed on the farm. Understandably, they were never able to reconcile themselves to the loss of their son. When the Veterans Administration wanted to name a new center in San Luis Obispo after Elwyn, Mom would not allow it. In the event he ever returned, she did not want him to think that the family had given up hope. She passed away in 1959. Pop followed her in 1963.

Sister Elizabeth had married in 1936 and except for two years in the Sacramento Valley, spent the rest of her life in the San Luis Obispo area where she and her husband raised four children. She loved to garden and entertain, and developed a real talent for artwork—especially watercolors—and was a charter member of the San Luis Obispo Art Association. She was well-respected as an administrator for several superior court judges and finished her public service as the county jury commissioner. She passed away in 2009 at age 95.

Family stalwart Ernie Righetti stayed on the ranch until passing away in 2014 at age 97. He left a wife and four sons. Perhaps the steadiest and hardest-working man the family ever produced, he continued to grow the ranching operation and in 1967 was the first to introduce avocado farming to the area. He remained active with 4-H and with the Future Farmers of America and served in many community organizations. Like his brother, he was a man of action and operated a bulldozer for the State of California as a contract firefighter, once having to shelter under his machine as fire overtook his position. His love of hunting continued, and he traveled internationally to take mountain sheep from several different continents.

Like Elizabeth and Ernie, both Lorraine and Doris stayed close to San Luis Obispo following the war. Doris married a local businessman and ran the bookkeeping side of their plumbing business. They lived for many years in a house they built on their portion of the original ranch, and raised two sons and a daughter. She remarried after her first husband passed. She died, at age 93, just as this epilogue was being written. Like Doris, Lorraine also raised a family and still lives near where she and her siblings grew up.

Brother Maurice finished the war with the 40th Bomb Group as a B-29 copilot on Saipan, and separated from the USAAF in 1946. Impetuous and fun-loving, he was a favorite with subsequent generations of Righettis. He owned an AT-6 Texan after the war and, as a certified flight instructor, kept aviation in the family through plane rides and instruction. Among several jobs, he worked for the Southern Pacific Railroad and the Rapid Transit District in Los Angeles. He died in 2002, leaving two daughters.

Cathryn—"Katydid"—had two children with Robert Mailheau, but the marriage did not survive. During the late 1950s she brought Kyle and Kyle's new brother and sister to San Luis Obispo, close to Elwyn's family. She eventually married a rancher and lived happily before passing away too young in 1979.

All the family was hurt by the loss of Elwyn, but perhaps the most unique hurt was endured by his daughter, Kyle.

My father vanished from my life before I was three years old, too young to remember much about him; a memory here or there or a story told me often enough that it seemed like a memory. There is, however, one incident that I consider a true recollection. We were probably living on base at Randolph Field in San Antonio, Texas. It was daylight and I was seated between big feet, big legs, and riding low to the ground and holding onto those legs around the calf. No faces, only the sound of the scooter being driven on the street. I don't know where I was going, but I know I was with my father. This is a preverbal memory ... and it is what I have.

The "missing in action" years as I was growing up seemed to pass in interminable days, weeks and months. Scattered here and there throughout the years were hopes and new stories. My mother, aunts and uncles and grandparents were waiting for word, as well. There were fading expectations that he would return although those were only the change from "when" to "if" and never really spoken about. And since we do not know what happened even now, we who remain continue to wait and wonder.

His legacy to us has been kept alive with loving recollections and respect for his contributions to all of us. Having a hero in the family is an honor ... but I missed having a dad.

AUTHOR'S COMMENTS

This is obviously a story about Elwyn G. Righetti who spent his combat career with the 55th Fighter Group. Accordingly the focus of the effort is on him rather than the 55th as a whole. Although there was a great temptation to write more about the 55th and its men, I felt that doing so would have taken the emphasis too far from Righetti. Accordingly, I covered the group's history and the men who made it only enough to allow me to put Righetti's service into context.

As this work is intended to be a popular history rather than a particularly academic or scholarly treatise, I sometimes edited official documents or personal quotes for clarity and readability. I believe these edits improve the reading experience and do nothing to diminish the meaning or intent of the original material or the interviewee.

I considered "novelizing" this story but ultimately took great pains not to do so. There is already too much confusion about Righetti, and cluttering it further with make-believe elements would do him and his family a disservice. Accordingly, there is no dialogue outside of what I found in Righetti's letters or other reliable sources. The actions described are largely based on eyewitness accounts, interviews, mission summary reports, encounter reports and, of course, the letters written by Righetti and his family. Consequently, the book has a real or even raw, character, as I let his words and ideas stand and did not make the man something that he was not. Righetti, as described in these pages, is a person based on evidence.

Much of the material that was used to set context for the story is footnoted. However, I did not footnote the letters between Righetti and his family. Doing so would have added no value for the typical reader, especially as the letters are not in the public domain and, if footnoted, would list nothing beyond the correspondents and the dates.

To be sure, Righetti's legacy is to a minor degree disadvantaged by the fact that I had no alternative but to recreate him using the sources I noted above. In comparison, the most compelling combat accounts to come from World War II are autobiographies. Most of those were written long after the fighting and from vantage points seasoned by the maturity and grace that is developed after living the greater part of a lifetime. Righetti obviously never had that opportunity.

Righetti's words are often sensitive, but sometimes seem coarse or unfeeling. Again, this might be due to the fact that I never met him. However, his words and attitude are not atypical for a man in his late twenties at war with a grim, brutal and deadly enemy. So far as he knew, his letters were private and would always remain so. He definitely did not write them for public consumption by an audience of thousands more than seven decades after the events described.

One problem with relying so heavily on his letters is that I was not part of the close-knit tribe that was his family. Where there was nuance, it is possible that I did not detect it. Where there was sarcasm or a shared family perspective it might not have been apparent to me. Where it was obvious to the family that his words had meanings other than what was written, it was not necessarily so to me. And although his brash, devil-may-care writing style was popular during the 1940s, it can sometimes seem cartoonish to the modern ear. I ran a risk then, in misinterpreting the man.

Further complicating my task was the fact that only a couple of the many letters that Righetti and his wife Cathryn exchanged are known to exist. These lost letters, no doubt, would have exposed his more tender and temperate side. Certainly they would have been more private. But Cathryn married two more times following Righetti's death and, compelled by a need to protect the intimacy they once shared, or perhaps by the sensitivities of her subsequent husbands, she might have destroyed them. Regardless, they are apparently lost.

Nevertheless, I feel that my experience as a fighter pilot who went to war at the same age—admittedly to a very different and certainly less dangerous fight—helped me develop an empathy and understanding for his occasional bravado and bellicosity. Moreover, I had the benefit of history at my fingertips; the air war in which Righetti fought is now well understood whereas it wasn't even finished at the time he presumably perished. And finally, a few of his friends and family members remained to help me in my interpretation of the man.

I hope I have done him justice. As one of the war's most aggressive, charismatic and effective fighter group commanders, his legacy deserves it.

ACKNOWLEDGEMENTS

Firstly, heartfelt thanks go to the extended Righetti family for giving me the opportunity to tell this story. Elwyn's daughter Kyle was especially helpful, albeit understandably nervous about how the project might turn out; I hope this work meets her expectations. David Middlecamp, sister Betty's grandson, is a professional photographer and journalist who has also written about his great uncle's combat career. He is perhaps more familiar with Elwyn's service than most of the family, and pointed me to articles, documents and photographs that I would otherwise not have found. David's father Bob, Elwyn's nephew, liaised with other members of the family to help me winkle out details that were important to the overall story. Sister Doris was gracious enough to interview with me, and sister Lorraine also shared information.

I have already identified Tony Meldahl as the individual who made me aware of this story. This book would not have happened had he not done so. Kenneth Renkert, cousin to the Righettis, was very interested in Elwyn's life and career and collected a good deal of information that he shared with Tony Meldahl who subsequently passed it to me. John Gray's book *The 55th Fighter Group vs the Luftwaffe*, helped me put the 55th Fighter Group's activities in context, and I enjoyed corresponding with him as I did so.

Likewise, Robert Littlefield's book, *Double Nickel-Double Trouble*, provided details about many of the 55th's men that were not available elsewhere. And Frank Olynyk, inarguably the world's foremost expert on American aces and victory credits, was very generous with his time and knowledge. My friend Dr. James Perry has always been my "go-to" man when I feel that the first draft of a book is ready to be seen by someone. As usual, his comments were on the mark, and very helpful. Lieutenant General (Ret) Michael Linnington, the head of the DPAA, was very helpful in getting public release authority for information that Dr. Nicole Eilers prepared for me. Thanks to both of them.

Steve Smith, the acquisitions editor at Casemate, recognized the value of this story and was quick to bring it on board. When other opportunities took him elsewhere he ensured that the project was left in capable hands. Those capable hands belonged to Clare Litt, Tara Lichterman, Ruth Sheppard and Hannah McAdams, among others. It was their final polish that made this book as good as it is.

The preservation of the 55th's records, maintained by the Air Force Historical Research Agency at Maxwell Air Force Base in Alabama, was apparently performed by eight-year-olds. Badly reproduced and terribly organized long ago, the condition of the group's official documents is consistent with the official records of most of the USAAF organizations I have researched. It is something about which the government should be greatly ashamed.

Finally, I have a German Shepherd dog. Her name is Frankie and she is big and beautiful and loyal and has a huge personality. She had nothing to do with this book, but she adores me and makes me happy. My no-good wife and daughters are rolling their eyes as they read this.

NOTES

Introduction: "I'll See You When I Get Back"

1. John M. Gray, *The 55th Fighter Group vs The Luftwaffe* (North Branch: Specialty Press Publishers and Wholesalers, 1998), 120. All references to, and quotes by, Downes are from this source.
2. Compilation of various correspondence between Anthony C. Meldahl and Paul Reeves, 1993. Unless otherwise noted, all subsequent quotes by Reeves are derived from this collection.
3. Telephone interview, Jay A. Stout with Frank Birtciel, February 8, 2015.
4. Compilation of various correspondence between Anthony C. Meldahl and Carroll Henry, 1996. Unless otherwise noted, all subsequent quotes by Henry are derived from this collection.

"I Now Have Cancer"

1. Gray, *The 55th Fighter Group vs The Luftwaffe*, 133.

"He Loved Flying More than Anything"

1. Interview, David Middlecamp with Elizabeth Righetti Middlecamp, April 20, 2004. All other quotes by Elizabeth Middlecamp are derived from this interview.
2. Interview, Jay A. Stout with Doris Righetti Dixon Ahrens, April 11, 2015. All other quotes from Ahrens are derived from this interview.
3. Patrick S. Pemberton. "A Fertile Heritage," *San Luis Obispo Tribune* (June 8, 2008), A1.
4. "Young Rider Injured," *The Morning Tribune* (October 25, 1897), n.p.
5. "Fall of Tree Takes Life of S.L.O. Pioneer," *San Luis Obispo Daily Telegram* (September 7, 1929), 1.

6. Letter, Ernie Righetti to Anthony C. Meldahl, June 5, 1995.
7. "Deaths, Fights Mark Lumber Salvaging," *San Luis Obispo Daily Telegram* (September 13, 1938), 1.
8. Letter, Ken Renkert to Anthony C. Meldahl, November 23, 2011.

"My Flying Has Been Pretty Good Lately"

1. Patrick S. Pemberton, "A Fertile Heritage," *San Luis Obispo Tribune* (June 8, 2008), A1.
2. Advertisement, "Ryan School of Aeronautics," *Popular Aviation* (April 1936), 235.
3. Henry Arnold, *Global Mission* (New York: Harper and Brothers, 1949), 181.
4. Ibid.
5. Bruce Ashcroft, *We Wanted Wings: A History of the Aviation Cadet Program* (Maxwell AFB: Air Education and Training Command, 2005), 30.
6. Arnold, *Global Mission*, 190.
7. Ibid., 192.

"I'd Rather Fly than Eat"

1. Linton Weeks, "The 1940 Census: 72-Year-Old Secrets Revealed." NPR (April 12, 2012). Accessed March 31, 2016. http://www.npr.org/2012/04/02/149575704/the-1940-census-72-year-old-secrets-revealed.
2. Navy Cyberspace, "Military Pay Chart 1922–1942." 1922–1942 U.S. Commissioned Officer Pay Chart. 2016. Accessed March 31, 2016. https://www.navycs.com/charts/1922-officer-pay-chart.html.
3. Office of Statistical Control, *Army Air Forces Statistical Digest, World War II* (Washington: Headquarters USAAF, 1945), 308.
4. Ibid., 16.
5. Arnold, *Global Mission*, 206.
6. Franklin D. Roosevelt: *Address at University of Virginia* (June 10, 1940). Online by Gerhard Peters and John T. Woolley, The American Presidency Project. http://www.presidency.ucsb.edu/ws/?pid=15965.
7. "Wings Awaiting 200 U.S. Flyers," *Sweetwater Reporter* (July 25, 1940), 1.

"I'm Really Enjoying This All"

1. Arnold, *Global Mission*, 200.
2. Wesley Craven and James Cate, *The Army Air Forces in World War II, Volume VI, Men and Planes* (Washington: Office of Air Force History, 1955), 429.
3. Craven and Cate, *The Army Air Forces in World War II, Volume VI, Men and Planes*, XV.

4. Franklin D. Roosevelt: *Proclamation 2487—Proclaiming That an Unlimited National Emergency Confronts This Country, Which Requires That Its Military, Naval, Air and Civilian Defenses Be Put on the Basis of Readiness to Repel Any and All Acts or Threats of Aggression Directed Toward Any Part of the Western Hemisphere*, May 27, 1941. Online by Gerhard Peters and John T. Woolley, The American Presidency Project. http://www.presidency.ucsb.edu/ws/?pid=16121.

"The Chance of a Skunk Picking on a Lion"

1. Office of Statistical Control, *Army Air Forces Statistical Digest, World War II*, 16.
2. Letter, Elizabeth Righetti Middlecamp to Anthony C. Meldahl, July 13, 1995.
3. Office of Statistical Control, *Army Air Forces Statistical Digest, World War II*, 62–63.
4. Rebecca Hancock Cameron, *Training to Fly: Military Flight Training, 1907–1945* (Bolling AFB: Air Force History and Museums Program, 1999), 425.
5. "Squeezing Last Ounce From Plane Helps Pilot to Keep Out of Jams," *Abilene Reporter-News* (August 31, 1944), p.8.

"I'm Going off to War Now, Mom"

1. Compilation of various correspondence between Anthony C. Meldahl and Leedom Kirk John, 1992 and 1993. Unless otherwise noted, all subsequent quotes by John are derived from this collection.
2. Compilation of various correspondence between Anthony C. Meldahl and Russell Haworth, 1995. Unless otherwise noted, all subsequent quotes by Haworth are derived from this collection.
3. Robert Littlefield, *Double Nickel-Double Trouble: KIAs, MIAs, POWs & Evaders of the 55th Fighter Group in WWII* (Visalia: Jostens Printing & Publications, 1993), 15.
4. Littlefield, *Double Nickel-Double Trouble*, 52–53.
5. Bernard Boylan, *Development of the Long Range Escort Fighter*, USAF Historical Study 136 (Maxwell AFB: Research Studies Institute, 1955), 180.
6. Telephone interview, Jay A. Stout with Frank Birtciel, February 8, 2015.
7. Compilation of various correspondence between Anthony C. Meldahl and Herman Schonenberg, 1995. Unless otherwise noted, all subsequent quotes by Schonenberg are derived from this collection.
8. Compilation of various correspondence between Anthony C. Meldahl and Darrell Cramer, 1993. Unless otherwise noted, all subsequent quotes by Cramer are derived from this collection.
9. Compilation of various correspondence between Anthony C. Meldahl and Edward Giller, 1993. Unless otherwise noted, all subsequent quotes by Giller are derived from this collection.

10. Compilation of various correspondence between Anthony C. Meldahl and John Cunnick, 1993. Unless otherwise noted, all subsequent quotes by Cunnick are derived from this collection.

11. Joe Christy, *Luftwaffe Combat Planes & Aces* (Blue Ridge Summit: Tab Books Inc., 1981), 82.

"Have My Own Squadron Now"

1. Adolf Galland, *The First and the Last: The Rise and Fall of the German Fighter Forces, 1938–1945* (New York: Bantam Books, 1978), 206.

2. Pilot's Personal Encounter Report, Elwyn Righetti, November 2, 1944.

3. Headquarters, Army Air Forces Office of Assistant Chief of Staff, *Pilot Training Manual for the Thunderbolt, P-47N* (Washington: Headquarters, Army Air Forces, Office of Flying Safety, 1945), 52.

4. Bernard Boylan, *Development of the Long Range Escort Fighter, USAF Historical Study 136*, 180–181.

5. Compilation of various correspondence between Anthony C. Meldahl and Millard "Doak" Easton, 1992. Unless otherwise noted, all subsequent quotes by Easton are derived from this collection.

6. Raymond F. Toliver and Hanns-Joachim Scharff, *The Interrogator: The Story of Hans-Joachim Scharff, Master Interrogator of the Luftwaffe* (Atglen PA: Schiffer Publishing, Ltd., 1997), 213–214.

7. Ibid., 223.

"Everyone Looks So Well"

1. Pilot's Personal Encounter Report, Frank Birtciel, March 22, 1945.

2. Colin Heaton and Anne-Marie Lewis, *The German Aces Speak: World War II through the Eyes of Four of the Luftwaffe's Most Important Commanders* (Minneapolis: Zenith Press, 2011), 64.

3. Smithsonian National Postal Museum. "Victory Mail—Online Exhibit." *Victory Mail—Online Exhibit* (accessed April 01, 2016); http://postalmuseum.si.edu/victorymail/letter/better.html.

4. Rosemary Ames, "Sabotage Women of America", File E-NC-148-57/181; OWI Intelligence Digests, Office of War Information, Record Group 208; National Archives at College Park, Maryland; 4–5. http://postalmuseum.si.edu/victory-mail/letter/better.html.

"We Try Not to Hit the Crew"

1. Klaus Grabmann recollections, via Anthony C. Meldahl, undated.

2. Mission Summary Report, 55th Fighter Group, February 25, 1945.

3. Johannes Steinhoff, *The Final Hours* (Dulles, VA: Potomac Books, 2005), 123–124.

4. Piet G. M. Truren, *The U.S. 8th Air Force's Microwave Early Warning (MEW) Radar at Greyfriars, Suffolk, and Eys, Netherlands During 1944–1945. November 2012.* Accessed April 1, 2016. http://www.dunwichmuseum.org.uk/reslib/ PDF/20130531141206Article2012,MEWSRadaratDunwich,PietTruren,4Mb.pdf.

5. Richard Davis, *Carl A. Spaatz and the Air War in Europe* (Washington: Center for Air Force History, 1993), 521.

6. Mission Summary Report, 55th Fighter Group, December 24, 1944.

7. Pilot's Personal Encounter Report, Elwyn Righetti, December 24, 1944.

8. Littlefield, Robert, *Double Nickel-Double Trouble*, 164.

9. Paul Reeves, *A Christmas Story*, Unpublished memoir, undated. All other quotes by Reeves about this incident are derived from this source.

10. Undated statement by Walter Konantz, 338th Fighter Squadron.

11. Pilot's Personal Encounter Report, Russell Haworth, December 24, 1944.

"Tonite This Lad is a Tired Guy"

1. *Narrative History for January 1945*, 38th Fighter Squadron, 55th Fighter Group, AAF Station F-159, England.

2. Missing Air Crew Report (MACR) No. 11525. Pilot Statement, Robert Jones, January 4, 1945.

3. Littlefield, *Double Nickel-Double Trouble*, 184.

4. Headquarters, 65th Fighter Wing, *Light, Intense and Accurate: U.S. Eighth Air Force Strategic Fighters Versus German Flak in the ETO* (Saffron Walden: 65th Fighter Wing, 1945), 53.

5. VIII Fighter Command, *Down to Earth: Fighter Attack on Ground Targets* (Bushey Hall: VIII Fighter Command, August 30, 1944), 14.

6. Headquarters, 65th Fighter Wing, *Light, Intense and Accurate: U.S. Eighth Air Force Strategic Fighters Versus German Flak in the ETO*, 29.

7. Ibid., 72.

8. Ibid., 79.

9. VIII Fighter Command. *Down to Earth: Fighter Attack on Ground Target*, 7.

10. Office of Statistical Control, *Army Air Forces Statistical Digest, World War II*, 263.

11. Headquarters, 65th Fighter Wing, *Light, Intense and Accurate: U.S. Eighth Air Force Strategic Fighters Versus German Flak in the ETO*, 53.

12. Gerhard Oberleitner, *You Up There—We Down Here* (Andelfingen: History Facts Time Capsule, 2011), 163.

13. Roger P. Minert, *In Harm's Way: East German Latter-day Saints in World War II* (Provo, UT: Religious Studies Center, Brigham Young University, 2009). https:// rsc.byu.edu/archived/harm-s-way-east-german-latter-day-saints-world-war-ii/ berlin-district/berlin-moabit-branch.

14. Mission Summary Report, 55th Fighter Group, January 14, 1945.
15. Headquarters, 65th Fighter Wing, *Light, Intense and Accurate: U.S. Eighth Air Force Strategic Fighters Versus German Flak in the ETO*, 10.

"It All Happened Pretty Fast"

1. Mission Summary Report, 338th Fighter Squadron, 55th Fighter Group, January 13, 1945.
2. Missing Air Crew Report (MACR) No. 11856. Pilot Statement, Kenneth Schneider, January 13, 1945.
3. Consolidated Encounter Report, 38th Fighter Squadron, 55th Fighter Group, January 13, 1945.
4. Littlefield, *Double Nickel-Double Trouble*, 168.
5. F. A. Borsodi, *Pilot's Comments on Me-109G, AAF No. EB-102*, Inter-Office Memorandum, Army Air Forces, Material Command, Dayton, Ohio, March 1, 1944.
6. F. A. Borsodi, *Pilot's Comments on Me-109G, AAF No. EB-102*.
7. Christy, *Luftwaffe Combat Planes & Aces*, 128.
8. Thomas Toll, *Report No. 868: Summary of Lateral Control Research*, National Advisory Committee for Aeronautics, Langley, 1947, Figure No. 47.
9. Christy, *Luftwaffe Combat Planes & Aces*, 45.
10. Ibid., 77.
11. Jay A. Stout, *Unsung Eagles: True Stories of America's Citizen Airmen in the Skies of World War II* (Mechanicsburg: Casemate, 2013), 257.
12. Littlefield, *Double Nickel-Double Trouble*, 42.
13. Memorandum, 1st Central Medical Establishment, Eighth Air Force to Headquarters, 66th Fighter Wing, *Berger Anti-G Suits*, August 29, 1944.

"Jerry Went Out of Control"

1. Letter, Frank Stich to Kenneth Renkert, October 8, 1982.
2. Pilot's Personal Encounter Report, Elwyn Righetti, 338th Fighter Squadron, 55th Fighter Group, February 3, 1945.
3. Pilot's Personal Encounter Report, William Lewis, 343rd Fighter Squadron, 55th Fighter Group, February 3, 1945.
4. Pilot's Personal Encounter Report, Elwyn Righetti, 343rd Fighter Squadron, 55th Fighter Group, February 3, 1945.
5. *Combat Thrills*, radio interview, Elwyn Righetti with Larry Freeman, Broadcast date unknown.
6. Pilot's Personal Encounter Report, Richard Gibbs, 338th Fighter Squadron, 55th Fighter Group, February 3, 1945.

7. Forsyth, Robert, *Luftwaffe* Mistel *Composite Bomber Units* (Oxford: Osprey Publishing, 2015), 57–59. All references to, or quotes by, Lorbach are from this source.

8. Memorandum, *Comparative Statistics: 55th Fighter Group with Other Groups in 66th Fighter Wing.* George Crowell, Commanding, Headquarters, AAF Station F-159, February 13, 1945.

"Seems Like an Excellent Break for Me"

1. Compilation of various correspondence between Anthony C. Meldahl and Frank Birtciel, 1993. Unless otherwise noted, all subsequent quotes by Birtciel are derived from this collection.

2. Commendation, George Crowell, Commanding Officer, 55th Fighter Group, AAF Station F-159, to Lieutenant Colonel Elwyn G. Righetti, February 21, 1945.

3. Letter, George Crowell to Kenneth Renkert, August 11, 1982.

4. Telephone interview, Jay A. Stout with Edward Giller, December 2, 2015.

5. Compilation of various correspondences between Anthony C. Meldahl and Richard Gibbs, 1993. Unless otherwise noted, all subsequent quotes by Gibbs are derived from this collection.

6. Pilot's Personal Encounter Report, Millard Anderson, 38th Fighter Squadron, 55th Fighter Group, February 25, 1945.

7. Headquarters (France), United States Strategic Air Forces in Europe, Public Relations Office, February 25, 1945, #10,206.

8. Ed Malone Radio Show, *Top of the Evening*, Westinghouse Overseas Program, December 6, 1944, Blue Network.

9. Pilot's Personal Encounter Report, Robert Cox, 38th Fighter Squadron, 55th Fighter Group, March 3, 1945.

10. Missing Air Crew Report (MACR) No. 12898. Pilot Statement, Marvin Satenstein, March 5, 1945.

11. Pilot's Personal Encounter Report, Robert Cox, 38th Fighter Squadron, 55th Fighter Group, March 3, 1945.

12. Joint Victory Credits Board, 65th, 66th and 67th Fighter Wings, April 17, 1945.

13. Headquarters (France), United States Strategic Air Forces in Europe, Public Relations Office, March 3, 1945, #10,256.

14. Telephone interview, Jay A. Stout with Frank Birtciel, February 8, 2015.

"I Hit the Deck"

1. Pilot's Personal Encounter Report, Thomas Kiernan, 338th Fighter Squadron, 55th Fighter Group, March 18, 1945.

2. Pilot's Personal Encounter Report, Archie Dargan, 338th Fighter Squadron, 55th Fighter Group, March 18, 1945.

3. John J. Pullen, "You Will Be Afraid." *American Heritage.* June/July 2005: 29.

4. Pilot's Personal Encounter Report, Elwyn Righetti, 38th Fighter Squadron, 55th Fighter Group, March 21, 1945.
5. Pilot's Personal Encounter Report, Dudley Amoss, 38th Fighter Squadron, 55th Fighter Group, undated.
6. Sworn Statement, Dudley Amoss, witnessed by Harold Benner, May 25, 1945.
7. Joint Victory Credits Board, 65th, 66th and 67th Fighter Wings, June 12, 1945.

"I'm Pretty Much Tired"

1. Letter, Roy Cooper to Ken Renkert, October 21, 1982.
2. Letter, Jack Ilfrey to Anthony C. Meldahl, May 4, 1993.
3. Colin Heaton and Anne-Marie Lewis, *The German Aces Speak: World War II through the Eyes of Four of the Luftwaffe's Most Important Commanders*, 60.
4. Alfred Price, *The Last Year of the Luftwaffe* (London: Arms and Armour Press, 1991), 130.
5. Ibid.
6. Telephone interview, Jay A. Stout with Frank Birtciel, March 24, 2015. All other quotes from Birtciel related to this incident are derived from this source.
7. Fritz Markscheffel, *Schulungslehrgang Elbe*. Unpublished paper. March 28, 2008. Via Anthony C. Meldahl.
8. Adrian Weir, *The Last Flight of the Luftwaffe: The Suicide Attack on the Eighth Air Force, 7 April 1945* (London: Cassell, 1997), 42.
9. Ibid., 45.
10. Ibid., 57.
11. Dietrich Alsdorf, *Auf den Spuren des "Elbe-Kommandos" Rammjäger* (Friedberg: Podzun-Pallas-Verlag, 2001), 25.
12. Fritz Markscheffel, *Commentary on Air Interrogation Report dated, April 26, 1945, A.D.I. (K) & U.S. Air Interrogation*, June 20, 2012. Via Anthony C. Meldahl.
13. Ibid.
14. Philip Kaplan, *Behind the Wire: Allied Prisoners of War in Hitler's Germany* (Mechanicsburg: Casemate, 2012), 25.
15. History Channel. "Dogfights—Kamikaze Aired on HISTP—Ark TV Transcript." April 1, 2010. Accessed April 4, 2016. http://tv.ark.com/transcript/dogfights-(kamikaze)/5916/HISTP/Thursday_April_01_2010/241943/.
16. Letter, Klaus Hahn to Karl-Heinrich Langspecht, March 25, 1993. Via, and translated by, Anthony C. Meldahl. All other quotes by Hahn related to this incident are derived from the same source unless noted otherwise.
17. W. Budd Wentz, MD. "Rammed Over Germany, Target: Parchim." Accessed April 4, 2016. http://home.earthlink.net/~tom.mccrary/TargetParchim-RammedOverGermany.htm.
18. Ibid.

"Don't Be a Fool"

1. Richard Davis, *Carl A. Spaatz and the Air War in Europe*, 539.
2. Pilot's Personal Encounter Report, Edward Giller, 343rd Fighter Squadron, 55th Fighter Group, April 9, 1945.
3. Joe Christy, *Luftwaffe Combat Planes & Aces*, 52.
4. Consolidated Encounter Report, Edward Giller, 343rd Fighter Squadron, 55th Fighter Group, April 9, 1945.
5. Pilot's Personal Encounter Report, Elwyn Righetti, 338th Fighter Squadron, 55th Fighter Group, April 9, 1945.
6. Richard Davis, *Carl A. Spaatz and the Air War in Europe*, 584.
7. Hermann Buchner, *Stormbird* (Manchester: Crecy Classic, 2000), 238.
8. Werner Girbig, *Six Months to Oblivion: The Defeat of the Luftwaffe Fighter Force over the Western Front, 1944/45* (West Chester: Schiffer Military History, 1991), 205–206.
9. David Middlecamp, "Remembering Elwyn Righetti on Memorial Day." Photos from the Vault. May 21, 2015. Accessed April 04, 2016. http://www.sanluisobispo.com/news/local/news-columns-blogs/photos-from-the-vault/article39533085.html.
10. Mission Summary Report, April 16, 1945, 38th Fighter Squadron, 55th Fighter Group.
11. Confidential statement, John Kavanaugh, 38th Fighter Squadron, 55th Fighter Group, April 16, 1945.
12. Oral history interview, Harold Ide with Edward Giller, November 22, 1991. All other quotes by Giller related to this incident are derived from this source.
13. Missing Air Crew Report (MACR) No. 13941. Pilot Statement, John Kavanaugh, April 17, 1945.
14. Missing Air Crew Report (MACR) No. 13865. Pilot Statement, Walter Strauch, April 20, 1945.
15. Missing Air Crew Report (MACR) No. 13866. Pilot Statement, Walter Strauch, April 20, 1945.
16. United States v. August Kobus, A German National, February 6, 1946, Case No. 12-1155, Deputy Theater Judge Advocates Office, War Crimes Branch, United States Forces, European Theater.
17. Littlefield, *Double Nickel-Double Trouble*, 171.

"One More Pass"

1. Missing Air Crew Report (MACR) No. 13920. Pilot Statement, Robert Welch, April 19, 1945.
2. Pilot's Personal Encounter Report, Richard Gibbs, 343rd Fighter Squadron, 55th Fighter Group, April 17, 1945.

3. Missing Air Crew Report (MACR) No. 13916. Pilot Statement, Carroll Henry, April 21, 1945.

4. Ibid.

5. Mission Summary Report, 55th Fighter Group, April 17, 1945.

"Your Little Daughter is Sure Getting Cuter"

1. Telephone interview, Jay A. Stout with Edward Giller, December 2, 2015.

2. Letter, Carroll Henry to Elizabeth Righetti, November 24, 1945.

3. Arthur Thorsen, *The Fightin' 55th* (Unpublished manuscript, 1984), 222.

4. Letter, Konrad Rudolf to Anthony C. Meldahl, April 27, 1993.

5. E-mail, Robert Righetti to Jay A. Stout, February 1, 2016.

6. Letter, E. A. Bradunas, Major, Air Corps, Chief, Notification Branch, Personnel Affairs Division, Deputy Chief of Air Staff, to Cathryn Righetti, May 31, 1945. Individual Deceased Personnel File (IDPF), Righetti, Elwyn G., Colonel, O-396412. Page 170 of 230. Complete copy of Individual Deceased Personnel File. Original housed at the Washington National Records Center, Suitland, Maryland.

7. Letter, Tom Welch to Righetti Family, July 5, 1945.

8. Letter, Lorraine Righetti to Associated Press War Desk, New York, August 20, 1945.

9. Letter, Headquarters, U.S. Forces, European Theater, Office of the Commanding General, to Elizabeth (Mom) Righetti, October 4, 1945.

10. Letter, Tom Welch to Righetti Family, October 4, 1945.

11. Letter, War Department, The Adjutant General's Office, to Elizabeth "Mom" Righetti, January 2, 1946.

12. Letter, Lieutenant Colonel Jack Hayes, Headquarters, 55th Fighter Group, to Staff Sergeant Lorraine Righetti, March 7, 1946.

13. Letter, Fred Gray to Elizabeth (Mom) Righetti, November 13, 1946.

14. Marija Wakounig and Karlo Kessler-Ruzicic, *From the Industrial Revolution to World War II in East Central Europe* (Berlin, LIT Verlag, 2011), 217.

15. Letter, Konrad Rudolf to Anthony C. Meldahl, April 27, 1993.

16. *Narrative of Investigation*, Riesa, Germany, June 21, 1948. Berlin Detachment (Prov), First Field Command, American Graves Registration Command. Individual Deceased Personnel File (IDPF), Righetti, Elwyn G., Colonel, O-396412. Page 198 of 230.

17. False [Unsuccessful] report, Schmorkau, August 6, 1947. Headquarters, 95th Quartermaster Battalion, American Graves Registration Command, Berlin. Individual Deceased Personnel File (IDPF), Righetti, Elwyn G., Colonel, O-396412. Page 45 of 230.

18. Letter, Office of the Quartermaster General to Commanding Officer, 7770 USAREUR QM Mortuary Service Detachment, May 5, 1953. (IDPF), Righetti, Elwyn G., Colonel, O-396412. Page 196 of 230.

"I Felt Bad"

1. *Wer Kann Angaben Dazu Machen?* handbill, Rudolf Daum, Riesa, Germany, 1993.
2. Interview, Rudolf Daum with Werner Struck, 1993. All other quotes from Struck related to this incident are derived from this source.
3. Interview, Rudolf Daum with Karl Augusten, 1993. All other quotes from Augusten related to this incident are derived from this source.
4. Interview, Rudolf Daum with Hildegard Wachtel, 1993.
5. Interview, Rudolf Daum with Wilfried Treppe, 1993.
6. Missing Air Crew Report (MACR) No. 13919. Pilot Statement, Frederick Wirth, April 17, 1945.
7. Interview, Rudolf Daum with Klaus Neidhardt, 1993.
8. Interview, Rudolf Daum with Werner Schäfer, 1993.
9. Interview, Rudolf Daum with Reiner Proschwitz, 1993.
10. *Mismanagement of POW/MIA Accounting*, United States Senate, Senate Hearing 113-293, August 1, 2013.
11. *Proceedings of Board of Review*, April 9, 1947. Headquarters, 7887 Graves Registration Detachment, Operations Division, APO 757, Liege, Belgium.
12. Manfred Mueller, "Die Neue Gedenk-tafel—Das Informationsportal." Amerikaner Fahnden Nach Verschollenen Piloten -. August 23, 2007. Accessed April 09, 2016. http://www.gedenk-tafel.de/forum/index.php?topic=3390.0.
13. Sandro Rahrisch, "Amerikaner Suchen Nach Vermissten Piloten." SZ-Online. April 15, 2009. Accessed April 9, 2016. http://www.sz-online.de/nachrichten/amerikaner-suchen-nach-vermissten-piloten-2157893.html.
14. Compilation of various correspondence between Anthony C. Meldahl and William Cullerton, 2011.
15. Gunter Von Niehus, "Spruensuch Die Mission des Richard A. Ingles, Ein Amerikanischer Pilot Sucht Bei Riesa Nach Spuren Seines Onkels Elwyn G. Righetti," *Saechsische Zeitung, Riesa* (July 31, 2004), p.1.
16. Mission Summary Report, 55th Fighter Group, April 17, 1945.
17. Historical Data, April 1945, Frederick Pickens, Historical Officer, 55th Fighter Group.
18. Missing Air Crew Report (MACR) No. 13916, April 17, 1945.
19. Joint Commission Support Directorate of the Defense POW-MIA Office, International Security Affairs, Office of Secretary of Defense, *Comprehensive Report of the U.S. Side of the U.S.–Russia Joint Commission of POW/MIAs* (Washington: OSD, 1996), 7.
20. Ibid., 80.
21. Ibid., 141.
22. Letter, Major General Edward Witsell, Adjutant General, to Senator William Knowland, April 11, 1946. (IDPF), Righetti, Elwyn G., Colonel, O-396412, 145–147 of 230.

23. Letter, Ruth Briggs, Secretary to the Ambassador, Foreign Service, to Elizabeth (Mom) Righetti, August 9, 1946.
24. Internal memorandum, *Releasable statement to author, Jay Stout, writing book about Col Elwyn Righetti, O-396312*, Defense POW/MIA Accounting Agency, Washington, Dr. Nicole Eilers, undated.
25. Ibid.
26. Ibid.

BIBLIOGRAPHY

Books

VIII Fighter Command. *Down to Earth: Fighter Attack on Ground Targets.* 1944.

Alsdorf, Dietrich. *Rammjager: Auf Den Spuren Des "Elbe-Kommandos": Neuzeit-Archaologie: Schicksale - Schauplatze - Funde.* Wölfersheim-Berstadt: Podzun–Pallas, 2001.

Army Air Forces Statistical Digest; World War II. Washington: Office of Statistical Control: 1945.

Arnold, Henry Harley. *Global Mission.* New York, NY: Harper, 1949.

Ashcroft, Bruce. *We Wanted Wings: A History of the Aviation Cadet Program.* Randolph Air Force Base, TX: HQ, AETC, Office of History and Research, 2009.

Baumbach, Werner. *The Life and Death of the Luftwaffe.* Costa Mesa, CA: Noontide Press, 1991.

Bekker, Cajus. *The Luftwaffe War Diaries: The German Air Force in World War II.* New York: Da Capo Press, 1994.

Boylan, Bernard Lawrence. *Development of the Long-range Escort Fighter.* Maxwell AFB, Ala.: USAF Historical Division, Research Studies Institute, Air University, 1955.

Buchner, Hermann. *Stormbird: One of the Luftwaffe's Highest Scoring Me262 Aces.* Manchester: Crecy Publ., 2010.

Caldwell, Donald L. *JG 26, Top Guns of the Luftwaffe.* New York: Ballantine Books, 1993.

Caldwell, Donald L., and Richard Muller. *The Luftwaffe over Germany: Defense of the Reich*. London: Greenhill, 2007.

Caldwell, Donald L. *Day Fighters in Defence of the Reich: A War Diary, 1942–45*. Barnsley, South Yorkshire: Frontline Books, 2011.

Cameron, Rebecca Hancock. *Training to Fly: Military Flight Training, 1907–1945*. Washington, D.C.: Air Force History and Museums Programs, 1999.

Cawthorne, Nigel. *The Iron Cage*. London: Fourth Estate, 1993.

Christy, Joe. *WW II: Luftwaffe Combat Planes & Aces*. Blue Ridge Summit, PA: TAB Books, 1981.

Colgan, Bill. *Allied Strafing in World War II: A Cockpit View of Air to Ground Battle*. Jefferson, N.C.: McFarland, 2010.

Craven, Wesley and Cate, James, *The Army Air Forces in World War II, Volume VI, Men and Planes*. Chicago: The University of Chicago Press, 1955.

Craven, Wesley Frank, and James Lea Cate. *The Army Air Forces in World War II, Volume VI: Men and Planes*. Washington, DC: Office of Air Force History, 1984.

Davis, Richard G. *Carl A. Spaatz and the Air War in Europe*. Washington, D.C.: Center for Air Force History, 1993.

Davis, Richard G. *Bombing the European Axis Powers: A Historical Digest of the Combined Bomber Offensive, 1939–1945*. Maxwell Air Force Base, Ala.: Air University Press, 2006.

Faber, Harold. *Luftwaffe: An Analysis by Former Luftwaffe Generals*. London: Sidgwick and Jackson, 1979.

Freeman, Roger Anthony, Alan Crouchman, and Vic Maslen. *The Mighty Eighth War Diary*. Osceola, WI: Motorbooks International, 1990.

Freeman, Roger Anthony. *The Mighty Eighth: A History of the Units, Men, and Machines of the US 8th Air Force*. Osceola, WI: Motorbooks International, 1991.

Forsyth, Robert. *Luftwaffe Mistel Composite Bomber Units*. Oxford: Osprey, 2015.

Galland, Adolf. *The First and the Last: The Rise and Fall of the German Fighter Forces, 1938–1945*. New York: Holt, 1954.

Girbig, Werner. *Six Months to Oblivion: The Defeat of the Luftwaffe Fighter Force over the Western Front, 1944/1945*. West Chester, PA: Schiffer Pub., 1991.

Gray, John M. *The 55th Fighter Group vs. the Luftwaffe*. North Branch, MN: Specialty Press, 1998.

Hannig, Norbert. *Luftwaffe Fighter Ace: From the Eastern Front to the Defense of the Homeland (The Stackpole Military History Series)*. Stackpole Books, 2009.

Headquarters, 65th Fighter Wing, *Light, Intense and Accurate: U.S. Eighth Air Force Strategic Fighters Versus German Flak in the ETO*. Saffron Walden: 65th Fighter Wing, 1945.

Heaton, Colin D., and Anne-Marie Lewis. *The German Aces Speak: World War II through the Eyes of Four of the Luftwaffe's Most Important Commanders*. Minneapolis: MBI Pub., 2011.

Heaton, Colin D. *The ME 262 Stormbird: In the Words of the German Aces Who Flew It*. Grand Rapids, MI: Zenith, 2012.

Hess, William N. *Down to Earth: Strafing Aces of the Eighth Air Force*. Oxford: Osprey, 2003.

Hilton, Fern Overbey. *The Dachau Defendants: Life Stories from Testimony and Documents of the War Crimes Prosecutions*. Jefferson, NC: McFarland, 2004.

Kaplan, Philip, and Jack Currie. *Behind the Wire: Allied Prisoners of War in Hitler's Germany*. Barnsley: Pen & Sword Aviation, 2012.

Littlefield, Robert M. *Double Nickel, Double Trouble*. Carmel, CA: R.M. Littlefield, 1993.

Minert, Roger P. *In Harm's Way: East German Latter-day Saints in World War II*. Provo, UT: Religious Studies Center, Brigham Young University, 2009.

Mitcham, Samuel W. *Eagles of the Third Reich: Men of the Luftwaffe in World War II (Stackpole Military History Series)*. Stackpole Books, 2007.

Musciano, Walter A. *Messerschmitt Aces*. Blue Ridge Summit, PA: Aero, 1989.

Neillands, Robin. *The Conquest of the Reich: D-Day to VE-Day, a Soldier's History*. New York, NY: New York University Press, 1995.

O'Leary, Michael. *VIII Fighter Command at War: 'The Long Reach'*. Oxford: Osprey Aviation, 2000.

Oberleitner, Gerhard, *You Up There—We Down Here*. Andelfingen: History Facts Time Capsule, 2011.

Olynyk, Frank J. *Stars and Bars: A Tribute to the American Fighter Ace, 1920–1973*. London: Grub Street, 1995.

Parker, Danny S. *To Win the Winter Sky: The Air War over the Ardennes 1944–1945*. Conshohocken, PA: Combined Publ., 1999.

Pilot Training Manual for the Thunderbolt P-47N. Washington: Published for Headquarters, AAF Office of Assistant Chief of Air Staff, Training by Headquarters, AAF, Office of Flying Safety, 1945.

Price, Alfred. *Luftwaffe Handbook, 1939–1945*. New York: Scribner, 1977.

Price, Alfred. *The Last Year of the Luftwaffe, May 1944 to May 1945*. London: Arms and Armour, 1991.

Schuck, Walter. *Luftwaffe Eagle*. Ottringham: Hikoki, 2008.

Spick, Mike. *Luftwaffe Fighter Aces: The Jagdflieger and Their Combat Tactics and Techniques*. New York: Ivy Books, 1997.

Spick, Mike. *Aces of the Reich: The Making of a Luftwaffe Fighter-pilot*. London: Greenhill Books, 2006.

Stedman, Robert F., and Karl Kopinski. *Jagdflieger: Luftwaffe Fighter Pilot 1939–45*. Oxford: Osprey, 2008.

Steinhoff, Johannes, and Dennis E. Showalter. *Final Hours: The Luftwaffe Plot against Göring (Aviation Classics)*. Potomac Books, 2005.

Stout, Jay, A., *Unsung Eagles: True Stories of America's Citizen Airmen in the Skies of World War II*. Mechanicsburg: Casemate, 2013.

The Rise and Fall of the German Air Force, 1933–1945. Kew, England: National Archives, 2008.

Thorsen, Arthur. *The Fightin' 55th*, Unpublished manuscript, 1984.

Toliver, Raymond F., and Hanns-Joachim Scharff. *The Interrogator: The Story of Hanns-Joachim Scharff, Master Interrogator of the Luftwaffe*. Atglen, PA: Schiffer Pub., 1997.

Wakounig, Marija, and Karlo Ruzicic-Kessler. *From the Industrial Revolution to World War II in East Central Europe*. Berlin: LIT Verlag, 2011.

Watry, Charles A. *Washout!: The Aviation Cadet Story*. Carlsbad, CA: California Aero Press, 1983.

Weir, Adrian. *The Last Flight of the Luftwaffe: The Suicide Attack on the Eighth Air Force, 7 April 1945*. London: Cassell, 2000.

Wells, Mark K. *Courage and Air Warfare: The Allied Aircrew Experience in the Second World War*. Essex, England: F. Cass, 1995.

Westermann, Edward B. *Flak: German Anti-aircraft Defenses, 1914–1945*. Lawrence: University Press of Kansas, 2001.

Newspaper/Journal articles

"Deaths, Fights Mark Lumber Salvaging." *San Luis Obispo Daily Telegram*, September 13, 1938: 1.

"Fall of Tree Takes Life of S.L.O. Pioneer." *San Luis Obispo Daily Telegram*, September 7, 1929: 1.

Pemberton, Patrick, S. "A Fertile Heritage." *San Luis Obispo Tribune*, June 8, 2008: A1.

Pullen, John, J., "You Will Be Afraid." *American Heritage*, June/July 2005: 29.

"Squeezing Last Ounce From Plane Helps Pilot to Keep Out of Jams." *Abilene Reporter-News*, August 31, 1944: 8.

Von Niehus, Gunter. "Spruensuch Die Mission des Richard A. Ingles, Ein Amerikanischer Pilot Sucht Bei Riesa Nach Spuren Seines Onkels Elwyn G. Righetti." *Saechsische Zeitung, Riesa*, July 31, 2004: 1

"Wings Awaiting 200 U.S. Flyers." *Sweetwater Reporter*, July 25, 1940: 1.

"Young Rider Injured." *The Morning Tribune*, October 25, 1897.

Websites

Ames, Rosemary. "Sabotage Women of America." File E-NC-148-57/181; OWI Intelligence Digests, Office of War Information, Record Group 208; National Archives at College Park, Maryland; 4–5. http://postalmuseum.si.edu/victorymail/letter/better.html.

History Channel. "Dogfights - Kamikaze Aired on HISTP - Ark TV Transcript." April 1, 2010. Accessed April 4, 2016. http://tv.ark.com/transcript/dogfights-(kamikaze)/5916/HISTP/Thursday_April_01_2010/241943/.

Middlecamp, David. "Remembering Elwyn Righetti on Memorial Day." Photos from the Vault. May 21, 2015. Accessed April 4, 2016. http://www.sanluisobispo.com/news/local/news-columns-blogs/photos-from-the-vault/article39533085.html.

Mueller, Manfred. "Die Neue Gedenk-tafel - Das Informationsportal." Amerikaner Fahnden Nach Verschollenen Piloten -. August 23, 2007. Accessed April 9, 2016. http://www.gedenk-tafel.de/forum/index.php?topic=3390.0.

NPR. "The 1940 Census: 72-Year-Old Secrets Revealed." Accessed April 17, 2016. http://www.npr.org/2012/04/02/149575704/the-1940-census-72-year-old-secrets-revealed.

Rahrisch, Sandro. "Amerikaner Suchen Nach Vermissten Piloten." SZ-Online. April 15, 2009. Accessed April 09, 2016. http://www.sz-online.de/nachrichten/amerikaner-suchen-nach-vermissten-piloten-2157893.html.

Smithsonian National Postal Museum. "Victory Mail—Online Exhibit." Accessed April 01, 2016. http://postalmuseum.si.edu/victorymail/letter/better.html.

Truren, Piet G.M. "The U.S. 8th Air Force's Microwave Early Warning (MEW) Radar at Greyfriars, Suffolk, and Eys, Netherlands During 1944–1945." November 2012. Accessed April 1, 2016. http://www.dunwichmuseum.org.uk/reslib/PDF/20130531141206Article2012, MEWSRadaratDunwich,PietTruren,4Mb.pdf.

University of California, Santa Barbara. "Franklin D. Roosevelt: Address at University of Virginia." Accessed April 17, 2016. http://www.presidency.ucsb.edu/ws/?pid=15965.

University of California, Santa Barbara. "Franklin D. Roosevelt: Proclamation 2487 - Proclaiming That an Unlimited National Emergency Confronts This Country, Which Requires That Its Military, Naval, Air and Civilian Defenses Be Put on the Basis of Readiness to Repel Any and All Acts or Threats of Aggression Directed Toward Any Part of the Western Hemisphere." Accessed April 17, 2016. http://www.presidency.ucsb.edu/ws/?pid=16121.

US Navy "Military Pay Chart 1922–1942." 1922–1942 U.S. Navy Cyberspace- Commissioned Officer Pay Chart. Accessed March 31, 2016. https://www.navycs.com/charts/1922-officer-pay-chart.html.

Wentz, W. Budd, MD. "Rammed Over Germany, Target: Parchim." Accessed April 4, 2016. http://home.earthlink.net/~tom.mccrary/ TargetParchim-RammedOverGermany.htm.

Miscellaneous

Borsodi, F. A., *Pilot's Comments on Me-109G, AAF No. EB-102*, Inter-Office Memorandum, Army Air Forces, Material Command, Dayton, Ohio, March 1, 1944.

Combat Thrills, radio interview, Elwyn Righetti with Larry Freeman, broadcast date unknown.

Daum, Rudolf, *Wer Kann Angaben Dazu Machen?* Handbill, Riesa, Germany, 1993.

Ed Malone Radio Show, *Top of the Evening*, Westinghouse Overseas Program, December 6, 1944, Blue Network.

Eilers, Nicole, Dr. Internal memorandum, *Releasable statement to author, Jay Stout, writing book about Col Elwyn Righetti, O-396312*, Defense POW/MIA Accounting Agency, Washington. Undated.

Historical Data, April 1945, Frederick Pickens, Historical Officer, 55th Fighter Group.

Joint Commission Support Directorate of the Defense POW-MIA Office, International Security Affairs, Office of Secretary of Defense, *Comprehensive Report of the U.S. Side of the U.S–Russia Joint Commission of POW/MIAs* (Washington: OSD, 1996), 7.

Markscheffel, Fritz, *Schulungslehrgang Elbe*. Unpublished paper. March 28, 2008. Via Anthony C. Meldahl.

Markscheffel, Fritz, *Commentary on Air Interrogation Report dated, April 26, 1945, A.D.I. (K) & U.S. Air Interrogation*, June 20, 2012. Via Anthony C. Meldahl.

Mismanagement of POW/MIA Accounting, United States Senate, Senate Hearing 113–293, August 1, 2013.

Narrative History for January 1945. 38th Fighter Squadron, 55th Fighter Group, AAF Station F-159, England.

Proceedings of Board of Review, April 9, 1947. Headquarters, 7887 Graves Registration Detachment, Operations Division, APO 757, Liege, Belgium.

Toll, Thomas, *Report No. 868: Summary of Lateral Control Research*, National Advisory Committee for Aeronautics, Langley, 1947, Figure No. 47.

United States v. August Kobus, A German National, February 6, 1946, Case No. 12-1155, Deputy Theater Judge Advocates Office, War Crimes Branch, United States Forces, European Theater.

INDEX